Praise for *Curable*

"Travis Christofferson provides a compelling strategy for curing our broken health care system based on 'moneyball' logic, common sense, and validated science. Why is the logic and science supporting this strategy ignored? Every member of our society should address the questions posed in *Curable*, especially those in the health care industry and in the US congress."

—**Thomas N. Seyfried**, PhD, author of *Cancer as a Metabolic Disease*

"We cannot expect the health care industry to change on its own. We have to take ownership of our own choices, look at the research with a critical eye, and compel the change that we so desperately need. Nobody provides the evidence-based rallying cry like Travis Christofferson, and *Curable* is a perfect blueprint for some of the ways we can start to make real improvements to the health of our nation, now."

—**Aubrey Marcus**, CEO, Onnit; *New York Times* best-selling author of *Own the Day, Own Your Life*

"Travis Christofferson's highly anticipated new book does not disappoint. Our current medical system (I find it difficult to call it 'health' care) is defective, and *Curable* goes into great detail as to why and offers an intelligent approach to the future of medicine. A growing number of doctors are finding ways to support their patient outcomes by repurposing drugs as well as changing their thinking in order to approach the challenge of chronic illness with entirely new methods. However, with the average clinical study costing millions of dollars and taking 17 years to go from bench to bedside, patients often don't have the luxury of time nor the financial resources to utilize these expensive treatments. Christofferson encourages us to look beyond the dogma and leads us down an entirely new path. I anticipate this book will be an important wake up call for physicians, patients, and biotechnicians to come together and return 'health' to health care."

—**Dr. Nasha Winters**, coauthor of *The Metabolic Approach to Cancer*

"*Curable* is exceptionally well written, captivating, and convincing. It's true that the existing problem with health care is psychological and systemic, and there are numerous examples and stories to support this. Travis Christofferson advances the idea of repurposing drugs in innovative ways, which has the potential to revolutionize a profit-driven and incompetent health care system. The off-label use of generic drugs can be highly efficacious and an adjuvant to augment existing therapies. For examples, see the recent studies on the use of metformin for cancer or the use of ketamine for drug-resistant depression. There are many ideas presented in this book that are incredibly important for researchers, health care professionals, and educators to understand and disseminate. *Curable* is incredibly informative, and I will be sure to recommend it to all my colleagues and students."

—**Dominic D'Agostino**, PhD, associate professor,
USF Morsani College of Medicine

"Travis Christofferson elegantly details why and how Western medicine is failing us and, more importantly, gives us a road map for recovery. We already have the tools of the trade to change direction, we simply need a new driver to effect those changes. *Curable* helps to properly inform those that wish to take control of their health to identify interventions that are biologically plausible and which have a proper scientific basis. These are time-tested therapies with minimal side effects and maximal outcomes that can give us all the power to change direction. As Lao Tzu said, 'If you do not change direction, you may end up where you are heading.' Read this book and steer yourself back to good health."

—**Dr. Sarah Myhill**, author of *Sustainable Medicine* and *Diagnosis and Treatment of Chronic Fatigue Syndrome and Myalgic Encephalitis*

"Travis Christofferson seamlessly weaves together psychology, medicine, history, and insight in this page-turning book, providing a compelling case for improving the quality of life of patients in efficient and effective ways. Christofferson has an exceptional ability to synthesize the work of others, and in *Curable* he brings it all together in a gripping narrative that's both informative and entertaining."

—**Bob Kaplan**, MS, MBA, medical research analyst

CURABLE

CURABLE

How an Unlikely Group of
Radical Innovators Is Trying to
Transform our Health Care System

TRAVIS CHRISTOFFERSON, MS

Chelsea Green Publishing
White River Junction, VT
London, UK

Editor: Makenna Goodman
Project Manager: Sarah Kovach
Copy Editor: Jennifer Lipfert
Proofreader: Deb Heimann
Indexer: Nancy Crompton
Designer: Melissa Jacobson

Printed in the United States of America.
First printing September 2019.
10 9 8 7 6 5 4 3 2 1   19 20 21 22

Our Commitment to Green Publishing
Chelsea Green sees publishing as a tool for cultural change and ecological stewardship. We strive to align
our book manufacturing practices with our editorial mission and to reduce the impact of our business
enterprise in the environment. We print our books and catalogs on chlorine-free recycled paper, using
vegetable-based inks whenever possible. This book may cost slightly more because it was printed on
paper that contains recycled fiber, and we hope you'll agree that it's worth it. *Curable* was printed on paper
supplied by Sheridan that contains 100% postconsumer recycled fiber.

ISBN 978-1-60358-926-0 (hardcover) | ISBN 978-1-60358-927-7 (ebook) | 978-1-60358-928-4 (audiobook)

Library of Congress Cataloging-in-Publication Data is available upon request.

Chelsea Green Publishing
85 North Main Street, Suite 120
White River Junction, VT 05001
(802) 295-6300
www.chelseagreen.com

Contents

Is Health Care Fixable?

When Michael Lewis published the book *Moneyball* in 2003, no one predicted the impact it would have. The book told the compelling story of the Major League Baseball franchise the Oakland Athletics and their nontraditional, data-driven approach to picking undervalued players. Using this radical methodology, the Athletics were able to far exceed the expectations of a small-market team with very little money. Nobody saw it coming. After all, baseball was steeped in a century and a half of wisdom. Yet the Athletics had done something remarkable; they discovered a disruptive new way to dramatically improve the process of picking players using a data-driven approach known as *analytics*, a technique that relies on analysts to sift through the trail of statistics accumulated over a player's career in order to determine his or her ultimate value. In 2002, the first year the Athletics fired their talent scouts and fully committed to the methodology, they won a record-breaking 20 games in a row and finished first in the American League West with a record of 103 wins and 59 losses.

In the wake of Lewis's *Moneyball*, however, a lingering question remained: How could the traditional method of using talent scouts to pick players have been so flawed in the first place? The talent scouts had been getting something wrong. But what? Why was raw, apathetic data better than the intuition of the expert mind? There had to be another story to tell. This story within a story might have been lost on Michael Lewis if not for a review of *Moneyball* published in the *New Republic* in the summer of 2003 by Richard Thaler and Cass Sunstein, two academics at the University of Chicago. Thaler and Sunstein pointed out that the questions about human intuition that *Moneyball* raised were, in fact, questions that two Israeli psychologists, Daniel Kahneman and Amos Tversky, had been grappling with since the 1960s.

Of course, Michael Lewis has a preternatural gift for sniffing out interesting stories. Tipped off by the *New Republic* review, he followed the trail of crumbs to Kahneman and Tversky. Here, Lewis realized, was a fascinating story about two irreverent psychologists who had quietly changed the very foundation of the social sciences. Their research centered largely on a single question: How does the human mind make decisions? Over decades, their research uncloaked a shocking number of hardwired glitches, firewalls, and irrational shortcuts inherent to the human mind. Kahneman and Tversky's work had alone reversed a long-standing assumption within the social sciences that people are mostly rational.

These findings, of course, have consequences far beyond explaining why talent scouts often get it wrong when deciding which players to draft for a baseball team. The consequences affect the very fabric of society: politicians deciding on tax policy or whether or not to go to war; investors deciding which stock to buy or sell; doctors making diagnoses or deciding on a treatment for a sick patient. If the human mind was so flawed, whom could we trust? And more importantly, how could we fix it?

Throughout the 1960s, '70s, '80s, and '90s, Kahneman and Tversky's work didn't travel far outside the narrow world of academia. Within academia, however, their careers experienced a meteoric rise. As the twenty-first century neared, they were showered with awards—a list that includes numerous honorary degrees, a MacArthur Fellowship, a Guggenheim Fellowship, the Grawemeyer Award, and the Nobel Prize, to name just a few. But in truth, neither of them cared much for awards. They had always sought something more inclusive. Something beyond the confined ecosystem of academia. They hoped their work would penetrate the world at large and make it a better place. That it would serve as a template for humanity to improve by recognizing its innate flaws and devising systems to bypass them.

All at once their wish came true. With the help of Lewis's 2016 book, *The Undoing Project*, and Kahneman's 2011 *New York Times* best-seller, *Thinking Fast and Slow*, Kahneman and Tversky's research was thrust into the public consciousness. The consequences of humans' deeply flawed intuition were not lost on important luminaries across a multitude of disciplines. And "the *Moneyball* approach" offered a solution. A societal revolution to improve human decision-making with systems was underway. "Making systems work is the great task of my generation of physicians and scientists," announced surgeon and best-selling author Atul Gawande. The word "moneyball" morphed into a viral meme that wove itself into the cultural vernacular. There are few places it hasn't penetrated. Moneyball has swept through all the major sports leagues, including the National Basketball Association (NBA) and the National Football League (NFL), and far beyond. Moneyball for education; moneyball for markets; moneyball for government, farming, start-ups, churches, banking. and presidential campaigns. Suddenly everyone was moneyballing. Governments, institutions, and corporations have recognized the failings of the human mind and are building systems to correct for it: checklists, redundancies, process-improvement protocols, artificial intelligence, and behavioral incentives. Almost every nook and cranny of society is becoming more efficient by recognizing the flaws in human intuition and installing systems to mitigate them.

With one glaring exception: health care.

I became part of the health care system in the summer of 2017. Three years earlier I had published a book titled *Tripping over the Truth: How the Metabolic Theory of Cancer Is Overturning One of Medicine's Most Entrenched Paradigms*. The book illuminates the emerging work of a small group of scientists who are offering an alternative explanation for the origin of cancer and, critically, a new treatment paradigm centered on targeting cancer though metabolism rather than genetics. The book's modest success led me to all sorts of interesting people and interesting opportunities. One such opportunity occurred while I was giving a talk for a small charity event in London. The charity had organized a one-day event focused on the promise of metabolically active cancer treatments. One of the other speakers was Ndaba Mazibuko, a practicing medical doctor at a start-up called Care Oncology Clinic located in London. He began his talk by explaining that the clinic had been conceived to address a well-characterized problem in oncology. That is, that there are numerous off-patent, generic medications with regulatory approval for the treatment of other diseases that could be "repurposed" to treat cancer.

There was no good reason why this had not yet been done, other than lack of financial incentive. The research to support using these drugs for cancer was vast, yet because the medications had aged off their patents the health care system provided no incentive either for physicians to prescribe them or for pharmaceutical companies to usher them through the necessary trials to win formal approval for their use in cancer. To address this problem, Care Oncology made the bold decision to open a clinic and offer a combination of four carefully selected, metabolically acting, generic medications to patients with cancer. The medications, Mazibuko explained, had to meet several criteria. Because cancer patients are going through so much already, they had to have very minimal side effects; minimal interaction with standard-of-care therapies (they don't get in the way, in other words), and abundant evidence to suggest they could help improve outcomes when added to the standard therapeutics the patients would also be receiving. From a patient's perspective, especially those with a dire prognosis, it made lots of sense—very little risk and a potentially large benefit.

The doctors at Care prescribed the medications in their Care Oncology Clinic protocol (COC Protocol) "off-label," meaning the drugs were being prescribed for a disease other than that for which they had received formal regulatory approval. Importantly, the four-drug protocol was administered only as an *adjunctive* therapy, meaning the treatment was to be taken alongside the standard of care, never competing with or replacing it. And the mechanistic data unequivocally backed this strategy: By targeting critical metabolic pathways exclusive to cancer cells, the drugs weakened the cells in a way that made standard therapies more effective. In addition to treating patients, Care Oncology would also conduct a formal "real-world" clinical trial to measure the outcomes of their patients, adding to the existing body of evidence supporting the treatment.[1] Additionally, and this is critical, in using off-label drugs in their trial Care could take advantage of the generic price of the medications. A sort of clinical trial in reverse. If it worked, eventually enough data could be accumulated to win US Food and Drug Administration (FDA) approval for a treatment comprised of a handful of generic drugs. This had never been done. A generic drug had never won FDA approval for a new disease indication without a pharmaceutical company first tinkering with it in a way that garnered them a new patent (varying the arrangement of a few atoms in the drug or switching the delivery method, for example). By cutting pharmaceutical companies out of the loop, the savings would all pass directly to the patients.

I loved this model.

In the end, we struck up a collaboration. I would help bring Care Oncology to the United States. I had already started a research foundation in 2012 to support the "financially stranded" therapies I had highlighted in my book: the ketogenic diet, exogenous ketones, fasting before the administration of chemotherapy or radiation, repurposing off-patent drugs, and hyperbaric oxygen, to name a few. All these therapies hold tremendous promise yet linger in a financial purgatory—again, mostly because it is difficult to patent them. My foundation supported research for the *future* use of these therapies. But here, with Care, there was an opportunity to do something tangible and immediate, to offer patients one of these promising treatments *right now*. I was all in. But I didn't realize how difficult it would be.

A year later a close friend and I opened the first US clinic in my hometown of Rapid City, South Dakota. Rapid City is a small, conservative community, but I had hoped the oncologists at the local cancer center would embrace this new treatment option for some of their patients, especially those with an almost always terminal diagnosis such as glioblastoma, the viciously aggressive form of brain cancer that took the life of John McCain. The director of the cancer center was receptive. He set up a time for me to present to the oncologists and other staff. In a small room packed with nurses, the head pharmacist, the medical director, and numerous medical and radiation oncologists, I went through a twenty-minute slide presentation detailing the logic and data supporting the use of the drugs in the COC Protocol. Immediately after I finished, one of the radiation oncologists sitting to my right launched into a rant that had nothing to do with the presentation. "We have all gone through medical school, we understand clinical trials, and, frankly, I'm offended you don't think we do," he said. I had no idea how I had offended him. I had simply presented the rationale behind Care's treatment and the data that supported it. The director, who seemed slightly taken aback, intervened to diffuse the tension. Even so, the oncologist flung another accusation. "I see what you're doing here. You're taking advantage of desperate people." I was befuddled by his reaction and didn't know what to say. The fee Care charged was minimal, the four drugs combined cost patients $60 per month. The mission of the company was to "capture" the generic price of the meds through their off-label use. From a cost perspective, operating within the current "patent-centric" health care system, Care's model seemed to be a revelation. And we had just gone through slide after slide of massive blocks of data, including internal data from Care's ongoing trial in the U.K., that suggested that the four drugs could improve outcomes with very little risk and few side effects.

The tension was palpable. After a flurry of questions from the other attendees, the radiation oncologist, still apparently smoldering, spoke up again about one of the medications in the COC Protocol, a drug approved for type 2 diabetes called metformin. "And why would you use a drug for type 2 diabetes in cancer?" he asked. Before I could answer, a medical oncologist, standing in the far corner, said, "I sometimes prescribe it to help prevent recurrence."

This disturbing encounter sparked my motivation for writing this book. Who was on the right side? Was Care Oncology doing the right thing? Were we solving a problem that was truly in patients' best interest? Oncology—and medicine as a whole—is only about measuring the effectiveness of a treatment and weighing it against the risk. Yet, as easy as this sounds, it is anything but. How often is this delicate equation subverted by human irrationality? And, in this modern medical era that we like to believe we live in, how could such a massive chasm in knowledge exist between two oncologists—in the same room, from the same hospital? One baffled by why a type 2 diabetes drug would ever be prescribed for cancer and another sufficiently confident in the data supporting its off-label use in the prevention of recurrence.

As you will see in the following pages, the answers to these questions can be uncomfortable. In medicine, an antiquated culture that has always protected a physician's autonomy, intuition, and self-reliance above all else, the fallibility of the human mind often goes unchecked. The truth is we have an extraordinarily complex health care system that often relies on a physician's intuition in making critical decisions—an intuition that, as psychologists Kahneman and Tversky have shown, can at times be terribly flawed.

No one is questioning the ability of our nation's doctors, and this book does not aim to demonize doctors for making the "wrong" decisions. This country's physicians are incredibly well-trained, smart, and well-intended people. They are our nation's best. But we are at a turning point in the history of medicine at which the complexity of medicine is challenging the capability of the human mind. As we move into the future, medicine will require evidence-based systems to answer these increasingly difficult questions. My hope is that this book will help, even in a small way, to clarify the path forward.

––––––––––

While almost every arena of human activity has become more efficient through use of a systems approach, health care has become less so. Costs have continued to rise while outcomes have remained stagnant. Health care has become a full-blown national crisis. In 2016 three iconic American businesses —Amazon, JPMorgan Chase, and Berkshire Hathaway—announced that they had had enough. The American health care system had become a pernicious parasite that was dragging their companies' competitiveness down relative to the rest of the world. Together they would start from scratch and create an internal health care system for their employees. If the politicians couldn't fix it, they reasoned, perhaps they could.

Clearly the chief executive officers of these companies must have had a plan. They must have first recognized that health care was *fixable*, that there were inefficiencies that could be corrected. Two of the men involved, Warren Buffett and Charlie Munger, the chief executive officer and vice chairman of Berkshire Hathaway, respectively, had spent their entire careers at Berkshire recognizing the flaws in human reasoning and the resulting inefficiencies in financial markets. They were moneyballing, in the truest sense of the word, long before it was a verb. Their story is remarkable. Buffett and Munger, two kids from Omaha, Nebraska, transformed an outmoded, nearly bankrupt textile manufacturer into an iconic American corporation—the fourth-largest company by market capitalization in the United States. There was no obvious reason why. They didn't have rich parents or deep connections. They didn't invent or hold the patent to anything revolutionary. In fact, their meteoric rise was due mostly to their investments in the stock market. The advantage they had wasn't obvious to anyone at the time.

Yet Buffett and Munger's approach was remarkably similar to that of the Oakland Athletics. Early on, Munger and Buffett recognized something few others did—that humans were not rational, and, moreover, that our irrationality appeared to follow a pattern. Furthermore, they saw that the field they were playing on—the stock market—was a magnified expression of this irrationality. Investors, they observed, were taken by irrational waves of euphoria followed by bouts of desperate gloom. When investors, panicking irrationally, dumped stocks hand over fist, Buffett and Munger were there to buy them. And when investors bid stocks up to insanely high levels, like during the dot-com boom, they patiently bided their time. Their system worked, and Berkshire Hathaway's rise was dazzling. And, according to economic theory, impossible.

An economic theory called the *efficient market hypothesis* claims that people are rational and, therefore, stocks are always priced perfectly. If a multitude of expert investors panics and sells a stock, it is for logical reasons. Likewise, if they buy a stock it is also based on calculated, logical reasons. In other words, there is no way to beat the market. Berkshire Hathaway, economists said, was nothing more than the product of luck. Yet year after year Berkshire Hathaway continued to beat the market, and not by a small amount. Like the Oakland Athletics would do decades later, Buffett and Munger recognized the patterned failing of human intuition and built a system to exploit it.

If anyone can fix health care it is Buffett and Munger. And health care desperately needs these types of reformers—those who have long recognized the failing of the human mind and discovered ways to do better. Buffett and Munger, alongside Jeff Bezos of Amazon and Jamie Dimond of JPMorgan, have a unique opportunity to prove that health care can also be moneyballed. The section titled "A New Culture" (page 161) tells the story of this triumvirate and its potential to create inspired solutions to solve our health care crisis.

How did we get where we are? How did health care become so inefficient in the first place? What are the inefficiencies? The answer to these questions can best be understood through a historical lens. Historical narratives have a remarkable way of crystalizing complex issues. As you will see in the following chapters, the rise of medicine has been a continual struggle between statistical data and the premium placed on the physician's intuition. A struggle similar to the one the Oakland Athletics' management faced: a confrontation between the value of the talent scout's intuition and empirical data.

Chapter 1 of this book is a brief look at how the systems approach is revolutionizing society. It is the tale of the Oakland Athletics, Tversky and

Kahneman, and Buffett and Munger. If you've read *Moneyball* and *The Undoing Project*, you will have a *much* richer appreciation of these topics.

Chapter 2 focuses on the institution of health care. I discuss the history of medicine though the story of an iconic American surgeon, William Halsted, often called "the father of modern surgery." The span of Halsted's career saw medicine go from a collection of pointless, almost mystical procedures, such as bloodletting and leeching, to highly technical surgeries and effective medications, such as antibiotics. Halsted was a pioneer. Early in his career he recognized the importance of utilizing sterile surgical technique and forced it upon a reluctant American medical system that was seemingly content to remain in the Dark Ages. Halsted's career also witnessed the fitful rise of the clinical trial as a way to measure a medical intervention's effectiveness. And here is where Halsted's career took a turn. His name had become inextricably synonymous with a surgery he pioneered for breast cancer called the "radical mastectomy." This brutal, disfiguring procedure was based more on Halsted's intuition than convincing data. When the value of the procedure first began to be questioned, Halsted and his followers defended it with zealot-like fervor. But in the end, irrefutable data would prove the procedure pointless. The story of the rise and fall of the radical mastectomy illustrates the struggle between pure data and human intuition in medicine—a struggle that is still going on today; a struggle between an antiquated culture and the new, systems approach; a struggle at the heart of health care reform.

In chapter 3 I discuss the remarkable story of the fecal transplant, a surprisingly effective and incredibly low-tech procedure that has struggled to be adopted as a treatment for *Clostridium difficile*, a relentless intestinal infection that kills over fifteen thousand people every year. This section then launches into an examination of other simple, cheap, and effective treatments and procedures that often fall through the cracks of our disjointed health care system. It is shocking how many of these procedures get ignored. Many of these procedures, if broadly adopted, would immediately save countless lives.

The book then turns to the reformers in chapter 4. Just as Buffett and Munger of Berkshire Hathaway and the management of the Oakland Athletics had each done for their respective institutions, there are a handful of health care reformers, including Brent James of Intermountain Healthcare, who have adopted a moneyball-type approach to health care. They have recognized the patterned fallibility of a doctor's intuition and worked to install systems to correct for it. The results have been nothing short of remarkable. They serve as a signpost for a way forward.

And last, while writing this book I couldn't resist delving into the relationship between our intrinsic irrationality and our individual health. Of course, this relationship, evidently vast, necessitated narrowing to a singular focus. In chapter 5 I explore how the same patterned irrationality that leads to inefficiencies in large institutions can lead to misconceptions about our own individual health. In other words, what we *think* matters the most to our health may not be what *truly* matters. I hope to show you how the emerging fields of epigenetics and social genomics are redefining the variables that matter for a healthy and, importantly, a happy life. Here the story circles back to Daniel Kahneman, who has devoted the second act of his career to understanding the fickle emotion of happiness. Kahneman is able to reframe what happiness is in a way perhaps only he can—and in a way that may dramatically change how we think about our own lives.

CHAPTER 1

A New System

The Irrational Human Mind and the First Few Who Recognized It

Traditionally, talent scouts have been the ones to pick which players to draft in baseball. It's a time-honored position, steeped in ritual and lore, but it's also a position shrouded in the mysteries of human intuition. It is thought that talent scouts draw on a rich reservoir of experience to discern qualities in players that are imperceptible to the casual observer: a crisp swing of the bat, a quick step, or a fluidity to their movement. They carefully study the way the players carry themselves to detect a possible underlying confidence cloaked in subtle movements and expressions, verbal or nonverbal. They are craftsmen of human intuition. They see beyond the statistics. They quantify the unquantifiable.

Or so it was thought.

In 2002 the Oakland A's, a small-market team with a small-market budget, set about finding a better way to pick players. Their general manager, Billy Beane, began ignoring the advice from the team's scouts and turned to a purely data-driven approach to picking players. He zeroed in on the single metric that the data shouted mattered the most: the percentage a player gets on base. It didn't matter, Beane reasoned, whether the player was short, fat, slow, or appeared unathletic; whatever variables caused the scouts to pass them over were irrelevant. It didn't even matter *how* they got on base—whether it was by a hit or an unglamorous walk—*as long as they got on base.*

It was a daring move, to be sure, and everyone thought Beane and his management crew were crazy. The difference between a good athlete and a great athlete was *impossible* to capture through statistics, the scouts shot back. It was buried in deep and cryptic perception, an acuity measured in nanoseconds. And only a scout whose life was dedicated to picking up these subtleties could determine who would remain average and who would surface as the next star.

Yet Oakland's management was convinced that these differences left a statistical trail of breadcrumbs. Scouts were human after all, and humans are capable of all sorts of misjudgment and bias. Statistics, however, were not. In the spring of 2002 many of the players who ran onto the field for the Oakland A's were there because of a mathematical formula. The formula screamed that these players were undervalued. For the A's in 2002, acquiring a player for cheap wasn't just nice, it was a necessity. Out of the thirty teams in Major League Baseball, the Oakland A's budget was twenty-eighth, three times less than that of the New York Yankees. They were acquiring players who had slipped through the cracks. They were getting the rejects who had passed unnoticed through the net of collective wisdom cast by the league's talent scouts. But to the A's, they were mispriced gems. To the scouts, the fans, the announcers, the team appeared to be a joke, a collection of misfits. What happened next shocked everyone: *The Oakland A's began to win.*

Then, on August 13, 2002, the team of oddities broke the American League record with a winning streak of twenty consecutive games. They made it all the way to the American League divisional playoffs, a feat that stunned Major League Baseball and slayed a century of conventional wisdom. After their 2002 season the Oakland A's moneyball approach to picking players was noticed by the rest of baseball. In 2004 the Boston Red Sox copied the A's strategy and won their first World Series in almost a century. And won it again in 2007. And again in 2013.

Could a purely statistically driven approach to picking players really be better than the human intuition of the league's talent scouts? Or was the success of the A's and the Red Sox just dumb luck? Too much money was at stake not to find out, and sports franchises outside of baseball began to adopt the model. In the spring of 2006 Leslie Alexander, owner of the NBA team the Houston Rockets, hired self-proclaimed "nerd" Daryl Morey to apply to picking players an analytical model Morey had built over years of painstaking analysis. As had been true with Major League Baseball, the new importance placed on these "geeks" didn't go over well in the culture of professional basketball. NBA all-star and network announcer Charles Barkley even went on a four-minute tirade during an NBA on-air half-time show about the league's new courtship with data crunchers, zeroing in on Morey himself. Barkley described him as an "idiot" and said his analytics were a bunch of "crap." Barkley finished his rant by claiming that guys like Morey were working in basketball because they "never got the girls in high school and they just want to be in the game."

Yet, for better or worse, "geeks" like Morey had arrived, and if their models proved better at picking players than the NBA talent scouts, they weren't going anywhere soon. Morey's model rummaged through mountains of accumulated data and isolated the variables that appeared to matter, assigning a degree of importance to each one. The whole system was designed to sidestep the internal biases and misjudgments intrinsic to the reckonings of the NBA's talent scouts.

Building a mathematical model to pick players, Morey could attest, was not at all easy. It was the product of years of trial and error, and it seemed never to be finished; the model was in a perpetual state of refinement. For example, a college player might have a record of scoring lots of points, but sometimes this was because the player hogged the ball, and the high scoring came at the expense of winning the game. Another player might look great in college only because he was older and physically more mature. The pool of data was not straightforward; it was full of statistical traps that had to be recognized and accounted for. In the end, however, Morey was confident the model offered a slight edge over the scouts. And in a game often decided by a tiny percentage of overall points, even a slight edge was enough.

But where did the scouts go wrong? Morey thought that the most obvious way appeared to be a flaw in human reasoning known as *confirmation bias*. Humans tend to make very quick judgments about people, often based on a range of subjective beliefs. The shape of someone's face, a subtle expression, or a certain laugh might remind you of someone you like or dislike and will immediately color your impression of that individual. Research shows that when an impression forms in the human mind it's hard to undo. Once an impression of someone is established—typically very quickly—you then tend to notice more closely those things that confirm your first impression and discount those that may contradict it. Like the rest of us, talent scouts also fall victim to confirmation bias.

A scout has a deep well of memories that flood to the surface when he or she evaluates a player. A prospective player might subconsciously remind the scout of a current star player or one of their successful picks: the delicate way the wrist drops upon release of the ball, a barely perceptible double head fake, or perhaps simply the player's looks or physical build. These attributes have little to do with the player's potential, but nevertheless the impressions coalesce in the scout's mind, helping to form a rapid judgement: *I like that player*. Locked in a confirmation bias the scout begins to notice attributes that conform to his or her flawed first impression preferentially.

"Confirmation bias is the most insidious because you don't even realize it's happening," said Morey. For example, a Chinese-American named Jeremy Lin entered the NBA draft after graduating from Harvard in 2010. Lin didn't look like any of the NBA players anchored in the minds of the league's talent scouts. But Lin caught the attention of Morey's model. Lin's statistics were entered, and the numbers were crunched: Morey's model signaled that Jeremy Lin was a hot prospect. According to the model, Lin should have been drafted 15th. But, just like the other scouts, Morey was unable to surmount his internal bias: "Every fucking person, including me, thought he was unathletic," he said. The Rockets passed Lin over. As did every other team. And Lin went undrafted.[1]

Looking back, Lin had a history of going unnoticed. Both of Lin's parents were 5-foot, 6-inch Taiwanese immigrants. Yet Jeremy, the middle child of three sons, defied his genetic allotment and grew to 6 feet, 3 inches tall. When Lin was a boy, his father took him and his brothers to the local YMCA where he taught them to play basketball. Jeremy took to the game immediately. During his senior year Lin led his Palo Alto high school team to the Division II state title, ending the season with a record of 32 wins and 1 loss. For his efforts Lin was named First-Team All-State and Northern California Division II Player of the Year. Still, college scouts seemed to scarcely notice him. He was offered no Division I scholarships. Even though the scouts failed to recognize Lin's talent, his high school coach and teammates did not, and declared that he possessed a sort of preternatural sense of the game. "He knows exactly what needs to be done at every point of the game," said his coach. "He always knew how the defense was set up and where the weak spots were," added a former teammate.

Rejected by his two "dream" schools, Stanford and UCLA, Lin's 4.2 GPA helped to land him at Harvard. By his junior year he ranked in the top ten for scoring in his conference. During his senior year he was a unanimous selection for the All-Ivy League First Team, leading his Harvard team to a series of records. Lin left Harvard as the first player in Ivy League history to score more than 1,450 points. Still, despite his performance at Harvard, Lin again went unnoticed, with all thirty NBA teams passing him over in the 2010 draft.

Unwilling to give up, Lin managed to reach a partial contract with his hometown Golden State Warriors. Even so, he didn't play much his rookie year and was demoted to the Development League three times before finally being let go. He was picked up by the New York Knicks in early 2011, again played little, and again spent time in the Development League. But in 2012, everything changed. Lin was sleeping on his brother's couch in a one-bedroom, East Village apartment, on the verge of giving up on the NBA, when a series of injuries to key players left the Knicks in a desperate situation. They had lost eleven of their last thirteen games. In what appeared to be a final act of desperation, Lin was flagged from the bench and put in the game. That night he went out and lit up the court, singlehandedly leading a gritty turnaround win for the Knicks against the New Jersey Nets. Following his outstanding performance Lin was promoted to the starting lineup where he fronted a seven-game winning streak—even outscoring Kobe Bryant in a matchup against the Lakers. The Cinderella story instantly captivated both the media and NBA's fan base and then spread around the globe, sparking a worldwide craze that quickly became known as "Linsanity."

Later, after Lin underwent a battery of tests, Morey discovered that he was, in fact, incredibly athletic. Lin logged an explosive acceleration and change of direction rate that few in the NBA have matched. But because Lin didn't conform to the *mental* model of what an NBA player should look like, he was passed over by every single talent scout. A 2012 *New York Times* article on Lin summarized it this way: "Coaches have said recruiters, in the age of who-does-he-remind-you-of evaluations, simply lacked a frame of reference for such an Asian-American talent."[2] When the dust settled, however, despite his mistake in passing Lin up, Morey's system worked. And in the decade that followed, Morey's analytic approach led the team to the third-best record in the NBA—a decade without a single losing season. The turn of the century had ushered in the rise of the "nerd." And "nerd" was no longer considered a purely derogatory label; it had become a badge of success. Silicon Valley was minting fresh "nerdy" billionaires at an astonishing speed as new technologies spawned entire new industries. And now they were redefining sports, too. Morey gave his own definition of a nerd: "A person who knows his own mind enough to mistrust it."[3]

Yet talent scouts had nothing *but* their mind. That *was* their tool. And now Morey was claiming that had been the problem all along. Until now, "talent scout" had been a canonized title. They were believed to possess a preternatural instinct honed over years of experience. Like any highly skilled individual, they were bestowed with the title of *expert*. What Morey was claiming was not trivial. He was casting doubt on the fundamental belief that the scout's mind, *the human mind*, was a rational learning machine capable of real intuition. This raised an important question: How rational *is* the human mind?

Are People Rational or Irrational?

I'm smart enough to know that I'm dumb.

—RICHARD FEYNMAN

Early twentieth-century economists built theories organized around a single basic assumption: People are mostly rational when it comes to making decisions. And how could we not be? The exalted rise of humanity was anchored in rationality. Starting in caves, human beings had perfected the use of tools, agriculture, animal domestication, and architecture—leading to the origin of entire civilizations. The Dark Ages were illuminated by the Enlightenment. Embracing the scientific method gave rise to the Industrial Revolution and technologies beyond our wildest dreams: light bulbs, telephones, cars, airplanes, and computers. It seemed intuitively obvious that humans *rationally* evaluated information when pressed to make a decision; the edifice of civilization was clear testimony to that fundamental assumption.

The assumption that humans are rational seemed so obvious, so self-evident, that no one in the social sciences had ever meaningfully challenged it. That is, until 1959. At first it was a Johns Hopkins psychologist named Ward Edwards who, without overtly challenging the assumption, asked a simple question: How *do* humans make decisions? Surprisingly, before Edwards, no one had really ever asked.

The innocent question posed by Edwards stirred something deep within the minds of two Israeli psychologists, Daniel Kahneman and Amos Tversky. When Edwards posed the question in 1959, Kahneman and Tversky were both professors in their mid-twenties at Hebrew University in Jerusalem. Kahneman's childhood had been tumultuous. As a Jewish boy living in Paris when the war broke out, most of his memories are of his family's desperate maneuvering to avoid capture by the Nazis. He remembers fleeing, staying in rooms provided by his father's friends, hiding in barns and chicken coops. He recalls the Nazis pulling men off buses, stripping them naked to see if they were circumcised, and, if they were, killing them. He remembers his father's death, his mother's struggle, and that his only friend during those years was imaginary.

Then, suddenly, the war was over. One day, Kahneman recalled, a certain lightness filled the French air. Even so, the trauma of the war had left his mother with a festering unease with regard to Europe. They returned to their ransacked apartment in Paris for a while, but it no longer felt like home. In 1946 she moved her family to Jerusalem to start a new life.

Tversky, on the other hand, was born in Israel. His parents were among the early settlers hoping to build a new Zionist nation after fleeing Russia in the 1920s. Tversky's childhood was consistent with the struggles of building and defending a nation under constant threat. For young Tversky, his surroundings and the people around him were rich with mystery—he credits his father for instilling in him the gift of curiosity. "[He] taught me to wonder," Tversky would later write.[4] To his father, people and their stories were endlessly fascinating. As he grew up Tversky was sculpted by the growing nation. The fledgling Israeli state was weaving a society that was incredibly tightly knit—neighbors, friends, family, all had to rely on each other unwaveringly. Rather than develop outward into the suburbs as did postwar America, Israel was developing inward. While America was exhaling, Israel was inhaling. The gestating society was built on human connections. Even the architecture's density funneled people together; in the shops, at the barber, and in the cafés—there was constant interaction. One was rarely alone.

A grave obligation came with being an Israeli: Every able-bodied citizen, whether male or female, was mandated to serve in the military, first in active duty and then in the reserves. Kahneman and Tversky were no exceptions. Tversky volunteered to become a paratrooper, and Kahneman was conscripted into duty after graduating from college. Tversky quickly rose to the rank of platoon commander. Both men saw their fair share of combat. Neither man ever questioned his obligation.

In between wars, however, Kahneman and Tversky took off their military uniforms and entered a starkly different world as professors of psychology at Hebrew University. They traveled in different circles, and, although they occupied the same department, somehow maintained discrete orbits that never intersected. "It was the graduate students' perception that Danny and Amos had some sort of rivalry. They were clearly the stars of the department who somehow or other hadn't gotten in sync," said a graduate student.[5] The students who knew them both couldn't help but notice their differences. Kahneman, a traditional psychologist, was shy, racked with self-doubt, and almost pathologically pessimistic—a morning person who kept a messy office. Tversky, a mathematical psychologist, was gregarious, dripping with self-confidence, and extraordinarily optimistic. He was a night owl, and his office was always meticulous.[6]

They finally discovered each other in the spring of 1969. The question that Edwards had posed—how do people make decisions?—had captivated both men. Meanwhile, Edwards, now at the University of Michigan, was conducting experiments designed to address his question. His experiments showed that, at least when it comes to judging probabilities, people *were* mostly rational. But this finding didn't satisfy Kahneman.

Soon after they became acquainted, Kahneman invited Tversky to give a lecture at his graduate seminar, and Tversky gave a sheepish presentation summarizing Edwards's tepid results, agreeing with his conclusion that humans are rational decision-makers. Edwards's experiments suggested that human intuition is a decent judge of statistical probability and therefore could make rational predictions about the future. But, to Kahneman, Edwards's results were overly simplistic, even slightly absurd—they didn't reveal much, if anything, about *how* people make real-life decisions. Kahneman, who taught statistics at the university, could *see* the irrationality in his students. He was very surprised that Tversky appeared to accept Edwards's conclusion so passively. After the lecture, Kahneman and Tversky found a quiet spot and launched into a substantive discussion. Kahneman challenged the notion that Edwards's results represented anything meaningful. Tversky listened. The discussion that spring day would set in motion a lifelong partnership largely centered around a shared passion for a single, yet astonishingly complex question—a partnership that would blaze a trail through the social sciences.

Kahneman and Tversky began scheming. They wanted to capture the way people made *real-life* decisions. They wanted to avoid overly simplistic experiments that were scrubbed clean of the human mind's messiness, with all its biases, firewalls, false assumptions, associations, and glitches. They sought to uncover the human fallibility that seeps into our minds as we grapple with choices. They devised questions carefully formulated to capture irrational patterns that they then gave to groups of experts and college students. By design, the questions had logical answers but had been deliberately crafted in a way to allow the respondents' subtle mental biases to creep in.

For example, Kahneman and Tversky read a list of thirty-nine names to a group of students; twenty of the names were traditionally male names, and nineteen traditionally female. Among the nineteen female names, they sprinkled in a few famous ones—Elizabeth Taylor, for example. They then asked the students to report if the list contained more male or female names. The students overwhelmingly reported hearing more female names than male names. And when they performed the experiment in reverse—listing nineteen male names and twenty female names, with some famous male names interspersed—the students this time overwhelmingly reported hearing more male names. This simple exercise exposed what they would call the *availability heuristic*, the tendency for people to color their thinking, and decision-making, based on what they can remember, or what is immediately *available* to them for recall.

Kahneman and Tversky showed that people begin to misjudge probabilities based on what has happened before. Everyone knows a flipped coin has a fifty-fifty chance of landing "heads" or "tails" each time it is flipped. But if a coin lands heads a few times in a row, they showed, people begin to assign a higher probability that the next flipped coin will land tails—even though the coin still has an exactly 50 percent chance of landing heads or tails. Instinctually, most people adhere to the "lightning doesn't strike in the same spot twice" axiom, even though lightning has the exact same probability of striking *any* single spot each time it strikes, regardless of whether it has struck that spot before.

Their work was critical in defining what is known as the *anchoring bias*, or the tendency to place too much arbitrary importance on the first piece of information one is given in a situation. Anchoring biases affect how we perceive the world every day. For example, the price of gas was about $1.85 a gallon in the early 2000s and then began to climb. As the price rose above $2.00 and then neared $3.00, people reported having a negative sentiment toward gas prices. But then the price reversed, eventually settling at around $2.50 a gallon. Now, after being anchored at $3.00, consumer sentiment toward gas prices shifted to the positive—at the exact same price they felt negatively about only a few months earlier.

In a separate experiment a researcher asked an audience to write down the last two digits of their social security number and consider whether they would pay this number of dollars for an item whose value they did not know, such as a bottle of wine, chocolate, or computer equipment. They were then asked to place bids for these items. Invariably, audience members who wrote down higher two-digit numbers would submit bids that were between 60 percent and 120 percent higher than those with lower social security numbers. The higher number, although completely arbitrary, had become their "anchor."

Another experiment showed how the anchoring bias can even influence our other senses. A researcher at the University of Bordeaux in Talence, France, asked fifty-four oenology (the science of wine) students to describe two wines, one white and one red. The students all tasted both wines and wrote down their descriptions of each. In a second tasting the students were given the same white wine that now had secretly been colored red with a dye that imparted no taste. This time the description the students reported was vastly different. The students reporting tasting red wine characteristics in the white wine. *Seeing* a red-colored wine had "anchored" a bias into the minds of the students, directly influencing their perception of taste.

The partnership that developed between Kahneman and Tversky was as unique as the work they were generating. "They had a certain style of working, which is they just talked to each other for hour after hour after hour," said a colleague. Kahneman, of his time with Tversky, mostly remembers the laughter. "We laughed a lot," he would tell a reporter after Tversky had died. "We could finish each other's thoughts." The rate that they churned out paper after paper reflected the growing intensity of their relationship. "We had, jointly, a mind that was better than our separate minds. Our joint mind was very, very good," said Kahneman.[7]

They exposed the reality that people are terrible at recognizing when events are random. For example, Londoners during the Second World War were convinced that the 2,419 German V-1 rockets launched at London from the shores of France and the Netherlands were aimed to hit certain parts of the city more than others because certain locations were hit multiple times and others not at all. In other words, the Londoners were sure the bombing was *nonrandom*. However, subsequent analysis revealed that the unguided German rockets had landed in a perfectly random distribution. This simple study revealed something important: Human minds are wired to find *significance in randomness*. This is perhaps why patterns leap into our minds as clouds drift by. We are wired to find meaning when it may not be there.

Kahneman and Tversky uncloaked one bias and heuristic after the next: availability, anchoring, adjustment, and vividness. Human irrationality was not random, they showed, it was *patterned*, it was something deeply baked into the human condition—as much a part of us as our internal organs.

The next experiment they performed uncovered a critically important heuristic. They created this scenario for a group of students:

Out of a pool of 100 people, 30 are lawyers and 70 are engineers. A person from the pool is picked at random. What is the likelihood the person is a lawyer?

The students correctly assigned the probability to be 30 percent. But then Kahneman and Tversky introduced a twist. They kept the scenario the same—a pool of 100 people, 30 of whom are lawyers and 70 of whom are engineers—but added the following description to one of the people in the pool:

Dick is a 30-year-old man. He is married with no children. A man of high ability and high motivation, he promises to be quite successful in his field. He is liked by his colleagues.

They then asked the students to determine the likelihood Dick was a lawyer. This time the students judged that there was an equal chance Dick was a lawyer or an engineer. Merely adding a description had somehow changed the probability from 30 to 50 percent in the students' minds, even though the description had no information whatsoever that should have affected their answer.[8]

Tversky and Kahneman discovered that, as shown in the previous example, an arbitrary description can trigger associations to someone's own history, and the individual will then assign value to those associations. Any descriptive input sets the brain into an automatic effort to "represent" what the input matches. These connections then come to the surface and begin to color judgment. Tversky and Kahneman coined this cognitive phenomenon the *representation heuristic*. We humans are storytellers, and we run narratives when we are trying to predict outcomes. "The stories about the past are so good that they create an illusion that life is understandable, and they create an illusion that you can predict the future," said Kahneman.[9]

The significance of the representation heuristic in skewing judgment resulted in a 1973 paper titled "On the Psychology of Prediction."[10] In it Kahneman and Tversky wrote, "Consequently, intuitive predictions are insensitive to the reliability of the evidence or to the prior probability of the outcome, in violation of the logic of statistical prediction." In other words, even when people know the statistical probability of an outcome, say a 50 percent chance of something being true, they will still let arbitrary information sway their prediction. Worse, Kahneman and Tversky showed that the factors that lead people to be more confident in their prediction are the same factors that cause the prediction to be less accurate.

The 1973 paper put them on the map. After hearing a talk Kahneman gave at Stanford University, one psychology professor commented: "I remember I came home from the talk and told my wife, 'This is going to win the Nobel Prize in economics.' I was so absolutely convinced. This was a psychological theory about economic man. I thought, what could be better? Here is why you get all these irrationalities and errors. They come from the inner workings of the human mind."[11]

Still, Tversky and Kahneman were unsatisfied. They desperately wanted their work to expand beyond the confines of professional journals and permeate the real world. Their motivation wasn't fame or fortune but their conviction that their theory could have a huge impact on society at large. What they were exposing cut to the heart of the everyday occurrences that changed people's lives: judges determining sentences, politicians deciding whether or not to go to war, educators designing reform, and health care providers making countless medical decisions.

During the early 1970s Kahneman and Tversky's work gained intensity. They narrowed their focus to how real-life decisions are made under the cloud of uncertainty, decisions involving loss and gain, decisions that matter the most in our everyday lives. They presented the following scenario to subjects:

Imagine you are a physician working in an Asian village, and 600 people have come down with a life-threatening disease. Two possible treatments exist. If you choose treatment A, you will save exactly 200 people. If you choose treatment B, there is a one-third chance that you will save all 600 people, and a two-thirds chance you will save no one. Which treatment do you choose, A or B?

Kahneman and Tversky found that most respondents (72 percent) chose treatment A, which saves exactly 200 people. They then presented another scenario to the same subjects:

You are a physician working in an Asian village, and 600 people have come down with a life-threatening disease. Two possible treatments exist. If you choose treatment C, exactly 400 people will die. If you choose treatment D, there is a one-third chance that no one will die, and a two-thirds chance that everyone will die. Which treatment do you choose, C or D?

In this case, they found that most respondents (78 percent) chose treatment D, which offers a one-third chance that no one will die.[12]

If you compare the two questions carefully, you will notice that they are identical. Treatments A and C are identical, and so are treatments B and D. The only thing that changes are the way the options are presented, or *framed*, for the subjects. What Kahneman and Tversky were showing was that people evaluate gains and losses differently. Thus, while treatments A and C are quantitatively identical, treatment A is framed as a gain (that is, 200 people are saved) while treatment C is framed as a loss (400 people will die). It appeared that people are more likely to take risks when it comes to losses than gains. In other words, people prefer a "sure thing" when it comes to a potential gain but are willing to take a chance if it involves avoiding a loss.

These sorts of data exposed a critical feature of real-life decision-making involving perceived risks and rewards. Kahneman and Tversky were finding that people are constantly making internal judgments that have little to do with purely rational statistical assessment. In other words, people incorporate all sorts of arbitrary, internal biases when a decision calls for them to be purely rational. We hate to lose, memories readily surface to remind us of other times we have lost. So just a little nudge—the framing of an option to remind us of the possibility of a loss rather than a gain, even when the odds are the same—will skew our decision. The reason we are more averse to loss than attracted to potential gain, reasoned Kahneman, is deeply embedded in our biology. "This is evolutionary. You would imagine in evolution that threats are more important than opportunities. And so it's a very general phenomenon that bad things sort of preempt or are stronger than good things in our experience. So loss aversion is a special case of something much broader."[13]

A powerful, real-world example of this comes from the way doctors present treatment options to patients. In the 1980s lung-cancer patients were given two choices: surgery or radiation. Surgery had a better chance of extending the patient's life but also came with a 10 percent risk of death. When presenting the surgical option, if the doctor said, "You have a 90 percent chance of surviving surgery," the patients opted for surgery over radiation 82 percent of the time. However, if the doctor said, "You have a 10 percent chance of dying from surgery," the patients opted for surgery over radiation 54 percent of the time. In other words, life-and-death decisions are not determined by a raw assessment of the probabilities alone. They are influenced by arbitrary descriptions—by how the doctor "frames" the options.

The implications of this data were enormous. Tversky and Kahneman summarized their finding in a 1979 publication titled "Prospect Theory: An Analysis of Decision under Risk."[14] The work was a masterpiece, a combination of Tversky's fierce mathematical logic and Kahneman's ability to tease out the internal wiring of the human mind. Few, if any, other psychological theories had such far-reaching and important implications. "Prospect theory turned out to be the most significant work we ever did," said Kahneman.[15] Academically, the implications of prospect theory were also profound: If prospect theory was right, economic theory was wrong.

Of course, Tversky and Kahneman never intended to pit their theory against the entire edifice of economic theory. Their intent was innocent and pure: simply to reveal the true nature of man. But like it or not, their theory forced economists to contend with this new image of the human brain. Until the advent of prospect theory, psychology had not had much of an influence on economics. Anyone looking closely, however, could see something remarkable: The whole structure of most economic theory was propped up by a single psychological assumption. Psychology didn't play much of a role in the math-heavy field of economics, but the role it *did* play was foundational. For a century, economic theory had been built around the single assumption that people are rational. They seek out the best information and act on it sensibly. They continually measure costs and benefits and maximize pleasure and profit. Now two psychologists were claiming that people were *not* entirely rational. They were disrupting an entire century of thought. They were claiming the economic human being was flawed and made errors when given information to act on. And what's more, that these errors were not random but systematic; they were predictable, they were *hardwired* into us.

In the 1960s an economic theory called the "efficient market hypothesis" was introduced by Eugene Fama at the University of Chicago. Fama claimed that asset prices—stocks and bonds, for example—fully reflect all available information at any moment in time. In other words, the work of frenzied efforts of legions of professional investors poring over companies' financials, newspaper articles, and annual reports, for every scrap of information they can find—even insider information—is all acted upon rationally by market participants. This results in an efficient market where at any moment the price of an asset reflected its true value. Given that all the information was available to all the experts, all the time, no one could gain an advantage. Much as water spilled from a cup onto the ground will inevitably seep nonpreferentially into every nook and crevice it can find, markets like the stock market inevitably smooth out in a continuum of "true" and "efficient" pricing.

Of course, the efficient market hypothesis, like all of economics, was founded on the assumption that humans are mostly rational and will make rational decisions about asset prices when presented with all the available data. Thousands of people bidding on a piece of art, a car, or a stock will "discover" the asset's worth. The theory predicted that no one could gain an advantage in any market because there was no advantage to gain.

As the years passed, the two theories existed side by side in an uncomfortable truce, the older economists seemingly content to ignore the implications of Tversky and Kahneman's prospect theory. The fact that psychology was still considered the backwater of the social sciences at the time made it somewhat easier to ignore. Economics, on the other hand, was the golden child of the social sciences and boasted large departments in prestigious institutions with lots of money. The separation was strange, especially considering that prospect theory was built on the tenet that economics *was* psychology. By 2010, however, "Prospect Theory" had become the second-most cited paper in all of economics and had given birth to a new field known as "behavioral economics." Even so, the "hard form" of efficient market theory was still the dominant economic theory taught in every university across the country. "People tried to ignore it," said one economist of Kahneman and Tversky's work. "Old economists never change their mind."[16]

Indeed, the old guard refused to bend. "The efficient market theory is one of the better models in the sense that it can be taken as true for every purpose I can think of. For investment purposes, there are very few investors that shouldn't behave as if markets are totally efficient," said Eugene Fama, who won the Nobel Prize in Economics in 2013 for his work developing the hypothesis.[17] "There is no other proposition in economics that has more solid empirical evidence supporting it than the Efficient Market Hypothesis. . . . In the literature of finance, accounting, and the economics of uncertainty, the Efficient Market Hypothesis is accepted as a fact of life," said Michael Jensen, the Jesse Isidor Straus Professor of Business Administration, Emeritus, at Harvard University.[18]

But here's the rub: They could not both be right. Human beings were either one or the other, rational or systematically irrational.

Who Was Right? "Six Sigma"

The first principle is that you must not fool yourself—and you are the easiest person to fool.

—RICHARD FEYNMAN

In the spring of 1995 Charles T. Munger took the podium at his alma mater, Harvard Law School. Munger was there to give a speech. Since his graduation from Harvard a few years after the end of the Second World War,

Munger—along with his partner, Warren Buffett—had amassed a fortune at the helm of well-known investment company Berkshire Hathaway.

What Munger and Buffet had accomplished was extraordinary in the history of American business. Starting in 1964—five years after Buffett and Munger first met at the Omaha Club in Omaha, Nebraska—Berkshire Hathaway has averaged a return of 20.9 percent per year, while the S&P 500 index has averaged 9.9 percent per year. Put another way: $10,000 invested with Berkshire in 1964 is worth about $240 million today, as opposed to only $1.5 million if invested in the S&P. And, remarkably, Munger and Buffett accomplished this mostly through buying and selling stocks.

Even more remarkable was the fact that they accomplished this when economists at America's best universities said it was not possible. According to the efficient market hypothesis, the accomplishment of Berkshire Hathaway was a fluke, nothing more than the product of random chance. What Munger and Buffett had achieved, economists said, could not last—it would average out in the end; it had to. They could not gain an advantage in the stock market because there was no advantage to gain. Yet Munger and Buffett had done the impossible. Year after year, Berkshire Hathaway defied the economists in their ivory towers. They were able to find the imperceptible ripples in the surface of the smooth continuum of "perfect" market valuations and exploit them. How did they do this? What was their secret? The Harvard audience, now sitting in hushed silence before Munger, wanted to know.

Anyone close to Charlie Munger had a deep appreciation for what he had achieved in his lifetime. His accomplishments were not the product of advantage or luck. His life did not track a charmed trajectory right up to the Harvard podium where he now stood. Rather, Munger had had to surmount turmoil and unimaginable tragedy that would take him to the brink of crushing despair and, ultimately, sculpt him into the person he became.

Charlie Munger was born in Omaha, Nebraska, in 1924. His father, Al Munger, the son of a federal judge and a respected lawyer in his own right, had modest expectations for life, yet was "successful in any sense that really matters," according to Charlie. "He had exactly the marriage and family life that was his highest hope. He had pals he loved and who loved him. . . .

He owned the best hunting dog in Nebraska, which meant a lot to him."[19] The family lived in modest circumstances at the western edge of Omaha. At the time, Omaha was the gateway to the open-ended vastness west of the Missouri River and was being settled by a richly diverse population. Neighborhoods of Germans, Italians, Irish, and Bohemians, together with a packing-house district, made up the town. The diversity didn't manifest in pockets of isolation; an overriding sense of community enveloped the citizens of Omaha—kids roamed freely, and doors were left unlocked. "There was no crime at all," said one resident. "There were better behavior standards in school and everywhere else," recalled Munger. Even among the richly diverse inhabitants of the midwestern town, the Munger family stood out. They had developed a sort of aristocratic, statesmanlike way about them, with high expectations and an emphasis on discipline and learning. Reading, expected in the Munger household, was a proclivity that would stay with Charlie his entire life. His children and grandchildren would often refer to him as "a book with legs."

As a boy Charlie read a sweeping range of subjects: science, medicine, and biographies of such great men as Benjamin Franklin, Thomas Jefferson, and Isaac Newton, for example. Reading about their lives wasn't just of passing interest to Munger; the pages he consumed established serious values for Munger to live by and infused in him the flair of an old-world gentlemen—duty, honor, and a strong sense of fair play were instilled as his core operating system at an extraordinarily young age. "I like the idea of filial piety, the idea that there are values that are taught and duties that come naturally," said Munger.[20]

Young Charlie's precociousness extended socially, too. As a child he was naturally drawn to people. "He was always gregarious, friendly, social," said a neighbor. In Omaha, the Munger family grew close to another neighborhood family, the Davises. Mr. Davis, a surgeon and good friend of Charlie's father, became friends with Charlie, too. "Dr. Ed Davis was my father's best friend, and I did something unusual for a person as young as I was—five, eight, twelve, fourteen—I became a friend of my father's friend. I got along very well with Ed Davis. We understood one another," said Munger.[21] Charlie's developing personality, with its deep reservoir of knowledge, however, was often perceived by others as arrogance. When an acquaintance claimed prosperity was making Munger pompous, an old law-school friend of Munger's defended him: "Nonsense, I knew him when he was young and poor; he was always pompous."[22] Yet those who knew him well knew that the arrogance was nothing more than a veneer; at his core Munger was a fiercely loyal friend.

After graduating from high school at the age of seventeen, Munger left Omaha to study mathematics at the University of Michigan in Ann Arbor. Even as a teenager, Munger had developed a unique pattern of thinking. If most people have a tendency to repeat destructive patterns, or at least fail to learn life's lessons, Munger was the exact opposite. Any lesson that he deemed meaningful was sealed into a mental vault. Once he learned a lesson, it was learned forever. In Ann Arbor, an introductory physics class his freshman year made just such an impression. "For me, it was a total eye-opener," he would later confess.[23] In its search for fundamental physical truths, the field of physics employed a methodology that, by necessity, excluded human bias. For Munger, this was a revelation. It wasn't necessarily physics itself that captivated Munger, but the *process* of doing physics that entranced him. To reveal nature's laws, reasoned Munger, was to achieve a kind of exalted purity of thought, to scrub clean the messiness of the human mind.

However, the high-minded academic lessons would come to an abrupt end. A year into his studies, the Japanese bombed Pearl Harbor. Only a semester into his sophomore year, with battles now raging throughout Europe, Munger felt the call of patriotic duty and enlisted in the Army Air Corps only a few days after his nineteenth birthday. Like so many young American boys, Munger suddenly was thrust into a future of uncertainty. He recalls a poignant conversation he had with a fellow soldier during basic training as they lay in a tent somewhere in Utah. Their new reality stripped away all pretensions from the conversation as their circumstances led them to reflect on what truly mattered in life. "I want a lot of children, a house with lots of books, and enough money to have freedom," Munger remembers saying.[24]

Of course, expectations about the future were best kept modest for an enlisted private in 1942. But Munger was abruptly spared from the battlefield when he was ordered to take the Army General Classification Test. A score of 120 on the test automatically qualified a soldier to be commissioned as an officer. Munger scored 149. He was shipped off to the University of New Mexico and then to the California Institute of Technology in Pasadena to study meteorology. Munger liked California immediately. If being raised in the Midwest had put any sort of noose around his sense of possibility, the electric energy and air of boundless potential in California removed it. At the time, Munger's sister, Mary, enrolled at nearby Scripps College, was also living in Pasadena. She introduced him to the daughter of a Pasadena shoe-store owner named Nancy Huggins. The spark was instantaneous. Charlie and Nancy's impulsive whirlwind romance, intensified by youth and the intoxicating new environment—and the uncertainty of war—captivated them. At the age of twenty-one, Munger and Nancy impulsively married.

Munger now needed a career. This he approached in a more pragmatic manner. He had recognized early on that he lacked the mechanical skills necessary for a profession such as surgery, and instinctively knew his skill in mathematics was not on par with the upper ranks. So he settled on his father and grandfather's profession: the law. Using the GI bill, Munger applied to Harvard Law School, his grandfather's alma mater. With the help of family connections he nudged his way in. However, the type of profound revelations he had discovered in classes like freshman physics, Munger realized, were not to be found in law school. "I came to Harvard Law School very poorly educated, with desultory work habits and no college degree," he said. And, according to Munger, he left not much better off. "I hurried through school," he said, "I don't think I'm a fair example [of an ideal education]."[25]

After Munger graduated from Harvard Law School, he and Nancy and their new son, Teddy, returned to Nancy's hometown of Pasadena and settled in to start their lives. They chose California over Nebraska because it offered greater opportunity for Munger to realize his lofty ambitions. Los Angeles was undergoing dazzling post-war growth. So, too, was Munger's career. He became a partner in a successful law practice, joined LA's exclusive clubs, and began establishing important connections and friendships that would anchor him in the city. His family also grew, with the addition of two daughters, Molly and Wendy.

On the surface the Mungers appeared to be thriving, but below the surface things were not well—his whirlwind marriage was unraveling. In 1953 divorce was considered a disgrace, and Charlie and Nancy knew this. But their incompatibility, the fighting, and the silences had become intolerable to both. They agreed to end the marriage. Nancy stayed in the house, and Munger moved into a room at the University Club that his daughter later described as "dreadful." She also remembered the beat-up yellow Pontiac he drove. While still reeling from the repercussions of divorce, they received devastating news. Their son Teddy was diagnosed with leukemia—a disease that in the 1950s was 100 percent fatal. Day by day Munger watched his son fade. With no insurance, he was left with mounting medical bills. A friend recalled that Munger would go to the cancer ward of the hospital and hold his son for long stretches. Then, distraught and feeling helpless, he would walk the streets of Pasadena and cry. Still, without fail, he would steel himself to cheerfully pick up his daughters from Nancy's house every Saturday in his beat-up Pontiac. The stress was almost unbearable. By the time Teddy died, Munger had lost fifteen pounds.

The life he had envisioned as a private lying in a tent now seemed further away than ever. Yet, despite the overriding despair, Munger was able to analyze his situation objectively, learn from it, and file away another of life's lessons into his mental vault: "You should never, when facing some unbelievable tragedy, let one tragedy increase into two or three through your failure of will."[26]

Munger's daughter, Molly, remembers a lightness, a kind of buoyancy her dad always conveyed, even in the face of pain and difficult circumstances. His optimism and enthusiasm for the future, she remembered, were always bubbling just below the surface. "Now I see he was almost broke. I knew he drove an awful car. But I never thought he was anything but a big success. Why did I think that? He just had this air—everything was to be first class, going to be great. He was going to put a patio on Edgewood Drive. He was going to get a boat for the island. He was going to build a house, build apartments. He had these enthusiasms for his projects and his future—his present. It was not as if you had to deny yourself in the present for the future. The focus was on how interesting things are today, how much fun to see them built. It was so much fun being in the moment. That's what he always communicated."[27]

Daniel Kahneman once said, "When action is needed, optimism, even of the mildly delusional variety, may be a good thing."[28] Indeed, Munger didn't waste any time indulging in self-pity. His incessant optimism for the future, even if mildly delusional, carried him through the darkest moments. A year after Teddy died he remarried—to another Nancy, also recently divorced. His law practice was flourishing, and, through a series of real-estate development deals, Munger had accumulated $1.4 million. "That was a lot of money at the time," he recalled. Nancy brought two young boys into the family, Munger had his two girls, and together they had four more children. By his forties Munger had realized his goal: financial independence, a large family, a beautiful home with the constant noise of kids and friends, and stacks of books spilling off numerous bookshelves.

Munger had also developed a unique way of looking at problems—a unique way of looking at life for that matter. He had developed a habit of approaching problems in the inverse: Instead of asking how he could make a situation *better*, he would flip it and ask what is making it *worse*, and work to fix or simply avoid that. "Problems are usually easier to solve if you turn them around in reverse. In other words, if you want to help India, the question you should ask is not: How should I help India? It should be: What's doing the worst damage in India? And how do I avoid it?" When asked to give an opinion about something, the first thing Munger would do was make a mental list of all the counterarguments to his opinion. Only then would he offer an opinion. In life, he first cataloged the things that would make his life worse—sloth, unreliability, extreme ideology, and a self-serving bias, for example—and then tried to avoid them. Indeed, life had taught him this lesson the hard way. "Anytime you find yourself drifting into self-pity, I don't care what the cause, your child could be dying of cancer, self-pity is not going to improve the situation. . . . It's a ridiculous way to behave," said Munger. By focusing on how to not make a situation worse, Munger realized, it tended to passively make it better. His method was a systems approach that operated in the negative; a system that didn't focus on the light, but rather where the shadows would be cast. "You can say who wants to go through life anticipating trouble? Well I did. All my life I've gone through anticipating trouble . . . and I've had a favored life. . . . It didn't make me unhappy to anticipate trouble all the time, and be ready to perform adequately if trouble came, it didn't hurt me at all, in fact it helped me."[29]

Munger's intellectual doppelgänger, strangely, was also from Omaha, Nebraska. That a midwestern town would incubate two of America's most unique minds seems improbable, yet virtually every mutual friend of Warren Buffett's and Charlie Munger's was awestruck by their similarities. In the late 1950s Buffett had visited the Davis home to ask if they would like to put money into a new partnership he was forming. As he gave his pitch Mrs. Davis listened intently, asking many good questions, while Mr. Davis, Charlie's childhood friend, sat in the corner listening but not saying much. Later Buffett recalled, "When we got all the way through, Dorothy [Mrs. Davis] turned to Eddie and said, 'What do you think?' Eddie said, 'Let's give him a hundred thousand dollars.' In a much more polite way, I said, 'Dr. Davis, you know, I'm delighted to get this money. But you weren't really paying a lot of attention to me while I was talking. How come you're doing it?' And he said, 'Well, you remind me of Charlie Munger.' I said, 'Well, I don't know who this Charlie Munger is, but I really like him.'"[30]

Most of us have a moment in our lives that is defining, where everything from that moment on is changed. For Charlie Munger and Warren Buffett that moment was on a Friday in the summer of 1959. Buffett was six years younger than Munger, so they had never crossed paths in school and socialized in different circles. Mutual friends, however, finally insisted that they meet. Munger's father had recently died, and he was back in Omaha from LA to settle his estate. A meeting was arranged at the Omaha Club, an exclusive private club where the city's elite came to do business. The arched doors opened, and, dressed more for the big city than for Omaha, Munger walked in and up the curved mahogany staircase to meet the kid with a crew cut he had heard so much about.

Soon after the introductions and usual pleasantries, Munger and Buffett launched into a more substantive discussion. The friends who had arranged the meeting sat listening raptly as the pace of the conversation quickened. It was clear to all that Munger had found his intellectual soul mate. As had Buffett. The relationship was born of their shared love of business, shared madness for boundless conversations, and ambitions that ran wildly beyond the usual for two kids from Omaha. Just as Kahneman and Tversky had found, it was the joy of sharing a single mind.

"Warren, what do you do specifically?" asked Munger, during a lull in the conversation. Buffett explained that he formed partnerships where people put in their money and paid Buffett a fee to manage it. In 1957, explained Buffett, his partnership had made over 10 percent, while the stock market had dropped over 8 percent. The next year the partnership shot up over 40 percent. So far Buffett had made over $80,000 in fees. Munger was entranced by the idea of forming a similar partnership back in LA. "I had a considerable passion to get rich. Not because I wanted Ferraris—I wanted the independence. I desperately wanted it. I thought it was undignified to have to send invoices to other people. I don't know where I got that notion from, but I had it," recalled Munger.[31]

Munger returned to LA, but his new relationship with Buffett continued to evolve. Daily hour-long phone conversations turned into daily two-hour conversations. When Munger's wife asked why he was paying so much attention to the kid from Omaha, Munger replied, "You don't understand. That is no ordinary human being." But the business arrangement between Munger and Buffett was not formalized right away. Rather, it developed over time—discussion after discussion, deal after deal. But something else was happening that went beyond traditional business relationships. In one conversation after the next, Munger and Buffett were developing an intellectual framework for investing. The framework that grew from their time together was more psychological than analytical, steeped in a deep appreciation of human nature—what made people tick—rather than in economic theory. They were pinning down the variables that mattered and identifying those that did not. In doing so they were forced to grapple with their *own* human nature.

Right away they recognized that one of the most important qualities in an investor is temperament. "Investing is not a game where the guy with the 160 IQ beats the guy with the 130 IQ. Once you have ordinary intelligence, what you need is the temperament to control the urges that get other people into trouble in investing," said Buffett.[32] They were each observing their own mind—its urges, irrationalities and quirks, and mapping out the ways *not* to trust it. "How do you learn to be a great investor? First of all, you have to understand your own nature," said Munger.[33]

They noticed how others made mistakes. Usually, they observed, mistakes were made by investors not recognizing the difference between what they *truly* knew and what they *believed* they knew—wandering into areas outside of their core expertise. To avoid this, they resolved to draw tight borders around their own competence, thus avoiding the pitfalls outside of it. "The game of investing," said Munger, "is one of making better predictions about the future than other people. How are you going to do that? One way is to limit your tries to areas of competence."[34]

As it logged dizzying returns year after year, Berkshire Hathaway became a thorn in the side of the efficient market hypothesis. Because Berkshire's stunning returns were "impossible," reasoned the economists, they must be a product of luck. It stands to reason, the economists said, that out of the massive universe of investors, some would rise to the top due to nothing more than sheer luck. A friend of mine who has a PhD in economics from MIT described it this way: "Well, if you have a stadium with 50,000 people in it and ask them all to flip coins repeatedly, a few in the stadium will get heads or tails 15 or 20 times in a row." This is how economists explained the anomaly of Berkshire Hathaway. Berkshire Hathaway was, in their minds, an accident bound to happen.

During the 1970s, '80s, and into the '90s, the casual observer watching Berkshire Hathaway pile up mountains of money was convinced they had some secret algorithm, a highly sophisticated methodology for picking stocks. In truth, their system was shockingly simple. For the most part, it was simply to know their own thought patterns well enough to distinguish what was knowable from what was not—and thus avoid mistakes. "It is remarkable how much long-term advantage people like us have gotten by trying to be consistently not stupid, instead of trying to be very intelligent. There must be some wisdom in the folk saying, 'It's the strong swimmers that drown,'" said Munger.[35]

Over the decades Munger and Buffett watched the formation of such companies as Long-Term Capital Management, replete with the brightest mathematicians in the world, who developed impossibly sophisticated algorithms to predict the market, only to fail miserably. The dot-com boom came and went. They listened to the assertions that they had become outdated relics who didn't understand the "new" internet economy. And yet they continued to beat the market.

"Esoteric Gibberish"

Munger stood before the Harvard audience. It was bigger than he expected. They, too, wanted to know the secret. How had he accomplished what Nobel Prize–winning economists said was impossible? Munger was about to tell them. He swiveled his head as he scanned the audience. And he began:

"Although I am very interested in the subject of human misjudgment—and lord knows I've created a good bit of it—I don't think I've created my full statistical share, and I think that one of the reasons was I tried to do something about this terrible ignorance I left the Harvard Law School with. When I saw this patterned irrationality, which was so extreme, and I had no theory or anything to deal with it, but I could see that it was extreme, and I could see that it was patterned, I just started to create my own system of psychology, partly by casual reading, but largely from personal experience, and I used that pattern to help me get through life."[36]

For the next hour and a quarter Munger rattled through a homespun list of twenty-four cognitive biases he had documented over a lifetime. In long conversations with Buffett he had made dispassionate observations of human behavior—mulling over their own lives, the Great Depression, the Second World War, the irrational market booms and busts, they observed and learned and talked. Like Kahneman and Tversky, Munger and Buffett were students of human nature. Together they saw the absurdity in the pillar of modern economic theory. The efficient market theorists said stock prices were a smooth continuum of perfectly efficient pricing. Kahneman and Tversky claimed that if you looked closely, there were ripples in the continuum; ripples due to the fickleness of human nature. Munger and Buffet had found the ripples—and exploited them.

"Now let's talk about efficient market theory," Munger said to the Harvard crowd. "A wonderful economic doctrine that had a long vogue in spite of the experience of Berkshire Hathaway. In fact, one of the economists who won—he shared a Nobel Prize—and as he looked at Berkshire Hathaway year after year, which people would throw in his face as saying maybe the market isn't quite as efficient as you think, he said, 'Well, it's a two-sigma event.' And then he said we were a three-sigma event. And then he said we were a four-sigma event. And he finally got up to six sigmas—better to add a sigma than change a theory, just because the evidence comes in differently. And, of course, when this share of a Nobel Prize went into money management himself, he sank like a stone."[37]

In 2016 Berkshire Hathaway had grown to the fourth-largest company by market capitalization in the United States. Only Microsoft, Alphabet, and Apple had larger valuations. "I have a name for people who went to the extreme efficient market theory—which is 'bonkers,'" said Munger. "It is an intellectually consistent theory that enabled them to do pretty mathematics. So, I understand its seductiveness to people with large mathematical gifts. It just had a difficulty in that the fundamental assumption did not tie properly to reality."[38]

In the end Munger and Buffett knew that on any given day the stock market echoes nothing more than the average price of millions of individual transactions. Each transaction reflects mostly how the buyer and seller *feel* about the price at that moment in time. Buffett and Munger knew instinctively that these transactions were not made after careful fundamental analysis, even by the experts. They recognized that the pillar believed to be supporting the efficient market hypothesis was an illusion. Investors—consumed by a lollapalooza of cognitive discord—could convince themselves of anything. Indeed, investors were a *highly* irrational group. But it was a patterned irrationality. At Berkshire they installed an internal system. Emotion, greed, fear, hope, panic—every useless emotion that gripped the masses was extirpated from their minds. The system distilled into one simple rule that would gain them a huge advantage over time: Be fearful when others are greedy and be greedy when others are fearful. To Buffett and Munger, financial metrics and equations were less important than simply gauging the collective emotional pulse of the market's participants. And then running in the opposite direction of the irrational herd.

For the experts and average Americans, however, this seemingly obvious heuristic—the one both Munger and Buffett have been shouting from the rooftops for decades—is almost impossible to practice. There are very few who can resist the combined forces of greed and fear. Indeed, this has been known for a long time. In 1975 Charles Ellis, a consultant to professional money managers, wrote an article titled "The Loser's Game" that showed that even so-called "expert" money managers failed to beat the market 85 percent of the time.[39]

It's even worse today. Over the last fifteen years 92.2 percent of large cap funds, 95.4 percent of mid-cap funds and 93.2 percent of small cap funds, all managed by experts, have failed to beat a humble S&P 500 index fund. In 2017 Warren Buffett estimated conservatively that pension funds, endowments, and wealthy individuals had lost $100 billion over the preceding decade to expert money managers who promised to beat the market. According to Buffett, the root of this problem comes from a cognitive bias. "The wealthy are accustomed to feeling that it is their lot in life to get the best food, schooling, entertainment, housing, plastic surgery, sports tickets, you name it. Their money, they feel, should buy them something superior compared to what the masses receive. The financial 'elites'—wealthy individuals, pension funds, endowments and the like—have great trouble meekly signing up for a financial product or service that is available as well to people investing only a few thousand dollars."[40] Buffett calls the advice these experts give "esoteric gibberish."

Here it's worth pausing for a moment of consideration. Because, as you drive across this country, you can see that the resources bestowed on these "experts" dispensing their "esoteric gibberish" is enormous. They are everywhere. In every city, high-rise tower, and downtown office building. Legions of investment specialists and financial advisors pitching mutual funds, hedge funds, and individual stocks to pension funds, endowments, wealthy individuals, and the general public—clerks, tradespeople, teachers, and other hardworking people. They look the part, too, clothed in expensive suits, sitting in fancy offices with mahogany desks, CNBC playing on the TV in the waiting room. This is serious business, the optics say, and these are serious people. But, just like the baseball scouts Billy Beane fired, these legions of experts have constructed an edifice of fiction—an illusion of wisdom, expertise, and intuition. If you look closely, there is nothing. The numbers don't lie. Still, though their "esoteric gibberish" loses to a passive S&P index fund over 90 percent of the time, by the millions we are deceived. It is a massive financial fiction imposed on the real, hardworking people who *do* produce a net benefit for society. Still, they exist. This is the power of cognitive bias.

Yet, for the average person, bypassing the experts and trying to beat the market on their own is an even worse idea. Average investors lose to the market by a *huge* margin. Over the last 30 years an individual American investing in stocks has averaged 3.79 percent per year while the S&P 500 has averaged 11.06 percent per year. And it seems our minds have countless ways to deceive ourselves into continuing our poor performance. Humans are saddled with an *overconfidence bias*, meaning we consistently believe we are better than we are. We exaggerate our own abilities despite overwhelming evidence to the contrary. In one study, 81 percent of new business owners thought they themselves had a good chance of succeeding, but when asked about their peers gave them only a 39 percent chance.

One way around all of this is to embrace Munger's "inverse rule" of problem solving and simply not try to beat the market at all. A sort of cognitive-bias hack in investing that is gaining in popularity is a process called *indexing*. Buying a passive fund that tracks an index like the S&P 500 is a way to bypass the potential for unnecessary loss due to the human mind's failings. Buffett agrees: "Consistently buy an S&P 500 low-cost index fund, I think it's the thing that makes the most sense practically all of the time." Buffett described Jack Bogle, the creator of the index fund, as a "hero." Investor and author Tony Robbins wrote, "When you own an index fund, you're also protected against all the downright dumb, mildly misguided or merely unlucky decisions that active fund managers are liable to make."[41] In short, investing in an index fund will save you from yourself and the experts.

How difficult is it to do what Buffett and Munger have done? To beat the market (or the S&P index) consistently, decade after decade? Buffett offers a guess: "There are, of course, some skilled individuals who are highly likely to outperform the S&P over long stretches. In my lifetime, though, I've identified—early on—only 10 or so professionals that I expected would accomplish this feat."[42]

The "secret" of Berkshire Hathaway's success was in the title of Munger's Harvard talk itself: "The Psychology of Human Misjudgment." He and Buffett stuck to Feynman's first principle that "You must not fool yourself—and you are the easiest person to fool." They identified and avoided the myriad cognitive biases inherent in all of us. They learned their own minds. And, as Billy Beane would do years later for the Oakland A's, they implemented a system that bypassed the most common misjudgments.

While Tversky and Kahneman were reshaping the social sciences during the 1970s, '80s, and early '90s, Berkshire Hathaway provided a parallel, real-world example of everything Tversky and Kahneman were saying. Berkshire's success was a challenge to prevailing belief: the masses, even the experts, are *not* rational. They are systemically *irrational*. Berkshire offered seductive proof that the world as viewed by social scientists was upside down. While the social scientists claimed the broad swath of the population acted rationally, Berkshire was proof that they did not. Perhaps most importantly, Berkshire demonstrated how humanity could do better, be more efficient, and operate with less waste. Other institutions should have been paying attention. Berkshire's success was an epiphany that implementing systems to counteract cognitive biases could result in dramatically improved outcomes. It seemed obvious to Buffett and Munger that their market competitors were stuck in a cognitive closed loop, as if the biases that prevented them from beating the market also made them incapable of recognizing the flaws in their own logic. Yet if that loop could somehow be opened, almost every societal institution stood to gain: education, finance, government, health care, corporate America, even people's personal lives. "Making systems work is the great task of my generation of physicians and scientists," observed surgeon and author Atul Gawande. "But I would go further and say that making systems work, whether in health care, education, climate change, making a pathway out of poverty, is the great task of our generation as a whole. In every field, knowledge has exploded, but it has brought complexity, it has brought specialization. And we've come to a place where we have no choice."[43]

Indeed, one might imagine that if there were any institution able to identify cognitive biases and systematically build a framework to avoid them it would be the institution of health care. After all, there the stakes are measured not in winning games or piling up money but in human lives. Our health care system, perhaps more than any other enterprise, stands to gain from this approach. Because, in the end, medicine is supposed to be an exercise of removing bias, dispelling human folly, and systematically measuring which pills, procedures, and therapies work and which do not. Yet because it is an institution so irrevocably entangled with our deepest hopes and fears— bound to the essence of what it means to be human—it is fertile ground for cognitive biases to germinate and thrive.

CHAPTER 2

How Health Care Became a "Culture of Inefficiency"

Nobody knew health care could be so complicated.

—PRESIDENT DONALD TRUMP, *2017*

The history of medicine reveals a fitful struggle between empirical measurement (the clinical trial) and a physician's intuition—a struggle that is still with us today. The story of William Halsted, who, in the late 1800s pioneered the radical mastectomy in the treatment of breast cancer, epitomizes this struggle. Halsted's story is a poignant example of the fallibility of humans and the delicate tightrope that the practice of medicine can be. Halsted's name will be forever attached to the best and the worst side of medicine. He was a saint who introduced to America critical surgical techniques that would save an untold number of lives; and he was on the wrong side of history, putting faith in an seductively intuitive procedure that turned out to be unnecessary and caused an enormous amount of needless suffering. The story of the radical mastectomy is tangled up in the story of the clinical trial and the arrival of epidemiology in medicine. It is a story of medicine's ongoing struggle to recognize the value of data over human intuition, and of how much further we still have to go.

The Perfectionist

In the fall of 1852 William Stewart Halsted was born the son of a wealthy New York City textile importer. From his days as a Yale undergrad there were no obvious clues that young Halsted would go on to earn the title "father of American surgery." Athletically built and handsome, Halsted was far more interested in athletics than academics. He was the captain of the football team, played baseball, rowed crew, and even dabbled in gymnastics. Indeed, the Yale library had no record of him ever checking out a single book. If there was any hint of the brilliant surgeon to surface, it came much later in a prosaic statement written by Halsted himself regarding his college days at Yale: "Devoted myself solely to athletics in college. In senior year purchased Gray's *Anatomy* and Dalton's *Physiology* and studied them with interest."[1]

The obsession Halsted had with athletics seemed to be transferred to medicine all at once. He attended medical school in the 1870s at Columbia and started a surgical internship at Bellevue Hospital in New York City while still in medical school. It was there that Halsted began to develop a reputation for working a heroic number of hours with little sleep, often culminating in something like a nervous breakdown. This would necessitate a period of convalescence, after which he would return, only to repeat the same exhausting cycle. At the same time he was developing a reputation for surgical excellence, an insatiable appetite for learning, and perfectionism, a quality that would often blur into the realm of neurosis. "He was so fastidious about his dress that he had his shirts made at Charvet in Paris in large, large quantities, and then he sent his shirts back to Paris to be laundered because he felt no one in America could wash and iron his shirts. When he made coffee, he would pick coffee beans for size and color, and they had to all match precisely before he ground them and used them. And it goes on forever. That's the way he lived his life," said his biographer.[2]

When his internship at Bellevue ended, Halsted boarded a steamship to cross the Atlantic for a two-year tour of study in Europe. In the late nineteenth century, the medical clinics in Germany, France, Austria, and England were percolating with innovation. Medicine in America, however, remained a patchwork of trial and error: bloodletting; trephining (boring a hole in the skull "to release disease"); removal of the ovaries, testicles, and adrenal glands; leeching; and purging. In Europe, however, new and innovative procedures, medications, and surgical techniques were being forged with breakneck speed.

In the fall of 1878 Halsted arrived in Vienna. From there, he embarked on a whirlwind tour of the Austrian and German clinics. He bounced from Vienna to Würzburg, Leipzig, Berlin, Kiel, Halle, and Hamburg and then back again to Vienna. The vibrancy and creativity of European medicine was an epiphany to Halsted. He ravenously studied the newest discoveries in pathology, bacteriology, anatomy, and physiology. He learned the skillful use of a microscope and the emerging foundations of sterile surgical technique. He voraciously absorbed the latest surgical procedures and technologies. For Halsted, the tour was an awakening. When he returned home in the fall of 1880, he was a changed man, now infused with a feverish zeal to spread his new knowledge to America. He set off at a blistering pace founding new departments, working as a surgeon at Bellevue, Roosevelt, Presbyterian, and Charity hospitals, teaching anatomy at Columbia, and consulting other physicians on the procedures he had learned in Europe.

Despite Halsted's desperate attempt (and the efforts of others like him) to elevate medicine in America, it lagged far behind. Conditions in the New York hospitals were appalling. Sutures made from the guts of sheep, cows, and cats hung from dripping surgical wounds that stained the floors with blood. Dirty scalpels were often wiped with dirty rags just before surgery. While in Europe Halsted had been exposed to a new idea put forth by the brilliant chemist Louis Pasteur, who suggested that microorganisms might be the cause behind many illnesses, including plague, influenza, malaria, typhoid, and tuberculosis. Indeed, infectious disease was far and away humanity's number-one killer. In England, a shy, unassuming doctor named Joseph Lister had extended Pasteur's logic to the surgical theater. Perhaps, reasoned Lister, these disease-causing microorganisms were behind the surgical infections that killed so many patients after major operations.

Halsted was captivated by Pasteur's "germ theory." Lister had already begun documenting reduced infection rates when surgical wounds were dressed with bandages soaked in bacteria-killing carbolic acid. But the American physicians remained unconvinced by Pasteur's strange theory. Halsted pleaded with the staff at Bellevue that a sterile surgical room should be built, but, unconvinced about germ theory, they "laughed him out of the room." Undeterred, he raised $10,000 from friends, enough to erect his own private surgical tent in an unused area of the hospital. Gas and water were piped inside, a maple floor said to be "as fine as a bowling alley" was laid down, a central gutter installed, and ventilation and lighting put in.

Halsted's tent was a symbolic beacon of enlightenment in a sea of ignorance. Inside the tent, Halsted's perfectionist nature took over. He compulsively considered every possibility for lurking bacteria to infect his patients' surgical wounds. He incorporated rubber gloves, sterile instruments, and handwashing. Witnessing his success, his colleagues begrudgingly began to follow his lead. "He ranks among the first, if not the first to develop in this country on the basis of these principles a consistent and thorough antiseptic technique," wrote a colleague.[3] His practices would become standardized and taught to medical students across the country. Before Halsted's aseptic procedures, almost every surgical patient developed a serious infection; half of them died. After Halsted's practices became broadly adopted, the infection rate dropped precipitously.

The Radical Mastectomy Begins

For centuries, all disease was thought to emanate through some combination of mysterious, intangible, and invisible forces—imbalanced humors, spirits, fits, or hysterias. And medical intervention reflected this nebulous understanding. It first appeared as an assortment of made-up rituals purported to correct some ill-defined imbalance: purging, leeching, and bleeding and feeding to or injecting patients with inconceivable concoctions of plants, herbs, extractions, blood, and metals.

In the mid-1800s, a few decades before Halsted set foot on European soil, a new foundational understanding of disease was reverberating across the continent. First, in 1838, two scientists working in Germany proposed that all living organisms were made from a single unit: the cell. This modest suggestion inspired the brilliant German biologist Rudolf Virchow to ask the next logical question: How did all the cells that make up an organism arise in the first place? The answer, claimed Virchow, was from each other. *"Omnis cellula e cellula,"* wrote Virchow in 1855—Latin for "All cells come from cells."[4]

This basic tenet of biology is obvious now, but in 1855 the concept was revolutionary. For every branch of science, the discovery of a unique fundamental unit establishes a foundation from which to build. For chemistry, it was the atom; for optics, the photon; for particle physics, the subatomic particle; for genetics, the nucleotides in DNA. Virchow's modest statement, "all cells come from cells," abruptly launched medicine forward into a new era. It set in motion the birth of *pathology*, the understanding of how disease—all disease—begins at the level of the cell and progresses outward, marching up a hierarchy of functionality to tissues, then organs.

The new "cell theory" championed by Virchow would soon allow him to clarify one of the most mysterious maladies afflicting humans in recorded history: cancer. What Virchow saw under his microscope was *omnis cellula e cellula* in hyperdrive. Cancer was uncontrolled, pathological cellular division. Cancer appeared an extreme version of this new law—every cell arises from another cell—as if the normal checkpoints and controls internal to the cell had somehow been broken. Cancer was a disordered version of our fundamental units, Virchow reasoned.

With this new appreciation of cancer sweeping across Europe, the corollaries were easy to follow. If cancer was uncontrolled cellular division, then a tumor must begin with a few cells, or even a single cell, starting at a single location. And, if so, perhaps the tumor could be removed with a surgeon's knife before it began its relentless arc of growth. But as surgeons attempted to excise tumors with their scalpels, a vexing problem kept resurfacing: recurrence of the cancer. The surgeons would remove a tumor only to have the cancer return, this time seemingly more aggressive.

In 1860 an English surgeon named Charles Moore began keeping meticulous track of the location of recurrences after the surgical removal of breast tumors. It was a project born of frustration. Why did the cancer come back so often, he wanted to know? And where in the body was it coming from? Soon he noticed a pattern. Most of the recurrences appeared to spring forth near the surgical margins, as if his knife had traveled too conservative a path. To cut too cautiously, Moore warned other surgeons, was a "mistaken kindness."[5] Another Englishman, William Handley, performed research that tracked the path of Virchow's hyper-dividing cells in breast cancer. According to Handley, breast cancer followed a "centrifugal" pattern, emanating from a single location outward in all directions, following the lymphatic channels as it went. Out of Moore and Handley's observations arose a powerful corollary: To prevent recurrence, the surgeon must cut farther out from the primary tumor in all directions.

While in Germany, Halsted and Virchow did cross paths. And although the extent of their time together is unclear, it is evident that Halsted absorbed the theoretical basis of Virchow's powerful new biological dictum. In Germany Halsted worked alongside Richard von Volkmann, who fully appreciated the significance of Virchow, Moore, and Handley's hypothesis and had already begun more aggressive surgeries—expanding the surgical margins, cutting out more tissue, even removing some muscle tissue under the breast.

Yet, even after Volkmann's aggressive mastectomies, a large percentage of women experienced both recurrence of the disease and death. Halsted extended the seductive line of reasoning further. Surgeons must extend the margins even more, he reasoned, and remove the "centrifugal" lanes through which the cancer traveled. He developed a procedure called the "radical mastectomy," which involved removing *all* the breast tissue as well as the overlying skin, the pectoralis muscles, and all the axillary lymph nodes. It was a severely disfiguring and painful procedure, leaving women with caved-in shoulders and collapsed chests, unable to move the arm on the affected side forward. With a severely impaired lymphatic drainage system, fluid would build up in the women's arms, often causing them to swell to twice the normal size. Recovery from the brutal procedure was measured in months, even years. Yet the women exposed to Halsted's more aggressive surgery *still* experienced recurrences. Despite Halsted's exhaustive procedure, the disease would often find a hiding spot and smolder there undetected until again leaping forth to resume its unrelenting growth and spread.

Undeterred, Halsted and his students returned to their linear line of reasoning: According to the centrifugal theory, as the disease cartwheeled outward through the lymphatic system, the surgeons should cartwheel their knives out even further, extirpating the only path the cancer could follow. They would do what centuries of armies had done when trying to isolate the enemy: destroy the roads, blow up the bridges, and scorch the earth behind them. For Halsted, the centrifugal theory was his guiding logic, his surgical North Star. And the vague notion of how cancer spread extrapolated outward into more and more aggressive surgeries.

Now, Halsted and his students removed the chains of lymph nodes under and above the collarbone, into the neck, and deep within the chest. Some surgeons in Europe, inspired by the same logic, had even gone so far as to remove the entire shoulder and ribs. If the disease was to return, it would not be due to lack of surgical resolve on their part; there would be no "mistaken kindness."

Theories of how cancer spread aside, there was only one reason the surgeons subjected women to the grisly procedures: saving, or, at the very least, extending their lives. In the spring of 1898, at the annual conference of the American Surgical Association in New Orleans, Halsted presented the results of seventy-six of his breast cancer patients whom he had treated with his radical mastectomy. At first the presentation sounded promising. Halsted was able to reduce the number of local recurrences when compared to the numbers reported from other clinics, such as Volkmann's in Germany. But there was another story to be told.

Deeply anchored in Halsted's mind—and the minds of the surgeons in his audience—was the centrifugal theory of cancer. Cancer didn't leap outward, or flow in the circulatory system to distant sites, bypassing the chains of lymph nodes that Halsted and his colleagues were diligently striving to harvest. Rather, it marched outward slowly, ploddingly, in an orderly manner—or so it was believed. If Halsted was preventing local recurrence, then his aggressive surgery should catch more of the malignant cells as they fanned outward. In a certain percentage of cases, it followed, the cancer had marched from its original location in the breast to the lymph nodes in the neck or deep in the chest, only to be caught "just in time" by Halsted's far-reaching knife. This was the only reason to justify disfiguring untold numbers of afflicted women. Ostensibly, these patients would be saved, and this would translate into a greater percentage of overall lives saved by the procedure—the only statistic that *truly* mattered. When Halsted presented the overall survival data, however, his radical mastectomy suddenly sounded much less radical. Of the seventy-six patients, *almost half* had died within three years of the surgery. The radical mastectomy might be able to eke out a slight decrease in the number of women experiencing a local recurrence; however, the death rate, the only number that mattered, appeared unchanged—as if the disease was somehow one step ahead of Halsted's aggressive knife.

The Rise of the Clinical Trial

If Halsted was trying to justify the radical mastectomy that night in New Orleans, he fell remarkably short. The survival data he presented had a conspicuous problem: It wasn't *compared* to anything. The data only raised more questions. Was the hyper-aggressive surgery saving anyone? Could a much less aggressive operation achieve similar results? Had Halsted's trial compared the radical surgery to a simpler form of surgery it might have revealed something useful. In truth, Halsted's presentation highlighted a problem that had plagued medicine since the dawn of time: *measurement*. Critically, how to measure the effectiveness of a medical intervention.

In reality, however, for much of medicine's history measurement mattered little. There was nothing *to* measure. Medicine consisted of little more than a cacophony of made-up salves, tinctures, mixtures, and such medieval procedures as bloodletting that were based on ritual, superstition, and spiritual belief. Hippocrates wrote that a "physician's judgment mattered more than any external measurement." And perhaps the best judgments a physician could make at the time were also suggested by Hippocrates: (1) "First do no harm"; and (2) "To do nothing is also a good remedy."[6]

One thousand years after Hippocrates, civilizations had risen and fallen, wars had been fought, empires won and lost, and, still, medicine had yet to make much meaningful progress. In the fourteenth century Italian Renaissance poet Petrarch, in a correspondence to Boccaccio, relayed a statement from an anonymous contemporary physician: "I solemnly affirm and believe, if a hundred or a thousand men of the same age, same temperament and habits, together with the same surroundings, were attacked at the same time by the same disease, that if the one half followed the prescriptions of the doctors of the variety of those practicing at the present day, and that the other half took no medicine but relied on Nature's instincts, I have no doubt as to which half would escape."[7]

If medicine was to advance, the burgeoning scientific method would have to be embraced. Three centuries after Petrarch's death, Flemish physician Jan Baptista Van Helmont was the first to attempt to quantify a medical intervention's effectiveness. Specifically, Van Helmont questioned the effectiveness of treating fevers by bloodletting. He resolved to challenge the medical orthodoxy of the time with a small study in which he divided a group of patients into two treatment arms: bloodletting and bed rest. The results Van Helmont obtained were clear: The group that was rested, not bled, fared better.[8] Yet Van Helmont's results were entirely ignored, and physicians, driven more by tradition than logic, continued undeterred, bloodletting patients with fevers for the next hundred years, late into the eighteenth century.

The next recorded clinical trial was performed by British physician James Lind in 1747. During the eighteenth century, due to new technologies, naval voyages increased in length, and sailors sometimes spent months at sea. Many, late into a voyage, were struck by a crippling disease known as scurvy. The symptoms were always the same. "Almost the whole crew," wrote a British Royal Navy commander, describing the symptoms experienced by his crew, "[has] luxuriancy of funguous flesh . . . putrid gums and . . . the most dreadful terrors." He noted many of his crew suffered "a strange dejection of the spirits" and lay still, while those who "resolved to get out of their hammocks, have died before they could well reach the deck." During the Seven Years' War the Royal Navy enlisted 184,899 sailors; 133,708 of these were declared "missing" or died from disease, scurvy being the main cause.

Remedies suggested for scurvy were based on little more than a series of conjectures. Captain James Cook, the famous British explorer, claimed the remedy was "malt and sauerkraut." Others declared the cures to be "elixir of vitriol" (dilute sulfuric acid), bloodletting, or applying a piece of turf to the patient's mouth to counter the "bad qualities of the sea-air."[9] In the late winter of 1747 Lind boarded the *Salisbury*, a fifty-gun warship commissioned by the Royal Navy for patrol during the War of Austrian Succession. According to the ship's log, while in the Plymouth harbor the following provisions were loaded: *"Rec'd 6 side fresh Beef, 170 Baggs of Bread, one Puncheon Pork, 3 Barrels Rasons, 3 Barrels & 1 Hogshead Rice, 15 Firkins Butter, 33 Cheeses and some Boatswain's and Carpenters Stores."*[10]

Months into the patrol, with no fresh, vitamin C–containing food, the crew began to demonstrate symptoms of scurvy, but Lind had an idea. He had devised a plan to test once and for all the various remedies that other sailors had sworn by. Lind selected twelve sickened sailors and divided them into groups of two. All twelve subjects displayed similar symptoms. "Their cases were as similar as I could have them. They all in general had putrid gums, the spots and lassitude, with weakness of the knees," wrote Lind. Isolated from the rest of the crew, the men were given the same rations, but each pair received a different test treatment: "Cider, a few drops of a weak acid, vinegar, sea-water, nutmeg and barley water, or oranges and lemons." Six days later the ship's supply of fruit was used up, but by then Lind had his result. Unmistakably, the two men fed the citrus had begun to recover. They were feeling so much better that they began helping to nurse the stricken crew. "The consequence was, that the most sudden and visible good effects were perceived from the use of oranges and lemons; one of those who had taken them, being at the end of six days fit for duty," wrote Lind.[11]

Six years later, now a practicing physician in Edinburgh, Lind published *Treatise of the Scurvy*, which contained the results of his trial. Inexplicably, it was not until 1795, almost half a century later, that the Royal Navy High Command ordered lemon juice to be part of a ship's provisions.

Measuring the Way Forward

Measurement in medicine, in the form of the nascent clinical trial, appeared to be having trouble penetrating the hidebound, heavily intuition-reliant profession. Physicians, it seemed, were hell-bent on preserving the old ways, exemplified by Hippocrates' guiding statement that a "physician's judgment mattered more than any external measurement." Society, meanwhile, was rapidly transforming. In Britain, the Industrial Revolution was reshaping the landscape and the way people lived. Here, too, and across Europe, a scientific revolution was underway. Advancements in mathematics, astronomy, physics, and chemistry reverberated across the continent.

Even beyond the development of clinical trials, if medicine—and biology in general—were to move forward, there was a much more fundamental problem to surmount. Physicists, astronomers, and chemists were clarifying the laws of sound, light, motion, and material at an astonishing pace. The contrast of progress in the natural sciences with that in the biological sciences, however, was exasperating. Natural science was about order, symmetry, abiding laws, whereas biology and medicine remained loose, chaotic, unlawful—unattached to the material world. Biology was still largely dominated by a theory called *vitalism*, a belief that "living organisms are fundamentally different from non-living entities because they contain some non-physical element."[12] Vitalism claimed the living and nonliving were governed by different dynamics. The living were infused with a "vitalistic" force that operated *outside* of natural law. The nonliving—light, atoms, gravity, planets, and electromagnetic forces—could be described by mathematical laws. The living, claimed the vitalists, existed in a different realm, a plane beyond human understanding. The corollary was this: If man was unable to understand the way our bodies worked, then medicine had no business applying the scientific method or comparative trials to measure whether a medical intervention worked or not. Medicine, it was thought, was best left to the mystics.

The irreverent French physiologist, Claude Bernard, fervently disagreed with the vitalists. Bernard, born in a small French village in 1813, was the son of a poor winegrower. With few educational opportunities, Bernard bounced from one tedious job to the next. He tried to be a playwright but failed miserably. After reading one of his plays, a Parisian critic presciently advised him to try medicine instead. Reluctantly, Bernard took his advice and entered medical school in the winter of 1834. There Bernard began to display the makings of a brilliant researcher. The ensuing years in the laboratory were remarkably productive for Bernard. He discovered the role of gastric juices, the pancreas, and the small intestine in digestion.

While Bernard was charting the process of digestion, his genius—one that would revolutionize medicine—would become apparent in his charting something else: the process of medical research. As a first principle, he rejected vitalism. He insisted that living creatures were bound by the same lawful rules as inanimate matter, and thus the understanding of their biology could be advanced through experimental measurement.

In 1860, with his health in decline, Bernard took the opportunity for a paid sabbatical. During this time away from the confines of the laboratory, he reflected deeply on how to pull medicine from the Dark Ages and into the Enlightenment that was burgeoning across Europe. More than anything, he reasoned, medicine needed to embrace the scientific method if it was to catapult forward as the physical sciences had. His reflections culminated in an 1865 book, *An Introduction to the Study of Experimental Medicine*.[13] The book was groundbreaking. Critically, he introduced the concept of the controlled clinical trial as a measure of a medical treatment's effectiveness. Carefully conducted experiments, he reasoned, were the arbiter of truth. They alone provided the points of light needed to prove whether a medical intervention worked or did not work. He railed against a medical system that refused to change and was content to ignore real evidence: "Comparative experiments showed, in fact, that treatment of pneumonia by bleeding, which was believed most efficacious, is a mere therapeutic illusion. . . . To learn we must necessarily reason about what we have observed, compare the facts, and judge them by other facts used as controls," wrote Bernard. Bernard's treatise was an admonishment to an impulsive field that refused to grow up. "When we meet a fact, which contradicts a prevailing theory, we must accept the fact and abandon the theory, even when the theory is supported by great names and generally accepted," wrote Bernard.[14]

Bernard knew that the clinical trial alone could transform medicine and change the course determined by Hippocrates' misguided proclamation that a "physician's judgment mattered more than any external measurement." But he also knew this would be no easy task. It was one thing for chemists and physicists to conduct experiments on inanimate material. It was another thing altogether for physicians to conduct experiments on human beings. Unlike atoms, photons, or planets, for example, human beings have emotions, alternative motivations, and biases. To obtain meaningful results, reasoned Bernard, the experimenter would have to dehumanize the process, create rules and procedures to transform the animate into the inanimate.

The potential confounding factors due to the human element were lurking invisibly everywhere. In 1898, inspired by Bernard, a Danish physician named Johannes Fibiger made the heretical suggestion that physicians *themselves* may be part of the problem. A physician, reasoned Fibiger, may have powerful incentives for a treatment to work: Money, fame, or even the desperation to prove a treatment could help suffering patients when there was nothing else. These incentives, then, could creep into the inner workings of the clinical trial. The physician, in selecting which patients to put in the test group and which in the control group, may, consciously or unconsciously, introduce a *selection bias*—selecting the patients who appear younger, healthier, or with less advanced disease for the test group, thus skewing the results in favor of the treatment. To counter this, Fibiger introduced the concept of *randomization*.

A random distribution of patients would ensure that both groups being compared were the same, provide an even testing ground. Randomization would guarantee that any improvement measured in patient outcomes would be due solely to the treatment being tested, reasoned Fibiger.

Fibiger introduced another critical concept into the design of the clinical trial—statistical power, a measurement based on the number of patients enrolled in the trial. The more patients, the higher the statistical power of the trial's results. Medical treatments are rarely perfect, after all. Few treatments are absolute cures, and most are measured in small degrees of improvement. A clinical trial is designed to measure the degree of a treatment's effect, and sometimes the effect is weak. For example, a drug might help only one out of every twenty patients treated. As such, if a trial enrolls only twenty patients there is a good chance the effect will be missed because the trial was "underpowered." If, on the other hand, a treatment is an absolute cure, like giving citrus to sailors afflicted with scurvy, the effect might be detected by a small trial, like the one Lind performed on the *Salisbury* with only twelve patients. Statistical power is defined this way: "The likelihood that a study will detect an effect when there is an effect there to be detected." If statistical power is high, the probability of missing the effect goes down.[15]

In 1898 Fibiger conducted what many consider to be the first partially randomized, controlled clinical trial (RCT). The trial was testing a new treatment for diphtheria. Fibiger, an obsessive planner, recognized the critical need to remove the possibility of a selection bias, which had tainted so many earlier studies: "Truly, the control cases in the earlier studies were selected to be as similar as possible to the ones treated with serum, but to eliminate completely the play of chance and the influence of subjective judgment, one had to use a different procedure. The only method which could be used rationally was to treat some patients with serum and every other patient in the usual way."[16] Fibiger also recognized the need for statistical power. He enrolled 484 patients, a massively powered trial for the time. If there was an effect from the treatment, even a weak one, his well-powered trial had a good chance of detecting it.

In the spring of 1898, Fibiger was just wrapping up his clinical trial for the treatment of diphtheria while Halsted was presenting his results on the radical mastectomy in New Orleans. The contrast between the two trials was striking. Fibiger's trial was elegant, controlled, and properly powered. Halsted's trial was chaotic, uncontrolled, and underpowered. Halsted's trial was flawed to the point of being meaningless. Without a control group, what was he comparing his treatment to? Without randomization, what biases may have influenced the results? And with so few patients in the trial, did he even capture the effect of the radical mastectomy?

Few physicians were as fastidious as Fibiger. And even fewer had his instinctive grasp of clinical trial design and statistics. The introduction of control groups, randomization, the placebo control (proposed by American physician Austin Flint in 1863), blinding (a method that eliminates bias by not allowing either the physician or the patient to know who is receiving the medication and who is receiving the placebo), and statistical power fell onto a field unprepared to receive it. It was a catch-22: The concept of the clinical trial was critical to advancing medicine, yet the majority of physicians, including Halsted, were not trained in experimental design, statistics, or the interpretation of results—and had little enthusiasm to learn.

In truth it didn't matter anyway. The way Halsted presented the results was good enough for the crowd of surgeons in attendance at the New Orleans conference and those throughout the country. After all, it appeared to them that he had reduced the rate of local cancer recurrence when compared to other surgeons, including Volkmann, who might have been doing a slightly less aggressive version of the radical mastectomy. That was good enough for them. The physician had become the archetype of professionalism, autonomy, and intellectual sovereignty—canonized in the image of Hippocrates—a revered expert with an intuition that transcended earthly explanation. "In nothing do men more nearly approach the gods than in giving health to men," said Cicero.[17] To the audience before him, and to his patients whose lives depended on him, Halsted was a god—omniscient, larger than life. His authority reigned supreme. They had faith in him.

In fact, Halsted, too, trusted his intuition more than the data. Statistics didn't help him on the operating table, intuition did; a gut instinct refined from thousands of operations. Why should anyone believe the statistics anyway? Medicine, perhaps more than any other profession, placed *absolutum dominium* on human intuition. After all, numbers could be manipulated, changed, made up, or skewed in any number of ways. "The surgeon interested in furnishing the best statistics may in perfectly honorable ways provide them," Halsted wrote, alarmingly.[18] For now, medicine remained a tug-of-war between experimental data and human intuition. And human intuition was winning.

If medicine was to progress it needed heroes—diplomats who could build a bridge between the physician's venerated intuition and the purely statistical side of medicine. A young Englishman named Sir Austin Bradford Hill would become such a hero. Hill began his career in the early 1900s and was on his way to becoming one of the insiders. He entered medical school when the First World War broke out. Infused with a sense of duty, Hill enlisted at the first opportunity in the Royal Naval Air Service. After training, he was posted to a Greek island to prepare for the pending invasion of the Dardanelles. While there Hill contracted pulmonary tuberculosis. With no good treatment options, Hill was sent home—believed most likely to die. After a few years of convalescence, however, he began to recover and to think again of his future. His lingering illness would still require long periods of convalescence, and a career in medicine was no longer an option. Concerned for the directionless young Hill, a friend of the family brought him a book on economics and persuaded Hill to consider it as a course of study. He would be able to study while in his sick bed as an "external student" of London University. Hill agreed. He fervently dove into the subject, voraciously consuming book after book and quickly obtaining a degree in economics while physically attending the University only twice to take exams.

But Hill never wanted a career in economics. He still longed to be part of the world of medicine. He was able to win a grant from the British Medical Research Council (MRC)—a government council dedicated to coordinating and funding medical research—to study the "distribution and cause of disease" across Britain. This was a problem for epidemiology, a discipline that hovered between statistics and medicine. A discipline that used statistics to track the health of populations and numbers to uncloak the invisible patterns of a disease, drawing lines from cause to effect. Epidemiology would bridge the gap between Hill's statistics-heavy education and the career he had longed for. Hill launched into his new job with a missionary's zeal, bouncing between the problems the MRC presented to him and advanced courses in statistics at University College London.

Hill recognized immediately what medicine was missing. In 1937 he published a series of revolutionary articles in the *Lancet* detailing the critically important methodology necessary for a clinical trial to achieve a meaningful result. The articles explained the importance of randomization, control groups, blinding of both physician and patients, and proper statistical power. The overriding message was this: Physicians, like all of us, are fallible, make mistakes, and are subject to cognitive bias. This wasn't an attack, but simply a recognition of human nature. Hill appreciated the delicate psychological nature of what he was trying to achieve, and feared that if he didn't do it correctly, he would suffer violent backlash. To the medical establishment, he was an outsider, a numbers guy, and his penetration of the inner sanctum of medicine must be subtle. Hill knew what he had to do. He wrote the *Lancet* articles for physicians, not other statisticians. For example, rather than using an esoteric symbol that only another statistician would know, he would explain the significance in plain language. Hill wasn't arrogantly thrusting statistics on physicians, but softly and unpretentiously massaging it into their consciousness. And Hill wasn't suggesting a wholesale rearrangement of medicine, he was delicately intimating that physicians begin to learn statistical methods—or at least allow statisticians like himself a seat at the table. "Tony was a quiet, unassuming, private person who sought to lead but not to drive,"[19] said a colleague. As it turns out, Hill's subtle approach worked. The *Lancet* articles were widely read and soon reprinted in a book, *The Principles of Medical Statistics*.[20] Hill's book, translated into many languages and sold throughout the world, had an immeasurable influence on medicine. "It may be difficult to appreciate how great an impact *Principles of Medical Statistics* had on the practice and interpretation of research results by what in 1937 was essentially an innumerate medical profession," wrote a physician.[21] And while Hill's book may have cracked the door for the clinical trial, soon a series of events converged with perfect timing to allow Hill to kick the door wide open.

The First "Well-Executed" Clinical Trial

Following the Second World War, the American pharmaceutical industry exploded. Infused with support from the War Production Board, drugs were being developed and produced at a dizzying rate. Synthetic vitamins, sulfon-amides, cortisol, and, especially, antibiotics flooded the market. Eleven US pharmaceutical companies were producing over half of the world's supply of penicillin after the war. In addition to producing drugs, pharmaceutical companies were employing a new mass-screening technology to discover new drugs with dazzling speed.

In 1944, through work funded by the pharmaceutical company Merck, a new antibiotic called streptomycin was discovered by microbiologist Selman Waksman at Rutgers University in New Jersey. It was quickly recognized that the new antibiotic might have activity against the gritty microorganism that caused tuberculosis, an organism against which penicillin had proved ineffec-tive. US pharmaceutical companies quickly ramped up production. In 1946, even with US production at full tilt, supply of the new, lifesaving antibiotic was constrained, with nearly all of it reserved for US military and domestic use. However, a gift was held back for a close wartime ally, a small allocation of streptomycin was sent across the Atlantic to Hill and the British MRC.

The clinical trial methodology Hill advocated contained an internal dilemma. Typically, if a promising treatment arose for a potentially fatal disease, physicians had an obligation to uphold the Hippocratic oath and administer the drug to all patients who might benefit from it. This presented an almost insurmountable problem for anyone trying to conduct an RCT, as it created the ethical dilemma of denying treatment to the control arm. For Hill, however, the tiny amount of streptomycin shipped over by the United States solved the problem. Because there was a vanishingly small amount, it *had* to be allocated. A colleague referred to the scenario as a "statistician's dream."

In 1947, after the initial planning, Hill and his colleagues at the MRC con-ducted the first-ever fully randomized, controlled clinical trial in history. The trial was a resounding success in two ways: First, it unequivocally established the ability of streptomycin to cure tuberculosis—a disease that in the 1800s had been responsible for 25 percent of all deaths. And second, it was a clear demonstration of the power of carefully planned and executed clinical trials to measure a medical intervention's effectiveness.

Selman Waksman was awarded the 1952 Nobel Prize in Sweden for his discovery of streptomycin. Yet Hill's influence on medicine, though less pal-pable than Waksman's, was perhaps more profound. One colleague wrote:

"It is no exaggeration to say that Tony Bradford Hill had more influence on the past 50 years of medical science than many winners of the Nobel Prize for Medicine. This is not because of the importance of particular pieces of research but because of the effect his teaching had on the way medical research has developed."[22]

There was another, more subtle consequence to Hill's streptomycin trial. For the first time, the role of the physician, previously the sole actor in every aspect of medicine, had been reduced. Even so, the backlash Hill feared didn't come. In truth, many doctors *wanted* what Hill was offering. A *Lancet* editorial written by a physician grappling with his changing role read, in part, "For most of us figures impinge on an educational blind spot. . . . This is a misfortune, because simple statistical methods concern us far more closely than many of the things we are forced to learn. Many of our problems are statistical; and there is no other way of dealing with them."[23] The clinical trial's ability to transform medicine was now apparent to everyone, and it was sweepingly adopted as the "gold standard" for measuring the efficacy of a drug. For the first time, outsiders had pierced the seemingly impenetrable fortress of medicine.

History tells a clear story: Statisticians like Hill had arrived just in time. Their tools were less obvious—they held no scalpel, prescribed no medications, had no interactions with patients. But they could tackle medical questions doctors had *no way* of answering. By the mid-1900s, for example, smoking cigarettes had become the norm for adults—including physicians, the majority of whom smoked. However, anxiety concerning cigarettes' effect on health was beginning to smolder. To assuage the growing concern, the public—and, ironically, the tobacco companies—turned to physicians for reassurance. In an ad featuring a white-haired, white-coated doctor with a reassuring smile, Lucky Strike stated brazenly that "20,679 physicians say 'LUCKIES are less irritating.'" Philip Morris one-upped Lucky Strike with their 1937 *Saturday Evening Post* ad claiming that research by independent physicians had concluded that their cigarettes were *proven* to be "less irritating." In 1946 the RJ Reynolds Tobacco Company kicked off an advertising campaign for Camel cigarettes. Their new campaign centered on the reassuring slogan "More doctors smoke Camels than any other cigarette."

In 1951 Hill and a colleague named Richard Doll, a physician turned epidemiologist, brainstormed a study to address the growing concern. The study would come to be recognized as a watershed moment for the power of statistical medicine. The study itself was drenched in irony. The time-honored doctor-patient relationship—with centuries of richly interwoven history and symbolism—was turned upside down in the study. This time, *doctors* were the subjects. The study, called the British Doctors' Study, followed 40,701 British physicians, smokers in one group and nonsmokers in the other, recording the rates of cancer and heart disease in each cohort.

By 1956 Hill and Doll had captured convincing statistical evidence linking smoking to both lung cancer and heart attacks. The study went on to show that smoking decreases life-span by up to ten years, and that over half of all smokers will die from a smoking-related disease.[24] It is difficult to quantify the effect the British Doctors' Study had on society. Over the ensuing decades of social change, how many lives were saved? The physician may be able to treat one patient at a time, but Hill, armed with the power of statistics, could save millions.

Skeptics Emerge

Take a moment to consider this fact: It took until 1947 for the first well-executed, fully randomized, controlled clinical trial to be performed. While the other sciences were sprinting, medicine had just begun to crawl. Chemists and physicists had long ago embraced experimental science with feverish zeal, and medicine was only now recording its first real measurement of a treatment. Over the previous century, new discoveries, one after another, filled volume after volume of textbooks. Chemical reactions, quantum mechanics, electromagnetic forces, gravity, sound, space, and time—the universe was being deconstructed and laid out before us by creatively thought out and carefully executed experiments—while medicine had just birthed its own version of experimental methodology.

Nevertheless, the incursion of statisticians into medicine had finally begun. Demonstrating how to measure the effectiveness of a drug was one thing, but the arrival of statisticians in the surgical theater—a tangled web of ego, ritual, and tradition—would prove not as smooth. As Hill and statisticians around the globe were emerging onto the scene in the 1940s and '50s, use of the radical mastectomy was just hitting its full stride. Legions of young surgeons trained in the "Halstedian" method stood, scalpels sharpened, ready to thrust the radical mastectomy upon thousands of women with breast cancer, year after year, in both Europe and the United States.

But amidst the din, a few heretical whispers of dissent could be heard. Radiation therapy had emerged and had proven capable of invoking responses that "softened" the breast tumors and, in some cases, even shrank them. Geoffrey Keynes, an English surgeon working at St Bartholomew's Hospital in London, wondered if combining radiation with a less extensive surgery might be just as effective as Halsted's radical procedure, and he began to experiment with the combination. The local recurrence rates Keynes achieved with the "kinder" combination seemed at least comparable to the percentages reported from Halsted in New Orleans. Keynes was cautiously optimistic that the procedure might spare women from the brutality of the radical mastectomy. He suggested modestly that the "extension of [an] operation beyond a local removal might sometimes be unnecessary."

Not surprisingly, Keynes's suggestion fell on deaf ears. Decades later, in 1953, however, a young American surgeon working at the Cleveland Clinic, George Barney Crile, began having his own doubts about the radical mastectomy. For Crile, the skepticism grew out of emerging laboratory research hinting that the centrifugal theory—the theoretical underpinning of the radical mastectomy—might be dreadfully wrong. Intrigued by the implications, Crile pored through Keynes's data. If Keynes was right, Crile reasoned, the radical mastectomy was completely unnecessary. Like Keynes, Crile began to treat women with a much milder procedure, the "simple mastectomy," a procedure that stopped short of the removal of blocks of pectoral muscle and distant lymph-node chains.

Crile found that, compared to the radical mastectomy, the simple mastectomy appeared to result in similar rates of recurrence, and he published his results in 1961. However, Crile's publication was met with "ridicule and scorn." Unable to convince his colleagues, a frustrated Crile turned to the patient. He became an advocate of empowering women to look at the data for themselves, publishing a book titled *Surgery: Your Choices, Your Alternatives*.[25] "He brought a simmering medical debate out into the open by encouraging patients to demand information so they might make informed decisions rather than be treated like children who would not understand," wrote a *New York Times* reporter.[26]

"Universal acceptance of a procedure does not necessarily make it right," Crile responded to his critics. But the colossal momentum of the radical mastectomy, the force of Halsted's reputation, and all those trained in his wake, eclipsed Keynes and Crile's heretical whispers of opposition. If the radical mastectomy was to be derailed, it would take an effort equal to its momentum.

"In God We Trust, All Others [Must] Have Data"

In the fall of 1957, a University of Pittsburgh–trained surgeon named Bernard Fisher received a phone call. On the other line was Fisher's mentor, I.S. Raven, also a surgeon, who was chairman of a clinical study panel. Raven invited a group of twenty-three surgeons to meet at Stone House, on the campus of the National Institutes of Health (NIH), to discuss the formation of a government-sponsored program to conduct clinical trials for the treatment of breast cancer. Initially Fisher had had little enthusiasm. But that day he would undergo a transformation. The concept of the clinical trial was still fresh—Hill's streptomycin trial was only ten years old. The new method of measurement captivated Fisher. He realized that carefully conducted trials were a "highly sophisticated methodology" and were a "major step toward transforming medicine from an art to a science." Fisher also had another epiphany: The entire logic justifying the radical mastectomy was based on the centrifugal theory of spread. But the procedure itself had never actually been proven.

As the meeting came to an end, Fisher was infused with a new sense of mission and, critically, a new fascination for the basic biology of how cancer spreads in the body, a phenomenon called *metastasis*. Fisher didn't return to the operating room, but instead dove straight into the laboratory where he launched a series of experiments that he hoped might shed light on how cancer spreads. In the years that followed, Fisher began to develop a new hypothesis about the behavior of tumor cells. Fisher's research suggested that tumor cells didn't march outward as Halsted had presupposed. Once a tumor established itself, reasoned Fisher, cells could break free and travel through the circulatory system, hopscotching over the lymph nodes. Cancer didn't travel a preordained path, as the centrifugal theory had suggested; it was darting erratically, and fleeting. If a surgeon was lucky enough to encounter a fully intact tumor, a simple, localized surgery was probably enough. But according to his new understanding of how cancer spread, if even only a few cells had broken free, the radical mastectomy was pointless, argued Fisher—like a desperate attempt to contain spilled water with one's hands.

By 1971 Fisher's laboratory work had left him deeply suspicious that the radical mastectomy was an entirely excessive procedure. Additionally, his time in the laboratory had infused him with a new appreciation for the power of data and how far medicine had fallen behind. "As a consequence of my laboratory research, I became familiar with the scientific method—the need for proper controls, the use of statistics, and other elements that contributed to a scientific gestalt. I looked upon clinical trials as an extension of my laboratory, and I appreciated that they could be used as a methodology for testing hypotheses. Until their use, anecdotalism was the primary source of information for determining treatment strategies."[27]

Fisher, more than anyone, knew that the only way to measure once and for all the value of the radical mastectomy was a clinical trial. In 1971 his consortium received $200,000 to carry out the necessary trial. The trial, given the clinical name "the B-04 trial," would randomize patients into one of three different treatments: radical mastectomy, simple mastectomy plus radiation, or simple mastectomy alone.

Fisher had no idea what he was up against. The trial was not like Hill's streptomycin trial—the "statistician's dream"—which had fortuitously circumvented the ethical dilemma inherent to most clinical trials. This trial *did* present an ethical dilemma: Surgeons were asked to *not perform* an operation they had been indoctrinated to believe would save a woman's life. And to obtain sufficient statistical power Fisher needed surgeons—lots of them. The resistance was fierce. His fellow surgeons even accused Fisher of potentially "murdering" the women receiving the simple procedures.

Yet Fisher doggedly persisted, driven by a scientific evangelism. "In God we trust, all others [must] have data," he shot at a journalist.[28] The search for surgeons willing to participate in the trial was a colossal nationwide effort, and even extended into Canada. In the end, Fisher was able to recruit 1,765 patients among thirty-four centers located across the United States and Canada staffed with surgeons willing to participate in the trial.

In 1985 the results of the B-04 trial were published in the *New England Journal of Medicine*.[29] The results led to a clear conclusion: There was *no difference* in survival between the three procedures. In other words, there was no advantage in performing a radical mastectomy compared to a much less severe, simple mastectomy. A twenty-five year follow-up, also published in the *New England Journal of Medicine*, continued to show no difference in overall survival in the three groups of women.[30] Over the span of nearly a hundred years, approximately half a million women with breast cancer had undergone a brutal, disfiguring, and completely unnecessary procedure. As physically disfiguring as the radical mastectomy was, it was perhaps even more so mentally. The nature of the procedure conferred a profound sense of helplessness. Often, after a lump was discovered, a patient was put under anesthesia while a biopsy was obtained and tested. If the biopsy results were positive, the surgeon proceeded to perform the operation immediately. Often only upon waking would patients discover they had received a radical mastectomy. Women were put to sleep not knowing what was going to happen to their bodies in the interim, yet powerfully held innate cognitive biases resulted in few questioning it. The seductive logic of the procedure was as potent as the anesthesia that induced a body to remain asleep and still throughout the brutal operation. Even the name resonated with an intrinsic logic—after all, a disease as relentless as cancer *had* to be fought with *radical* measures. In life we learn early on that a desired outcome always comes at a proportional price. Harder work and more suffering leads to a bigger payoff; why should this be any different? The pain endured from a radical mastectomy should be proportional to the outcome: more pain, more gain. But cancer, we now know, doesn't live by our rules. This time Fisher proved unequivocally that our own minds had deceived us. This time the extra suffering was pointless.

A Cowboy Culture

What failed these women was not the doctors, not even Halsted and his adherents—but the system. Or lack of a system, to be more precise. The story of the radical mastectomy and the lesson therein cannot be lost to history. Why? Because the same fatally flawed system that allowed the radical mastectomy to flourish still exists today.

Remember, Hippocrates wrote that a physician's judgment mattered more than any external measurement. That ethos has persisted in a health

care system that resembles nothing Hippocrates could have even dimly imagined. Medicine has been built on the autonomy of the physician's venerated
intuition—but something more is required. Still today medicine more closely
resembles a culture than it does a logically structured, evidence-based system. A culture inextricably shackled to the fallibility of the human mind with
its myriad biases. "Holding onto that structure we build around the daring,
independence, self-sufficiency of each [specialist], has become a disaster,"
said Atul Gawande in his 2012 TED talk "How Do We Heal Medicine?" "We
have trained, hired, and rewarded people to be cowboys. But it's pit crews
that we need. . . . We've come to a place where we have no choice but to
recognize, as individualistic as we want to be, complexity requires group
success. We all need to be pit crews now."[31]

Halsted hated clinical trials. He hated statistics and the tedious minutiae
involved in tracking patient outcomes. Survival data, statistics, graphs, charts,
and tables were all dreadfully dull to him. He loved surgery. The grandness
of the operating theater. The challenge. The artistry. It was where he was at
his best, where he rose to the level of the gods.

However, the lesson is clear: *Both* are critical. We need pit crews now—
comprised of the skillful surgeon *and* the expert statisticians. Medicine
needs the clinical trial experts to guide the surgeons, to capture the data
that instruct them what surgeries to perform and when to perform them.
Unfortunately, large gaps in knowledge—gaps that clinical trials, or even
carefully conducted analysis of data retrieved from electronic health
records, could address—continue to exist. The "Halstedian" dynamic that
allowed the radical mastectomy to persist unchallenged for a century lin-
gers now, to this day.

The problem can largely be attributed to incentives. Currently the health
care system offers no incentive to perform the clinical trials necessary to measure the worth of surgeries like the radical mastectomy. The uncomfortable
truth is that there are many procedures with only thin evidence to support
them—procedures that endure because of an antiquated culture. Procedures
that, like the radical mastectomy, persist because of tradition rather than
evidence-based knowledge.

For example, for the last thirty years, patients with advanced kidney
cancer have had their diseased kidneys surgically removed as the standard

of care. Yet a study performed on 450 kidney cancer patients in Paris and presented in the summer of 2018 at the annual America Society of Clinical Oncology meeting in Chicago showed that surgical removal of the kidneys in these cases provides no benefit over chemotherapy alone.[32] At the end of his presentation, the surgeon who presented the Paris data to the Chicago audience showed a cartoon depicting a man shooting himself in the foot, acknowledging the irony of the situation to the applause of the audience. This type of data is certainly not in the surgeon's self-interest.

Two additional studies presented at the same meeting also zeroed in on unnecessary procedures. The first showed no benefit from a certain chemotherapy regimen often used for advanced colon cancer—a regimen that has been used for the past fifteen years. The study is "an excellent example of how less is more" when it comes to certain treatments for cancer, commented an oncologist.[33] And the second, a massively powered study funded by the NIH, showed adjunctive chemotherapy (given after surgery to prevent recurrence) to have no benefit in treating the most common type of breast cancer (hormone-positive, HER2-negative). "We can spare thousands and thousands of women from getting toxic treatment that really wouldn't benefit them," said the author of the study.[34]

It is incumbent on governments to sponsor these types of critically important studies, because no one else will. There is simply no incentive to do so. Yet currently government funding is being slashed. Over the past decade the number of these types of studies funded by the US government has dropped from 575 to 143.

Examples like this (and the story of the radical mastectomy) show that once a procedure becomes established it develops a kind of institutionalized inertia, and it becomes difficult to reverse course. Even when there is published evidence against a given procedure, it can continue. For example, every year scores of Americans have stents surgically placed in their hearts to prop up narrowing cardiac vessels, even though in many cases there is clear research showing there is no benefit to the procedure. Still, it is estimated that one in ten stents are put in "inappropriately." The reason appears to be nothing more than the apparent logic of the procedure itself. "One of the beliefs among primary care physicians and cardiologists is that if you see a blockage and you open it, it must help in some way even if the data suggest otherwise," said Grace Lin, an associate professor of medicine and health policy at the University of California San Francisco School of Medicine.[35]

Extreme Variation and Extreme Overtreatment

Because medicine is often practiced under a cloud of uncertainty, it is deeply entangled with a multitude of cognitive biases. A keen eye can spot them everywhere. Daniel Kahneman, for example, believes there is a very clear pattern to when a doctor's intuition breaks down. "People are very willing to make an intuitive diagnosis even when they're likely to be wrong," said Kahneman. An experiment performed at the University of Oregon in 1968 offers disconcerting confirmation of Kahneman's statement.[36] The Oregon researchers presented a group of nine radiologists with a series of x-rays of stomach ulcers in 192 patients and asked them to rate the probability that the ulcer was cancerous on a scale of 1 to 7, a rating of 7 denoting "definitely malignant," while 1 denoted the ulcer to be "definitely benign." As a twist, the Oregon researchers, without telling the doctors, made many duplicate copies of the patients' x-rays and mixed them up in the pile of x-rays given to each doctor. Thus, each doctor unknowingly made a diagnosis of every x-ray twice. Stunningly, the diagnoses were wildly inconsistent. The radiologists rarely offered diagnoses that matched each others', and, what's worse, the radiologists almost always contradicted *themselves*, diagnosing the same x-rays differently.

Physicians are trained to intervene in the medical problems that are presented within their given specialty. There is an inherent human tendency to *want* to intervene, a desire to *fix* a problem. The adage attributed to Mark Twain holds true: "To a man with a hammer, every problem appears as a nail." The corollary is clear: The surgeon will operate, the oncologist will give chemotherapy, the pathologist will diagnose, and so on, even when many medical decisions are made under conditions of uncertainty—decisions that, as Kahneman and Tversky showed, exhibit a patterned irrationality. How a specialist determines to use his or her skills and tools also depends on the culture that has developed at the center where they work. And, as Kahneman pointed out, the prevailing tendency is to diagnose a problem and then act on it, even with little relevant data.

The result of these forces, however, is something that *is* measurable: wildly inconsistent health care across the United States. For example, you are way more likely to get a stent inserted in Davenport, Iowa, than in, say, Iowa City or Sioux City. You're three times more likely to get a stent placed in Elyria, Ohio, compared to Cleveland, less than fifty miles away. One study from 1992 showed a fifteen-fold variation in the rates of surgery for back pain across various counties in Washington State.[37] Inexplicably, some primary care doctors order twice as many CT scans as their colleagues in the same practice. These few examples barely scratch the surface of the massive variation in health care across the United States.

Late-stage cancer care, too, is all over the map. A cancer patient in New York City has a 43 percent likelihood of dying in the hospital, while a similar patient in Mason City, Iowa, has only a 10 percent chance of dying in a hospital. In a case like this, one might imagine that the difference boils down to the type of hospital: academic versus rural. Yet strangely, even when comparing similar, academic hospitals, inconsistency in care still surfaces. During their last month of life, 58 percent of cancer patients at UCLA spend time in the ICU, while only 18 percent of cancer patients at Johns Hopkins do. In some parts of the country people will see up to eighty specialists in the last six months of their life, while in other parts they will see only eighteen. "Most physicians don't resist understanding variation, they just don't know about it. We're not trained in medical school to ask questions about how my pattern of practice differs from yours. We're not given the tools through data or a continuous flow of information to study that. We remain oblivious to variation," commented one physician.[38]

The upshot of erratic care is erratic outcomes. The relationship is zero-sum. If, for the same patient, one physician would insert a stent and another would not, one decision must be better than the other. This is indeed the case. For example, a 2015 study done by researchers at Memorial Sloan Kettering Cancer Center, showed that the five-year survival rate for cancer is 53 percent at eleven so-called "PPS-exempt" cancer centers (institutions exempt from the Medicare payment system such as MD Anderson, Dana-Farber, and Moffitt, to name a few) compared to 44 percent at the 4,873 nonacademic, non-NCI (National Cancer Institute), community hospitals across the country —a difference that equates to thousands and thousands of lives.

The degree of difference in outcomes is chilling. In another example, if you were to receive care at a Kaiser Permanente hospital following an "acute coronary event," your chance of death drops by up to 76 percent when compared to being treated at most other hospitals across the country. And you are much less likely to have an adverse drug event or give birth to a baby with lung problems at a hospital within the Intermountain Healthcare system (a chain of hospitals in Utah and Idaho) than at most other hospitals.

The vastly inconsistent care that plagues our hodgepodge health care system is a confluence of many psychological dynamics. Group psychological forces, such as the *bandwagon effect* and the *conformity bias*, often come into play. An extreme case of this occurred in Redding, California, in the early 2000s. At that time Northern Californians with certain worrisome symptoms were referred to the Redding cardiac center by local doctors. There the patients underwent the usual radiological studies of their heart vessels. But then something strange happened: Even if the patient's cardiac vessels appeared almost normal, the Redding surgeons would operate. Any slightly perceived abnormality—cases in which a clear majority of surgeons across the rest of the country would not operate—resulted in the patient being shuffled off to surgery.

Heart surgery is no trivial procedure; huge risks are involved. And once regulators realized what was going on at the Redding center they came down like hammer, fining the facility $450 million. The media shredded the Redding facility, framing the fiasco as an example of money-grubbing doctors and administrators acting unethically in a fee-for-service payment system—a system that pays a doctor for every test and procedure performed. Yet the reporters who dug deeper found something fascinating: The doctors and administrators at the Redding hospital were in a state of shock. They truly believed they had done nothing wrong.

A misguided culture had developed at Redding. In an escalating loop of colleague-to-colleague reinforcement, the doctors involved in these cases had convinced each other that performing surgery, even when there was only the slightest presentation of blockage, was doing the patient a favor. The facility's head of medical ethics was so convinced of the logic behind the procedure that he even flew his own father in from Chicago to be diagnosed and operated on by the Redding doctors. One of the Redding surgeons even referred to abstaining from operating as "widow-making." And the culture was insidiously self-perpetuating. Because they were operating on healthier and healthier people, their mortality rates dropped precipitously.

Another example of the development of an extreme "health care culture" occurred in McAllen, Texas. In 2006 Medicare spent $15,000 per enrollee in McAllen, almost twice the national average. This was shocking. Especially considering that McAllen is a low-income region, where the annual per capita income is just $12,000. In other words, Medicare spends $3,000 more per person in McAllen than the average person there earns. Why was health care spending in McAllen so extreme? It wasn't because of demographics. If you drive eight hundred miles up the border to El Paso County, you would find the same demographics. Yet Medicare was spending half as much per enrollee in El Paso as in McAllen.

If it wasn't demographics, then what was it? Atul Gawande went to McAllen to find the answer to this very question. From the moment he arrived, Gawande began to ask almost everyone he encountered about McAllen's extreme health costs. He asked businessmen, desk clerks, even a police-academy cadet eating at McDonald's. It was only when Gawande sat down with six full-time, private-practice physicians that he began to get a glimpse of the answer. After batting around answers like "better service" and "malpractice expenses," one surgeon finally spoke up: "Come on, we all know these arguments are bullshit. There is overutilization here, pure and simple." The McAllen doctors were simply ringing up more of everything: treatments, procedures, and tests of all kinds.[39]

Gawande next turned to economists and private data-analysis companies to see if this was true. The data they uncovered were undeniable: "Compared with patients in El Paso and nationwide, patients in McAllen got more of pretty much everything—more diagnostic testing, more hospital treatment, more surgery, more home care," wrote Gawande. This, of course, prompted another question. *Why* were the doctors in McAllen overtreating their patients so extremely? The answer was not immediately obvious. At first impression, nothing seemed overtly different about the McAllen doctors, Gawande observed. Then a hospital administrator who met with Gawande one morning offered up an explanation. He said it was because the doctors in McAllen had developed a "culture of money."[40]

"In El Paso, if you took a random doctor and looked at his tax returns eighty-five per cent of his income would come from the usual practice of medicine," he said. But in McAllen, the administrator thought, that percentage would be a lot less. In other words, the McAllen doctors had an unusually strong entrepreneurial drive. The administrator had noticed how many doctors owned imaging and surgical centers, as well as real-estate investments such as apartments and strip malls. And this culture, he felt, bled over into their practice of medicine. They would ring up the cash register whenever they had a chance by ordering extra tests, operating when it might not be necessary, and so on.

The administrator said that doctors had even approached him for kickbacks. "I've had doctors here come up to me and say, 'You want me to admit patients to your hospital, you're going to have to pay me.'" One doctor asked for $500,000 dollars. As Gawande dug deeper, the explanation for McAllen's extreme overtreatment was the development of a culture. But unlike the culture that had developed in Redding, this culture was about the money.[41]

It would be easy to become outraged. Yet, in the end, Gawande looked at it through another lens. "The real puzzle of American health care, I realized on the airplane home, is not why McAllen is different from El Paso. It's why El Paso isn't like McAllen. Every incentive in the system is an invitation to go the way McAllen has gone. Yet, across the country, large numbers of communities have managed to control their health costs rather than ratchet them up."[42] Indeed, as Gawande said, every incentive in our health care system is an invitation to "go the way of McAllen." Our health care system has a mindbogglingly misguided incentive structure that encourages overtreatment in general. When speaking to the Harvard crowd that day in 1995, first on Charlie Munger's list of human misjudgments was the underestimation of the power of incentives. "All my life I've underestimated it," Munger said, "and never a year passes that I [don't] get some surprise that pushes my limit a little farther."

Our health care system puts doctors in a terrible position. The fee-for-service model of payment dangles a financial carrot in front of every test, scan, and procedure and forces upon our doctors a conflict between making money and the patient's best interest. The ultimate result: 30 percent of all health care dispensed is unnecessary, to the tune of over $200 billion per year. And physicians admit it. In a 2017 poll, 71 percent of physicians admitted that they are more likely to perform unnecessary procedures when they personally profit from them.[43] The consequence of this incentive structure is frightening. Studies have shown that the best predictor for the number of surgeries in a given region of the United States is not the rate of a given disease but rather the density of surgeons in the area. Implant more back surgeons in a city, and the number of back surgeries will increase.

Another study showed that in regions of the United States with fewer medical resources, people do, in fact, receive less medical care on average.[44] Yet, the study revealed something else, something that might be counterintuitive to most. The study showed that less care was not a bad thing; the people receiving less care were no worse off for it. Being on the short end of medical care, the study concluded, did not translate into reduced rates of survival. Economists analyzing Medicare spending have also uncovered this disturbing relationship. The more Medicare spends per person in a given state correlates to a lower ranking of patient care quality in that state. Louisiana, Texas, California, and Florida spend the most and are near the bottom of the national rankings for quality of patient care. This inverse relationship holds true for McAllen, too. Of the twenty-five metrics that Medicare ranks hospitals on, McAllen's five largest hospitals performed on average worse than El Paso's on all but two of these metrics. Medicare spent $7,000 more per person each year in McAllen than in the average American city. But, oddly, this didn't translate into better care.

Why is this? How could *less* access to medical care not translate into a less healthy population? The answer is straightforward. Medical intervention, whether it's surgery, chemotherapy, scans, or drugs always carries risks. More is not always better. For most of history luminaries have recognized that medicine was little more than the illusion of control, that, in many cases, it did more harm than good. "The art of medicine consists in amusing the patient while nature cures the disease," Voltaire is reported as saying.[45] William Osler, one of the founders of Johns Hopkins Hospital along with Halsted, wrote, "One of the first duties of the physician is to educate the masses not to take medicine."[46]

Modern medicine boasts a marvel of lifesaving surgical procedures, preventative measures, and medications. Unquestionably, medicine today can prevent an enormous amount of suffering and save an untold number of lives. If it is dispensed *appropriately*. To overtreat is to impose a risk without a benefit. The math is simple: Overtreatment takes a toll in pain, suffering, complications, and death. Entropy is a universal law. Things go wrong. Every pill, procedure, surgery, and radiographical scan carries some risk. Consider this: Two-hundred thousand Americans die every year because of medical error. Seven thousand Americans die from sloppy, unintelligible physician handwriting alone. Globally, following heart disease and cancer, prescribed medication is estimated to be the third most common cause of death. Just walking through the door of a hospital, even if you are perfectly healthy, carries risk. Overtreatment leads to many unintended consequences: "People suffer from more anxiety about their health, from drug side effects, from complications of surgery. A few die. And remember: these people felt fine when they entered the health care system," said Gilbert Welch, author of *Overdiagnosed: Making People Sick in the Pursuit of Health*.[47]

Overdiagnosis and overtreatment are problems that have run especially rampant in cancer. The focus on early diagnosis over the last few decades has had a startling outcome: Increased screening *has* led to increased diagnosis of cancer, but, strangely, this has not translated into increased rates of survival. Cancer screening with mammography, ultrasound, and blood testing has dramatically increased the detection of breast, thyroid, and prostate cancer during the past few decades. And this has resulted in doctors treating hundreds of thousands more people each year for these cancers than before. Yet only a vanishingly small reduction in death—if any at all—has resulted. The reason: Many of the tumors diagnosed early represent no threat to the patient. They are benign or extremely slow-growing masses.

The calculation here is straightforward. If more people are diagnosed with cancer and treated for it, yet death rates haven't budged, it means thousands upon thousands of people are being treated for tumors that pose no threat. Yet these early diagnosed patients are often subjected to surgery, chemotherapy, and radiation—all of which are very caustic and damaging and can even inflame a cancer that might otherwise have remained indolent. The solution to this overtreatment is not obvious. The process of metastasis is responsible for 95 percent of the deaths from cancer, and many of these early diagnosed tumors would never lead to metastasis. The problem lies in knowing which early diagnosed tumors will spread and which will not. This uncertainty breeds anxiety. Even when the risk of a tiny tumor, detected early on, is clearly explained to be extremely low, once a patient hears the word "cancer," fear overrides reason.

One policy change recommended by a physician group centers on how doctors "frame" an early diagnosis. They suggested doctors avoid using the term "cancer" to describe tumors that pose little threat. "When patients hear the word 'cancer,' they often demand further tests and treatment, even when medically unjustified, and physicians are too often eager to comply," wrote a *Scientific American* reporter.[48]

In their efforts to pin down the enormity of the problem, public health physicians writing in the *New England Journal of Medicine* estimated that in the year 2008 alone, seventy-thousand American women were overdiagnosed with breast cancer. The astonishing degree of overtreatment in breast cancer is "shocking and appalling and unacceptable," said Karuna Jaggar, executive director of Breast Cancer Action, a San Francisco–based advocacy group. "It's an example of how our profit-driven health system puts financial interests above women's health and well-being." And it's not just breast cancer: "[M]en who take the common prostate-specific antigen [PSA] test and receive a cancer diagnosis have been estimated to be 47 times more likely to get unnecessary, harmful treatments—biopsies, surgery, radiation, chemotherapy—than they are to have their lives extended."[49]

"We've learned these lessons the hard way," wrote Atul Gawande in a 2009 *New Yorker* article. "Over the past two decades, we've tripled the number of thyroid cancers we detect and remove in the United States, but we haven't reduced the death rate at all."[50] The sweeping problem of cancer overtreatment extends to the very end of life. Over 50 percent of patients with advanced cancers receive chemotherapy in their final months, even though it offers an exceedingly small chance of extending life. Study after study have shown that end-of-life chemo degrades what little time people have left and does nothing to extend life. But these frank discussions about incurable cancers are difficult for both the doctor and the patient, and are often avoided altogether. "We haven't asked about cure or how much time I have," confessed an advanced cancer patient, "We haven't asked, and he hasn't offered. I guess we have our heads in the sand."

"Communication is a two-way street; doctors and patients alike contribute to patients' failure to appreciate medicine's limited ability to treat advanced cancer," wrote a *New York Times* columnist upon learning her husband had stage IV lung cancer. Yet doctors who are frank can meet resistance from both their patients and the patients' families. "People have an optimistic bias," pointed out two physicians in the column. "Even with repeated discussions, about one-third of patients are not able to say they have a disease from which they will die in a year or so," remarked another oncologist.[51]

Patients who do have these difficult discussions with their doctors and are realistic about the benefit of further treatment, tend to fare far better. A study in the *New England Journal of Medicine* looked at 150 patients with lung cancer. Half of them received palliative care—in this case, physicians, nurses, social workers, and nutritionists offering support and counseling—in addition to medical treatment soon after they were diagnosed. The other half received standard medical care without palliative care consultations. Those receiving palliative care had fewer aggressive treatments at the end of their lives, reported better quality of life, less depression, and, surprisingly, lived an average of two months longer than those who did not.

Complexity

One of the biggest problems dogging medicine today is complexity. When Hall orchestrated the first RCT in 1948, it set in motion the spectacular rise of a new industry. Pharmaceutical companies had peddled various tinctures, salves, and mixtures in apothecaries for centuries, but large-scale clinical trials—combined with new government regulations separating over-the-counter drugs from patent-protected, prescription-only drugs—set the stage for a massive profit windfall by the pharmaceutical industry. The upshot was this: Clinical trials, previously performed haphazardly by physicians within their clinics, were effectively outsourced to a budding new industry that worked closely with the FDA to conduct the "gold standard" of measurement: randomized, double-blinded, placebo-controlled clinical trials. For the most part, this was good and led to a dazzling increase in the number of new medications.

The explosive growth of the pharmaceutical industry, however, also came with downside. As private insurance took over as the dominant payer of health care, the cost of drugs became buried in a fixed premium—effectively hidden from the consumer, on whom capitalistic markets depend to keep prices in check. With no one left to drive down the price, the cost of medications (and other devices and treatments) skyrocketed. Second, the blossoming industry churned out thousands of new drugs. For doctors, the influx of new medications and medical devices and procedures has ratcheted up the complexity and uncertainty of their trade immeasurably. Today, a physician is expected to navigate through 6,000 approved medications and 4,000 medical and surgical procedures. And the pace will not slow anytime soon. In the white-hot field of immunotherapy alone, there are currently more than 2,000 drugs in development.

Here is a good example of the complexity physicians face today. Imagine a man who has been told he has early stage prostate cancer. The oncologist lays out the five treatment options: watchful waiting, surgery to remove the prostate, and three radiation options, including a targeted form called "intensity-modulated radiation therapy" (IMRT) and the latest, proton radiation therapy, a new and extraordinarily high-tech and expensive form of radiation. But here's the catch: "No therapy has been shown to be superior to another," said Michael Rawlins, chairman of a British medical research institute.

At any given cancer center, however, the oncologists might emphatically endorse one therapy over another for early stage prostate cancer. But no physician can point to a definitive study saying *why* they endorse it. Now here's the second catch: The price difference in therapies is astonishing. Watchful waiting will cost a few thousand dollars. Proton-beam therapy costs close to $100,000. The others fall somewhere in between. And under the current fee-for-service payment system, the trend is decidedly moving toward the costlier therapies, with no evidence that they are any better. This single example highlights a systemic problem: Increasing treatment options with a relative lack of comparative data guiding decision-making.

To be sure, the adoption of the clinical trial was a godsend for medicine. "But there is one important way in which medicine never quite adopted the scientific method. The explosion of medical research over the last century has produced a dizzying number of treatments for different ailments," wrote *New York Times* reporter David Leonhardt in a piece titled "Making Health Care Better." "Yet once a treatment enters the mainstream—once we know whether it works in certain situations—science is largely left behind. The next questions—when to use it and on which patients—become matters of judgment, not measurement. The decision is, once again, left to a doctor's informed intuition."[52]

When you add up all the inefficiencies in America's health care system and put them in purely numerical terms, the story is stunning. "The US spends 17.1% of GDP on health care, that's a cool three trillion dollars a year," wrote Mario Schlosser, chief executive officer and co-founder of Oscar Health, a technology-focused health insurance company. "For comparison, the global mobile advertising market—that's the market that gives companies [like] Facebook and Google pretty much all their valuation—is $100 billion per year, the global handset market is $400 billion per year. In other words, a mind-bogglingly large number."[53]

And what do we get for that $3 trillion? Subpar health care compared to the rest of the industrialized world—which spends far less. Among the seven wealthiest nations, the United States ranks dead last in life expectancy for men, and second to last for women. And compared to other advanced nations, the United States ranks last in infant mortality. We also leave 10 percent of our population uninsured. "Right then and there, you see the absolutely incredible inefficiencies of our health care system. There might not be another economic system on the planet that is as dysfunctional with regards to what is 'normal' operations, as the US health care system is vs. the rest of the rich world," wrote Schlosser.

In the throes of the subprime-led financial crisis, as the government carefully scrutinized every line of the US balance sheet, President Obama summed up the enormity of the problem in a 2009 speech at the White House: "The greatest threat to America's fiscal health is not Social Security," Obama said. "It's not the investments that we've made to rescue our economy during this crisis. By a wide margin, the biggest threat to our nation's balance sheet is the skyrocketing cost of health care. It's not even close."[54]

"The Whole System Is Cockamamie"

My doctor constantly writes PSA test, prostate-specific antigen. I just cross it out. He says, "What the hell are you doing? Why are you doing this?" And I said, "Well, I don't want to give you an opportunity to do something dumb."

—CHARLIE MUNGER

Berkshire Hathaway's first annual meeting was held in 1973 in the employee lunchroom of an Omaha-based insurance company that Buffett had acquired a few years earlier. On the door, Buffett taped up a piece of paper printed with the words "Meeting in Progress" to avoid being interrupted by employees shuffling through to get coffee or a snack. From this modest beginning, annual meeting attendance exploded skyward, matching Berkshire's skyrocketing stock price. Buffett and a handful of shareholders made up that first lunchroom meeting, and by 1989, only sixteen years later, a thousand shareholders were in attendance. Thirteen thousand were attending by the turn of the century, and 40,000 by 2015.

These meetings are not your typical corporate annual meetings. Berkshire meetings spill over with flair. Thousands of journalists and expert investors sit listening intently, notepads at the ready to write down the pearls of wisdom dispensed from Buffett and Munger. Buffett likes to call it the "Woodstock of capitalism." Being at one of these meetings is like attending an improv show and an Ivy League lecture at the same time. The nature of the annual meeting speaks volumes: Buffett and Munger don't simply run a Fortune 500 company; they've created a unique culture, one rooted in fair-dealing, logic, and a rich understanding of human nature.

But in 2017 a new issue had surfaced, one that usually didn't come up at corporate annual meetings. The issue was health care. Rising costs had become such a problem that it had caught Buffett and Munger's attention. The cost had become a significant burden to Berkshire's companies. And it wasn't just Berkshire's problem. It was America's problem.

As a percentage of GDP, health care in most industrialized nations has gone from 5 percent in 1960 to 11 percent today. But in America the rise was faster. It didn't level off at 11 percent as it had in most other advanced nations, but continued to rise to 17 percent—and still continues to shoot upward. "I don't see anything necessarily in the horizon that will cause that number to go down," said Buffet, in one of a flurry of postmeeting interviews, this one with CNBC. "You better not count on it reversing itself from natural causes." The reporter then turned to Munger: "Charlie, let's get your perspective on this. You are the chairman of Good Samaritan Hospital so you know health care on a very first-hand basis when it comes to this, and . . ." But Munger cut her off mid-sentence. "The whole system is cockamamie," he blurted out. "It's almost ridiculous in its complexity. And it's steadily increasing in cost."[55]

It wasn't the pace of the increase that got Munger riled up but the reasons *behind* the spiraling cost. "It you look at it up close the amount of overtreatment of the dying is just disgusting. There is a lot wrong with the system. It's wrong to pour a load of chemotherapy into people that are all but dead. It makes them miserable, costs them a lot of money, does no good for anybody. . . . It's not too much to say that its evil." To Buffett and Munger, health care now resembled a parasite on American business. "We are at a huge competitive disadvantage in terms of our health care cost—it's $3.3 trillion a year," said Buffett in another postmeeting interview. "It really truly is a tapeworm on the economic system."

Munger and Buffett didn't get where they are today by dragging their feet. In the winter of 2018, Berkshire Hathaway, alongside corporate stalwarts Amazon and JPMorgan Chase, announced that they would form an independent health care company for their employees. The goal was simple: to deliver better health care at a cheaper price.

After the announcement, many immediately derided the new consortium. Gary Cohn, director of the Trump administration's National Economic Council, told CNBC the new company would not be doing anything the White House hasn't already done. The stock market, however, had a different opinion: Shares of the major insurance companies crashed after the announcement. Shares for Cigna fell by nearly 6 percent; Anthem's also fell 6 percent; UnitedHealth Group's slid 3.3 percent; and Aetna's, 2.5 percent. Clearly, those betting with their own money felt the consortium had the potential to disrupt the current market.

Although few details were given with the announcement, people familiar with those involved probably could have made a good guess as to the general

strategy. In a story reminiscent of Berkshire's, Jeff Bezos had stunned his colleagues at Amazon by the meteoric rise of the company, from a tiny online
bookseller in a garage to a nearly trillion-dollar company. "I had a very, very,
very high opinion of Jeff's ability when I first him, and I underestimated him,"
said Buffett. "I've watched Amazon from the start. I think what Jeff Bezos has
done is something close to a miracle."[56] What Bezos did with Amazon was
to disrupt the entire retail sector by offering a better and cheaper platform.
And now he wanted to repeat this strategy with health care—disrupt the
industry by finding a way to deliver better health care at a cheaper price. In
one critical sense, however, the health consortium was different: There was
no profit motive behind it. "The three companies, which bring their scale and
complementary expertise to this long-term effort, will pursue this objective
through an independent company that is free from profit-making incentives
and constraints," explained the press release. This single detail is critical.
Examples like the city of McAllen, Texas, illustrate that the fee-for-service
model motivates doctors to overtreat. And it stands to reason that for-profit
hospitals that answer to shareholders will have the same issue. Knowing the
value that Munger and Buffett place on incentives, the consortium's doctors
will operate under a different framework of incentives to be sure—one that
incentivizes them to deliver the best care at the lowest cost. Simply providing the proper incentives will chip away at overtreatment, the single biggest
problem in health care today.

The group also announced a general strategy beyond incentives. "The
initial focus of the new company will be on technology solutions that will
provide US employees and their families with simplified, high-quality, and
transparent health care at a reasonable cost." Indeed, this is what these
guys do best—simplify. They find the festering inefficiencies in a system
and extirpate them. Outdated medical record systems, poor patient-doctor
communication, the ordering of duplicate tests or unproven, expensive procedures, practicing reactive medicine rather than preventive medicine—all
these examples could be addressed through technology. But, admittedly, the
announcement made it clear that beyond a general strategy it was a work in
progress. "Our group does not come to this problem with answers," wrote
Buffett. "But we also do not accept it as inevitable. Rather, we share the belief
that putting our collective resources behind the country's best talent can,

in time, check the rise in health costs while concurrently enhancing patient satisfaction and outcomes."[57]

To get the answers, however, they knew they would need the right person to head up the consortium. "The job now is to get the right CEO," said Buffett. "This is critically important."

The search was on.

CHAPTER 3

How Simple and Effective Treatments Get Lost

The problem of wildly inconsistent treatment and overtreatment are now well documented, and widely known to those in the health care industry. But could our health care system also be flawed in other, less obvious ways? If we looked closely could we uncover percolating inefficiencies in the other direction as well? That is, in contrast to *over*treatment, what about missed or *under*utilized medications, treatments, and procedures? Perhaps our system is porous in a way that allows simple, cheap, and effective interventions— interventions that might have massive impact on our lives—to fall through the cracks.

"You Should Get Your Affairs in Order"

It was the spring of 2012, and Catherine Duff was at the end of her rope. The fifty-seven-year-old grandmother from Carmel, Indiana, had an insidious infection in her bowels that had become resistant to antibiotics. Eight times the doctor gave her a round of antibiotics; eight times the relentless bug came back. The infection first appeared after Duff had undergone surgery for diverticulitis, a condition where painful pouches form in the wall of the large intestine. Duff was given the standard round of postoperative antibiotics to prevent infection. The antibiotics, however, also wiped out the normal bacteria in her colon, clearing the way for a highly pathogenic bacterium called *Clostridium difficile* (*C. diff*) to take up residence. This is almost always how *C. diff* shows up—almost always in a hospital, almost always following a course of antibiotics.

C. diff infections have become a massive problem for hospitals and nursing homes. It is the number-one cause of hospital-acquired dysentery. And the rate of *C. diff* infections is rising at an alarming rate. The chance of contracting *C. diff* is 13 percent if you're in the hospital for two weeks—50 percent if you're there for longer than four weeks. Half a million Americans are infected every year. And, according to the Centers for Disease Control and Prevention (CDC), 30,000 deaths are linked to *C. diff* every year, 15,000 being directly attributable.

C. diff is difficult to kill, and hospitals go to incredible lengths to try to eliminate it. Despite their efforts, *C. diff* finds a way—lurking on doorknobs, surfaces, and hospital workers' hands. If it finds its way into the mouth of a patient who has just had her normal intestinal ecosystem of trillions of bacteria decimated by antibiotics, *C. diff* takes up residence. Once established in a patient's colon, *C. diff* emits two powerful toxins. The first clue of a *C. diff* infection is always the onset of diarrhea. "There is no mistaking the smell of *C. diff* diarrhea," one nurse told me. "You can almost always diagnose a patient just by the smell." The toxins also cause damage that can lead to a condition called pseudomembranous colitis: visible yellow plaques that populate the intestine walls. If the condition worsens, the colon swells and can perforate, causing feces to leak into the abdomen, possibly leading to a condition called *sepsis* (a systemic infection of the blood). The course of a *C. diff* infection can be relentless. Ironically, even though antibiotics are often the cause of *C. diff*, they are also the treatment. If a patient fails multiple rounds of antibiotic treatment, the downward spiral is horrible. A cancer patient who had acquired *C. diff* was asked if he could be cured of either his cancer or *C. diff*, which one would he choose. He said he "would choose to cure the *C. diff*."

When the test for *C. diff* came back positive, Catherine Duff's gastroenterologist did what the medical journals call for and prescribed more antibiotics. The first round of antibiotics, usually metronidazole, works for approximately 75 percent of people. Duff fell into the unlucky 25 percent who have a recurrence after the initial round of treatment. The standard of care for those who experience recurrent *C. diff* is even more antibiotics, but the chance the patient will be cured drops with every consecutive round: from 75 percent with the first round, to 40 percent with the second round, to 20 percent with the third, and so on. This is what happened to Duff. After each round of antibiotics, the *C. diff* kept returning. The only time she left her bed was to run to the bathroom—up to twenty times per day. Crushing fatigue set in from the lack of nutrients being absorbed by her inflamed intestine. "I wanted to die," she said. The relentless assault of the *C. diff* toxins so damaged part of her colon that sections of it had to be removed. More antibiotics. *C. diff* came back again. Now Duff's kidneys began to shut down. Her heart was showing signs of stress. Exasperated, her doctors said the only move they had left was to remove her entire colon, leaving her with a colostomy bag. But even this might not work. "You should get your affairs in order," they told her.

For about 15,000 Americans every year, this is the end stage of *C. diff*. But Duff's daughter refused to give up. A desperate internet search led her to something that sounded promising—a treatment called a fecal transplant. The procedure, she discovered, was just what it sounded like. Feces from a healthy person are transplanted via enema into the colon of the person with *C. diff*. The results, she read, were remarkable—almost always resulting in a cure.

Healthy feces are made up of lots of stuff: 75 percent water and 25 percent solid material, undigested fiber, protein, cells lining the intestine that have sloughed off, fats, salts, and mucus. But, importantly, of the solid material about 50 percent to 80 percent is comprised of *bacteria*, both dead and living. Strange as it sounds, feces *are* a probiotic, but they differ from traditional probiotics in an important way. Normal over-the-counter probiotics usually only have a handful of beneficial bacteria. Feces, on the other hand, comprise an *entire* ecosystem—a complete probiotic. The idea is simple and seems intuitively obvious in hindsight: Transfer the ecosystem back into the infected colon and let the normal bacteria "crowd out" the pathogenic species, thus restoring a healthy digestive tract. Remarkably, as Duff's daughter read, the procedure worked almost all the time and was associated with few, if any, side effects. But there was a catch: Only two doctors were doing it. One in Australia and one in Nevada. And Duff was too sick to travel.

"Re-establishing the Balance of Nature"

The idea of using fecal matter as medicine is not new. In 1941 the Nazis' North African campaign was nearing an end. They had won decisive battles over the British and were in control of the region. But an unanticipated adversary that threatened their victory emerged: a severe outbreak of dysentery. Because of Louis Pasteur's discoveries, the Nazi medical team knew that dysentery was caused by a microorganism. The pathogen swept relentlessly through the troops, who were living in close quarters. Hundreds of soldiers were dying by the week. In response, the Nazis flew in a team of physicians, chemists, bio-chemists, bacteriologists, and other experts to help. There were no antibiotics at that time; penicillin would not begin mass production until a year later.

The Nazi medical team made a curious observation: The local Arabs were not sick. Yet they *must* have been exposed to the same bacteria that were sickening the Germans through the local food and water, the medical team reasoned. Why were they not getting sick? The medical team observed them carefully. In fact, they discovered, the local Arab residents *were* getting sick, but at the first incidence of diarrhea the Arabs would do something that shocked the medical team. A sick Arab would go outside and wait patiently among the camels. Then, after a camel defecated, he would scoop up hand-fuls of steaming feces and eat them. The dysentery, the Nazis discovered, was *immediately cured*, often within hours. When the team asked the locals why they did this, the reply was always the same: "Because my father taught me, and his father taught him." The camel feces, the medical team reasoned, must contain a bacterium also—one that somehow countered the dysentery pathogen. A few desperately sick Nazi soldiers consumed the camel dung, and, like the Arabs, were immediately cured. The medical team set about creating a more palatable way to cure the troops. Using camel dung as a start-ing culture, they produced vats of a bacteria-laden broth for the dying troops to drink. They soon generated thousands of gallons of the murky liquid for the troops, curing hundreds of sick soldiers and halting the outbreak.

Later it was discovered the medicinal quality of the broth was due to a sin-gle bacterium: *Bacillus subtilis*. It is thought the effectiveness was due to this particular bacteria's aggressiveness. It engages in bacterial warfare, efficiently killing other bacteria, outcompeting for a niche environment. *B. subtilis* is able to establish its presence rapidly in the human gut, killing the bacterium responsible for dysentery in the process. The Germans soon figured out how to isolate and dry *B. subtilis* into a powder form that could be put into capsules and mass-produced. Sold under the brand name Bacti-Subtil, the capsules rapidly became the standard treatment for dysentery across the globe in the early 1940s.

In the meantime, commercial development of penicillin, discovered in 1928 in Alexander Fleming's unkempt Scottish laboratory, had stalled. The tantalizing possibility that the antibiotic produced by the fungus could be isolated and mass-produced was proving impossibly difficult. The fungus Fleming had discovered simply did not generate enough antibiotic to scale up for mass production. However, on a summer day in 1941, an assistant to two scientists who were attempting to increase the efficiency of penicillin production bought a cantaloupe covered in "a pretty, golden mold" at a local market. Back at the laboratory, the scientists tested the "golden mold" and discovered it was a hyperactive new strain of penicillin-generating fungus—producing 200 times more antibiotic than the species Fleming had discovered. They exposed the species to x-rays in the hope of producing mutations that might boost the production of antibiotic even higher. Eventually, they got lucky. A mutated strain emerged that produced 1,000 times more antibiotic than the original found on the cantaloupe. Manufacturing was quickly ramped up to meet wartime demand. By the end of the war, American pharmaceutical companies were producing 650 billion units of penicillin a month.

Once the war was over, the rapidly growing pharmaceutical industry needed new indications for the billions of units of "wonder drug" they were manufacturing. Dysentery became an obvious target for the drug's use, and physicians began preferentially prescribing penicillin over the camel dung–inspired Bacti-Subtil.

In the following decade, Big Pharma churned out new antibiotics with remarkable speed. In most cases the new drugs were considered medical miracles—curing patients of infections that only a few years prior had been fatal. "Substances that do deeds transcending all medical preconceptions," as Nobel laureate Payton Rous described them.[1] However, observant physicians began noticing a dark side to the new drugs. Antibiotics were the preferred treatment for dysentery, but, strangely, a few physicians began suspecting that antibiotics could also be *causing* dysentery. There arose a strange medical irony whereby a therapy appeared to be both the cure and the cause—like drinking more alcohol to cure a hangover. And worse, in difficult cases of dysentery, antibiotics sometimes didn't work. They would treat a patient with some success, yet the infection would return. This time, more aggressive; this time, more difficult to treat.

In 1958 Ben Eiseman, then chief of surgery at the VA hospital in Denver, was one of the physicians suspicious of antibiotics' role in causing dysentery in some cases. He had a hunch. As a matter of routine procedure, surgical patients were given a course of antibiotics preoperatively to prevent an infection from taking hold while on the operating table. Too often, noted Eiseman, his patients developed dysentery while recovering from their operation. In a flash of insight, he reasoned that the antibiotics might be the cause—they must be wiping out the normal bacterial ecosystem and thus allowing more virulent bacteria to take hold. His hunch was this: Perhaps if he transferred the fecal matter of a healthy person into the colon of a postoperative patient with severe dysentery it might "re-establish the balance of nature," curing them of dysentery. At the time, antibiotics were still hailed as wonder drugs, and Eiseman's idea was entirely heretical. Feces were viewed as nothing more than a vector for disease, and the importance of the gut biome was not yet appreciated. To be sure, Eiseman's hunch was just a vague suspicion, a gut instinct that ran decidedly against medical convention. To transfer feces into a patient was inconceivable. But in 1958 physicians operated under a different set of rules. "Those were the days that if we had an idea, we simply tried it," said Eiseman. Over the course of a year, Eiseman performed fecal transplants on four postsurgical patients who had developed pseudomembranous colitis (this was before the cause of this affliction was known to be *C. diff*). All four patients had been given preoperative antibiotics; all four had developed severe dysentery; all four were near death. Eiseman sent a resident to collect stool specimens from a nearby maternity ward. He reasoned that pregnant women had the best probability of being young, healthy, and, importantly, most likely not to have taken antibiotics recently. Eiseman transferred the feces into his patients, and all four recovered immediately. Eiseman published the astonishing results in the journal *Surgery*.[2]

Despite Eiseman's extraordinary results, the procedure would lie dormant for thirty years. That is, until 1988, when Thomas Borody, a bold and irreverent gastroenterologist in Sydney, Australia, read Eiseman's paper. Borody had a patient who had reached a dead end. The patient had returned from Fiji with an undiagnosed intestinal ailment that had failed to respond to any of the treatments attempted so far. After some discussion, Borody and his patient, agreeing there was little to lose, decided to duplicate the procedure Eiseman had performed thirty years earlier. The patient recovered. Impressed by such an immediate and robust recovery, Borody began to treat other patients with fecal transplants. Borody now estimates he has performed the procedure 5,000 times since he first read Eiseman's paper.

"Pretty Close to Miraculous"

In fact, Borody was the Australian doctor Duff's daughter had run across in her frantic internet search to help her mother in 2012. He was one of only a few in the world performing the procedure for desperately sick *C. diff* patients. By now, however, even though the medical community had yet to embrace Eiseman's therapy, desperately ill patients and their families were finding a way. Do-it-yourself fecal transplant videos had cropped up on the internet. Another online search led Duff's daughter to an instructional video. The title: "How to Do an At-Home Fecal Transplant."

Wary of attempting a do-it-yourself fecal transplant, Duff and her daughter presented the idea to a few local physicians in Indiana, but none were willing to try it. Again at a dead end, a desperate Duff and her family turned back to the internet. Now out of options, Duff faced a simple choice: Do the at-home fecal transplant or, most likely, die. Her kidneys were shutting down, her colon was inflamed, necrotic, and rotting, and her heart was greatly weakened. It was now or never. The instruction video made the procedure seem remarkably simple: A healthy donor's fecal sample is mixed in a blender with sterile saline, put into an enema bottle, and then squirted into the rectum. The supplies cost less than fifty dollars. Even though Duff's gastroenterologist refused to perform the treatment, he had at least agreed to screen her husband, John, as a potential donor.

When John's test came back clean, the Duffs went back to review the instructional video. They had now fully resolved to take matters into their own hands. In the upstairs bathroom John captured some of his stool in a sterile plastic bag. He then walked downstairs into the kitchen and, after putting on a pair of plastic gloves, followed the video's instructions on how to prepare the sample. He then took the gloves off and walked upstairs. Duff, who was lying on the bed, turned onto her left side and drew her knees up to her chest as John administered the enema. John had propped the foot of the bed up with a piece of lumber to let gravity help keep the enema in as long as possible. He kissed his wife on the forehead. And then they waited. The whole procedure scarcely took the whole morning.

"If you've ever made a milkshake, you can do it," said Michael Silverman, MD, chair of the infectious disease division at the Schulich School of Medicine and Dentistry at Western University in London, Ontario. As graphic as that sounds, it has been estimated that tens of thousands of do-it-yourself fecal transplants have been performed to date. About 10,000 people find the videos that have cropped up on blogs and social media sites like Facebook and YouTube every year. In fact, demand for the procedure has vastly outstripped the few doctors willing to perform it. For every procedure performed by a doctor, many, many more have been performed at home by people like Duff.

When she finally had to get up and go to the bathroom, Duff could tell she already felt different. That night she slept soundly. For the first time in months, she didn't have to rush to the bathroom in the middle of the night. "When I woke up I felt good enough to take a shower and dry my hair and put on makeup and jewelry—things I hadn't done in months!" Duff's recovery mirrored the testimonies of many of the DIYers on social media. The effects were almost instantaneous and enduring.

The handful of doctors performing fecal transplants in their offices observed similar results. "It's the closest thing to a miracle that I've ever seen in medicine," reported one gastroenterologist. "I've been in medicine for a little more than forty years, and I don't think I've ever done anything that has helped as many people and changed as many lives as fecal transplant has," said Lawrence J. Brandt, a gastroenterologist at the Albert Einstein College of Medicine in New York, and an early pioneer of the procedure. "We're dealing with something that is pretty close to miraculous."[3]

Brandt performed his first fecal transplant in 1999. He estimates that at the time he was the only doctor in the United States doing it. By 2012, when Catherine Duff underwent her at-home procedure, maybe a handful of other gastroenterologists had adopted it. But why not more? Strangely, the reluctance of the medical community to embrace the procedure wasn't necessarily from a complete lack of evidence. A 2011 review paper analyzing over 300 patients with *C. diff* who had undergone the procedure reported a cure rate as high as 92 percent.[4] Even so, the number of doctors willing to perform fecal transplants was bizarrely low. The math simply didn't add up. Thousands of people were dying from *C. diff* every year. How could modern medicine be failing these patients so badly? Especially considering there was a remarkably effective, low-cost, safe solution the medical community had known about since 1958. The fact that these people didn't have to die sparked something close to outrage in Duff.

Meanwhile, the FDA had no idea what to do with fecal transplants. In the spring of 2013, a year after her DIY fecal transplant, Duff drove her Chevy Tahoe to the NIH campus in Bethesda, Maryland, to attend a workshop. Passing through the security gates, she drove up to Lister Auditorium, a floor-to-ceiling glass building that stood out on the sprawling campus. Even though only a few doctors were performing fecal transplants, because of the meteoric rise in the number of DIYers, the FDA was being forced to reckon with the unusual procedure. The two-day workshop was entitled "Fecal Microbiota for Transplantation." The goal was to establish some sort of guideline for the procedure.

Conference attendees filled 150 of the 176 seats in the auditorium. One hundred and forty-nine were taken up by medical doctors, researchers, and affiliates of the CDC or FDA. And a single seat was filled by the only member of the public to attend: Catherine Duff. Wearing a black cardigan sweater, she sat in the back row. The 149 experts were there to make a circumspect evaluation of the procedure—the benefits and risks. Fortuitously, there was fresh evidence to consider. A few months prior, findings of the first randomized, controlled trial (RCT) of fecal transplants for *C. diff* were published in the *New England Journal of Medicine*. The results had been stunning. The trial had randomly assigned patients with recurrent *C. diff* into three groups: One group received a fecal transplant, and the other two groups received antibiotics alone, or antibiotics with bowel lavage. The trial was initially designed to include 120 patients, but it was stopped after only 43 patients had been treated. The doctors stopped the trial as soon as they saw that the fecal-transplant patients had a cure rate of 94 percent while the antibiotic group's cure rate was less than a third. In light of these results, the investigators considered it unethical to continue the trial and began administering fecal transplants to the antibiotic group. The author's conclusion wasted few words: "The infusion of donor feces was significantly more effective for the treatment of recurrent *C. difficile* infection than the use of vancomycin."[5]

·Duff listened as the speakers gave their presentations. The benefits seemed clear. The regulatory agencies, however, were mostly focused on the risks. To be sure, the published review papers on fecal transplants showed minimal risk. The reported side effects were mostly self-limiting and seemed to be related to the infusion itself. The symptoms most commonly noted were bloating, flatulence, belching, and abdominal cramps. When the procedure was done in a doctor's office, the stool sample was always screened for transmittable viruses, pathogenic bacteria, and parasites, which removed the most immediate risk of infecting the recipient. The other possible risks seemed far removed. There was a possibility that the donor might gain weight if the sample was donated by an overweight person, for example. As Duff listened, it became clear that the representatives of the regulatory agencies were more concerned with the unknown future risks that might surface years after the procedure. In her opinion, they had somehow lost touch with what mattered. Why were they so concerned with some nebulous future risk when people were dying *now*, today? Why had this meeting veered so far off track? As she listened, her smoldering anger grew in intensity.

By the second day of the workshop it was clear to Duff what the FDA intended to do: They would regulate fecal transplants like any other new drug. This meant bureaucracy. And lots of it. The few doctors performing the lifesaving procedure would now have to fill out an Investigational New Drug application, or IND, if they intended to continue doing it. This was no trivial task. Completing the lengthy IND (printed out and set on a scale, it weighs twenty-two pounds) can take a busy clinician up to a year, and that's with staff helping. In effect, this would shut down access to most people suffering from *C. diff*, forcing them to go the do-it-yourself route, like Duff.

Midmorning on day two it was Catherine Duff's turn to speak. She stood up immediately after Jay Slater, director of the FDA's Division of Bacterial, Parasitic and Allergenic Products, who had added additional emphasis for the need to classify the procedure under an IND. Duff nervously adjusted the microphone and began to speak: "I seem to be the only actual member of the public that's here at the public forum. I'm one of those people who call and email you every day." Duff went on to recount her story. Consumed with emotion, tears flowed down her face. "If your spouse, child, parent, sibling, or best friend were dying from antibiotic resistant *C. diff* I imagine that all of you would want them to be able to try a fecal transplant. People are dying every day, today, right now. I have a wonderful husband, three amazing daughters, and two small grandchildren, and I want to live. All of us just want a chance to live. Please, do something not only for me, but for all those around the country and everywhere who have no insurance, no financial resources, no computer with which to Google information, and no hope. Please do something quickly."

Until Duff spoke, the meeting had marched down a predictable path. The FDA almost always regulates new products as Investigational New Drugs, and it was treating fecal transplants no differently. Approval involves massive trials of hundreds to thousands of patients to prove safety and efficacy and costs hundreds of millions of dollars. It can take up to a decade before the FDA gives its blessing. But something was lost in the room, and Duff had brought it back. It was a simple risk-benefit analysis rationally applied to the procedure with all the available, existing data. The highly powered RCT that had finally dragged medicine out of the Dark Ages—decimating unnecessary procedures like the radical mastectomy and proving the efficacy of many others—had now somehow morphed into a dogmatic straitjacket, a religion, the Hippocratic oath taken to an extreme ideology. The pendulum had swung too far. What was desperately needed was old-fashioned common sense. People were dying, and a fecal transplant was the cure. This simple realization needed to come first, and the rest—the potential for long-term risks to be uncovered by large-scale clinical trials—could be sorted out later.

For the fifty-seven-year-old grandmother from Carmel, Indiana, however, common sense prevailed. Somehow, what seemed so clear to Duff became submerged and muddied as the experts debated. It was certain that fecal transplants saved lives; no one disputed that. What the real long-term risks were, though, no one could be sure. And that was the hitch. It was the FDA's job to safeguard the public from the long-term and unforeseen risk presented by new drugs and procedures. Period. They were just doing their job. But to

Duff, and the thousands like her, the equation was simple. The immediate risk was death by organ failure caused by *C. diff.* Anything else was inconsequential. "FDA and some others are concerned about the long-term effects. But my point was these people are getting ready to die now," said Brandt. "They're not going to survive long enough to develop the disease you're afraid they're going to get."[6]

As Duff took her seat there was a moment of complete silence. In that instant, an almost imperceptible shift occurred in the Lister Auditorium. Suddenly, the audience erupted into applause. Duff had reaffirmed something that had almost escaped them. And they felt it. The air was exchanged and then rushed back in. The room exploded in a new, vigorous debate, now restored—thanks to Duff—to its original purpose: how best to help real people suffering from a potentially terminal illness. The handful of clinicians who were treating patients with fecal transplants were saving lives, attenuating a massive amount of suffering, and witnessing few, if any, worrisome side effects. The practitioners in the room were emboldened by Duff's emotional testimony. "We don't have three years to wait, and there are a lot of patients like the one who just spoke," said a Mayo Clinic doctor. "How are we going to help these patients while studies are going on?" asked another.

Most patients desperately wanted the peace of mind of having a doctor perform the transplant safely. But the FDA was threatening to place a massive roadblock in front of patient access to the lifesaving procedure. The debate continued to rage as the facility staff shut down the lights in the auditorium and sheepishly attempted to usher them out. A few months later, however, the FDA reversed their decision requiring a doctor performing fecal transplants to fill out an IND. Instead, they announced, they would be exercising "enforcement discretion"—a vague way of saying that, for the time being, they would not prosecute anyone performing the procedure. Even so, many admit that the FDA's noncommittal position creates a cloud of uncertainty for doctors who might otherwise be willing to perform the procedure today.

The Low-Hanging Fruit in Health Care

The story of fecal transplantation raises a critical question: When it became clear that this was a cheap, safe, and incredibly effective procedure for a problem *with no other solution*, why was it not quickly adopted across the country? How was it overlooked by the medical community while thousands of people died from *C. diff*?

The answer is not straightforward. One problem is governance. Health care is not governed from the top down. There is no single, formal committee that could recognize the value of something like fecal transplantation and order it to be adopted at hospitals across the country. Our health care system is a fragmented arrangement that demands doctors operate as independent agents. In fact, most states have strict laws to ensure that physicians remain self-governing, uninfluenced by outside corporate entities. This is why most clinics and hospitals are either nonprofit or physician-owned so as to avoid "the corporate practice of medicine." Because health care is a loose system structured around the autonomy and self-sufficiency of the physician, the adoption of any new treatment is typically dependent on each doctor alone.

But the unavoidable truth is that any health care system that depends on individual physicians has outgrown itself. Because medicine has become so complex, doctors simply don't know everything. They can't. For most of history medicine was much less complex, and doctors had a good understanding of *all* the interventions and medications available to them. Today that is not the case. The complexity of medicine has exploded in recent decades. As previously mentioned, there are now 4,000 medical and surgical procedures and every doctor has a license to prescribe 6,000 drugs. "It looks like a completely different world. We have now found treatments for nearly all of the tens of thousands of conditions that a human being can have . . . and we've reached the point where we've realized, as doctors, we can't know it all. We can't do it all by ourselves," said Atul Gawande.[7]

A change in the culture of health care is desperately needed. And a simple acknowledgment of the human mind's capabilities is the first step. The enormous body of medical knowledge has outstripped the human mind's ability to catalog and implement it effectively. Consequently, such simple, cheap, and effective procedures as fecal transplants often slip through the cracks unnoticed by a system shackled to the fallibility of the human mind. "The most expensive care is not necessarily the best care. And the best care often turns out to be the least expensive," said Gawande. These are precisely the kind of issues, the proverbial "low-hanging fruit," that the Berkshire,

Amazon, and JPMorgan consortium have the unique opportunity to address, leveraging technology to create inspired solutions.

Surely there are many factors at play. There is a human cognitive bias, the *pro-innovation bias*, that assigns excessive optimism to newer technologies, often at the expense of interventions or medications perceived to be low-tech or outdated. And there is the time-tested *bandwagon effect*, the tendency to follow the herd. It's difficult to be the first one to start mixing poop in a blender when all your colleagues are prescribing the latest and greatest antibiotics.

Like fecal transplants—and for many of the same reasons—many low-tech, cheap medical interventions are left behind. For example, extracting the full potential out of many old medications has also fallen through the cracks in the system. In Big Pharma's frenzied quest to find the next block-buster medicine, old drugs that have lost patent protection—usually referred to as *generics*—get lost in a financial purgatory. But the truth is that many "off-patent," generic drugs hold tremendous promise to treat diseases other than those for which they were originally intended. In other words, there is a lot of *unrealized potential* in today's 6,000 existing drugs. And, like the fecal transplant, their latent potential is often left ignored and languishing due to myriad cognitive biases and badly structured financial incentives.

New Uses for Old Drugs

To explain why this is, we must briefly grapple with the molecular nature of small-molecule *pharmacodynamics* (the complex interactions between a drug and the human body). Most drugs on the market today fall into a category called "small molecules," a simple reference to the number of atoms that make them up. And small molecules tend to be highly *pleiotropic*—a fancy way of saying that they affect more than one cellular process, or *pathway*, as it is known in molecular biology. Picture it this way: The effect of a small-mol-ecule drug can be imagined to be like trying to stop a single gear inside an engine by throwing in a handful of ball-bearings machined to be the right size to fit into the teeth of the targeted gear. Yes, gumming up the targeted gear will give the desired result. But inevitably some of the bearings will also become lodged in whatever other gears, pulleys, and levers have similarly sized nooks and crannies, thus also inadvertently inhibiting the operation of the engine's other processes. In pharmacological terms, the biological effects that occur beyond a drug's intended result are known as *off-target*, or *off-label* effects. At first glance, nothing about off-target effects would seem good, and many off-target effects are indeed bad—cast into the bucket labeled "deleterious side effects" that adorn the packaging of every medication. Yet, some off-target effects can be therapeutic—binding up the gears and levers of an entirely different disease process.

Due to its remarkable pleiotropy, a typical small-molecule drug has been shown to affect, on average, six molecularly relevant cellular pathways. Simple arithmetic reveals that the number of FDA-approved indications per drug does not come close to reflecting the quantitative opportunity that exists in the current pharmacopeia (all 6,000 approved drugs). "My opinion is that we could actually get more if we stopped putting all our efforts into the new, and spent more time tinkering with what we already have," said Gauthier Bouche, director of clinical research of the Anticancer Fund, a Belgium-based not-for-profit with the mission of realizing the full potential of old medications.[8]

Occasionally, a clinically relevant "off-target" effect will fortuitously emerge at the right time, giving the pharmaceutical company an opportunity to "repurpose" the drug for the newly observed indication while it is still under patent protection. Case in point: Sildenafil (Viagra) came from a phase 1 trial of Pfizer's promising new compound labeled UK-92480 for angina (chest pain caused by reduced blood flow to the heart). The compound failed to relieve angina, but a different, off-target effect unmistakably was noted in the patient population: sustained erections. Similarly, minoxidil was in a phase 1 trial for hypertension when the patients noticed unexpected hair growth. Upjohn Pharmaceuticals realized the enormous potential and pivoted—the result was the famous branded product for hair loss, Rogaine.

But most of the "off-target" effects of drugs aren't noticed until much later, over decades of observing large patient populations on the drug. By then the drug has usually lost its patent protection. And herein lies the problem: When a drug loses its patent protection, pharmaceutical companies have zero incentive to do the required trials to win a new indication for the drug. They could never recoup the cost. These promising drugs then become known as "financial orphans"—drugs suspended in a financial purgatory. However, all is not lost. Thankfully, even though the pharmaceutical industry cares little for these orphan drugs, academia, nonprofits, and governments do fund research on nonpatentable compounds to determine their potential to treat new diseases. Academics are continually searching for interesting research leads that have a high probability of getting funded. Once a lead is identified, there tends to be a stampede toward the same promising research all at once. The upshot is a surprising amount of research supporting the off-label use of some old medications.

But then things get bizarre. Even with a substantial body of research supporting the use of certain old drugs for other diseases, the health care system has no mechanism to get these drugs onto the prescription pads of physicians. Most doctors rely on FDA approval and the pharmaceutical sales force to guide their prescription writing. They certainly don't have the time to sort through the thousands of studies pertaining to the off-label use of generic drugs, and, to be honest, have little incentive to do so. So for the most part, even with significant data supporting their use, these promising medications just sit. And sit.

For example, consider the type 2 diabetes drug metformin. Metformin was first approved in France in 1957 and then in the United States in 1995. It was a godsend for type 2 diabetics—a remarkably effective medication for the insidiously corrosive disease with very few side effects. Metformin is listed on the World Health Organization's (WHO) List of Essential Medicines. These are the medicines considered to satisfy the priority health care needs of the population and are the medications that WHO has determined people should have access to at all times in sufficient amounts.[9] Today, metformin is the most prescribed drug in the world for type 2 diabetes, and, according to a 2017 *Business Insider* article, the eighth most prescribed drug in the United States. (Vicodin is number one.)

Metformin was first discovered to have antitumor activity in hamsters in 2001. This led to a series of population studies that resulted in head-scratching conclusions: Type 2 diabetics taking metformin appeared to be diagnosed with many types of cancer significantly less frequently than the general population, and, if they were diagnosed, they tended to respond to treatment better and live longer. This befuddled researchers because, in general, type 2 diabetics are a less healthy group and are known to have higher rates of cancer. Yet somehow metformin appeared to be reversing this norm entirely. Some studies even suggested that metformin was piling on an additional protective effect, that diabetes patients on metformin were living longer with certain cancers than the healthy population of nondiabetics. These eyebrow-raising studies led to a frenzied explosion of research into metformin's anticancer properties—hundreds of studies, not one of them sponsored by Big Pharma. Why? Because the drug is off-patent a pharmaceutical company could never recoup the cost of the large trial that would be needed to win FDA approval for the new indication. There is no financial incentive.

The traditional way a drug gets into the "system" is like this: Big Pharma takes a promising drug candidate and ushers it though phase 1, 2, and 3 clinical trials, wins approval from the FDA, and then hands the new drug over to its massive nationwide sales force to knock on the doors of clinics throughout the country and pitch the new drug's virtues. With the fresh stamp of FDA approval, physicians are safe to prescribe the new drug to their patients. Because the research to support their use falls outside of this time-honored process, promising off-patent drugs like metformin get lost in the system—stranded in a financial neverland. "Even though there is no traditional phase 3 trial, there are hundreds of observational studies and phase 1 and 2 type of trials—I would argue that the existing evidence, cumulatively, is as convincing as any pharma-funded phase 3 trial," said Robin Bannister, PhD, the head pharmaceutical chemist for the SEEK group, a U.K.-based pharmaceutical company dedicated chiefly to making new use of old medications, speaking from his London office. "There is a shocking amount of data out there to support the use of some of these old drugs, it just seems that few doctors are really paying attention."[10]

Those who are paying attention, however, describe metformin's nontraditional entry into the oncology field as a pharmaceutical fairy tale. Lewis Cantley, director of the Cancer Center at Weill Cornell Medicine, stated in a 2017 *Wired* article about metformin: "Metformin may have already saved more people from cancer deaths than any drug in history."[11] That's a bold statement. In the same article, Nobel laureate James Watson suggested something equally profound, stating that metformin is "our only real clue into the business" of fighting cancer. In a 2016 *New York Times* article Watson had explained that the traditional method of targeting cancer through genes had been "remarkably unhelpful" and that the recent shift to targeting cancer through biochemical, metabolic pathways with drugs like metformin held extraordinary promise. And that if he were going into cancer research today, he "would study biochemistry rather than molecular biology."[12] This isn't just theoretical talk for Watson; he is so convinced of the preventive power of metformin that he takes it daily.

But it isn't only metformin. Another old class of drugs with mountains of data supporting off-label anticancer activity is the cardioprotective class of drugs known as statins. As with metformin, the off-label anticancer potential of statins has been hinted at in the medical literature for decades. For example, an RCT done at Osaka University Hospital and published in the *British Journal of Cancer* in 2001, showed that the addition of a simple statin drug to the standard treatment for eighty patients with liver cancer increased the median length of survival by 100 percent—from nine months in the group that received standard treatment alone, to eighteen months when a statin was added to the treatment. The drug is extraordinarily safe (especially in the context of having a potentially terminal cancer) and the cost is about the same as metformin: a nickel per pill. Even so, it is rarely, if ever, used in the treatment of cancer, because, like fecal transplants and metformin, it falls outside the current standard of care and lacks formal FDA approval.

In the summer of last year, the British newspaper the *Guardian* published an article titled "Statins Could Reduce Risk of Breast Cancer Death by 38%, Research Shows."[13] The article cited seven observational studies that had tracked tens of thousands of women with breast cancer. It compared those who started taking a certain class of statin (lipophilic statins, such as atorvastatin, or Lipitor) around the time they were diagnosed to those who did not. The results were eyebrow raising. The study showed that the women who began taking a lipophilic statin around the time of diagnosis had a 38 percent reduced risk of dying from their cancer. This is not trivial; these numbers represent real lives. As with the administration of fecal transplants and metformin, this simple, low-cost, low-risk intervention has the potential to save thousands and thousands of lives.

But how are statins actually doing this? "Cancer cells have membranes highly enriched in cholesterol. It is an important building block supporting growth. Cancer cells even manufacture cholesterol internally," explained

Bannister. "By reducing the cancer cells' ability to manufacture cholesterol, we are essentially reducing cancer's ability to grow." Yet the anticancer effect of statins extends further. Mechanistic studies show that, like all small molecules, statins are remarkably pleiotropic—binding multiple gears and levers that are activated in the cancer cell.

The opportunity in repurposing drugs has another dimension. Because these drugs are often prescribed together, observational studies can unveil drug-drug synergies. "When statins and metformin are combined, that data gets really interesting," says Bannister, referring to their effect on cancer cells. "The two drugs appear to synergize with each other, each enhancing the effect of the other." Indeed, when one sifts through the literature, the observational data speak loudly: Patients taking both a statin and metformin appear to have dramatically lower rates of developing cancer and better outcomes when they do get cancer.

The promise of repurposing drugs for cancer goes far beyond statins and metformin. There are approximately eighty drugs approved by the FDA for other diseases that have shown various degrees of promise as anticancer medications. Consider aspirin, one of the oldest drugs in the world. References to aspirin-containing plants appear as far back as ancient Egypt. Studies dating back to the 1950s have made the tantalizing suggestions that aspirin could help prevent some types of cancer, or help arrest the spread of the disease in people who do develop cancer. "When many of these drugs were developed, we had a very simplistic view of cancer, and all the focus was on finding ways of killing cancer cells," says Pan Pantziarka, whose son died at age seventeen from a rare type of cancer.[14] Today Pantziarka, PhD, is the joint coordinator of the Repurposing Drugs in Oncology (ReDO) project of the Belgium-based Anticancer Fund, which aims to identify the most promising medicines for repurposing and get them into clinical trials.

Indeed, for most of the twentieth century, researchers' basic understanding of cancer shaped the way they "framed" the disease, perhaps introducing a bias that allowed them to miss, or pass over, drugs that didn't fit into the theoretical framework. Today, however, a renaissance in the understanding of cancer's basic biology is underway. A new appreciation for targeting cancer through metabolic, inflammatory, and epigenetics pathways has surfaced. "The whole system depends on developing a supporting blood supply, subverting the immune system, and producing certain growth factors. A lot of these repurposed drugs address these other things that cancer is dependent on to survive," says Pantziarka. "Changing the microenvironment with anti-inflammatories or drugs that modulate the immune system or drugs that change the metabolic environment, we now know, has the ability to change the course of the disease," says Bannister. "We just didn't consider this before."

For Pantziarka and millions like him, the calculation is easy. Even if there is no phase 3 RCT to support the use of many of these drugs, the risk is often minimal. And the data that do exist, in many cases, can be compelling. "It just makes sense to try something that might weaken the tumors but wasn't going to have a big impact on me in terms of side effects," said a lung cancer patient in a 2016 *Guardian* article titled "The Cancer Drugs in Your Bathroom Cabinet." "If you've got a lethal diagnosis, then you're going to have to take some risks to beat it," said Ben Williams, a brain cancer survivor and author, who at one point was taking more than twenty repurposed drugs to combat his cancer.[15]

While it makes sense to the patients with potentially terminal diagnoses, it doesn't to most doctors. "My doctor was not very positive," said Pantziarka, when he approached his physician about prescribing some off-label drugs for his son. Other patients hoping to add drugs like metformin to their cancer fight often encounter similar skeptical sentiments. And the practitioners' caution is understandable. For doctors, prescribing drugs off label can come with career risks. Typically, doctors don't have any experience with the off-label use of these old medications, and if dangerous adverse events occur—even if unrelated to the medications—they could get in trouble. "I'm nearing the end of my career," one oncologist told me, "I've always been conservative, and, especially now, I don't want to do anything that might get me in trouble." Herein lies the heart of the problem. To be sure, medicine was slow to adopt the scientific method in the form of the RCT. And its broad adoption ushered medicine into a new era. But somewhere along the way the RCT transitioned into something else. It became an almost religious belief system, a cop-out of sorts, an excuse that any evidence outside an RCT and formal regulatory approval is invalid. Researchers often joke that the dogmatic belief in the RCT can be represented by a doctor about to skydive. Just before it is his turn to jump the doctor hesitates and asks the question:

"How do I know the parachute is going to work? It has never been tested in a randomized, controlled trial." And yet, from the perspective of human incentive, the situation is quite understandable. For a doctor to limit his or her practice to the comfortable confines of FDA-approved treatments, or the "standard of care," as it is commonly referred to, is to avoid the massively complex universe of non-RCT data that exist in the medical literature and to sidestep the career risk that comes with treating patients off label. It is the easier path. But our health care system desperately needs the flexibility and analytics to incorporate non-RCT data. Should fifty observational, phase 1 and 2 types of studies be considered the equivalent of a single phase 3 RCT? Should "real-world data" captured from interconnected electronic medical record systems guide off-label treatments? These sorts of questions need to be asked. And this is where smart reformers can have a meaningful impact. If a patient needs a parachute, it should be prescribed.

Indeed, non-RCT evidence—like that found through a thoughtful search of old medical records, for example—can reveal surprising opportunities for old drugs. We need a system flexible enough to capitalize on these opportunities. Consider the incidence of breast cancer: Two hundred thousand women are diagnosed with early stage breast cancer every year in the United States. Of the 40,000 women who die every year of their disease, 75 percent (30,000) had received their diagnosis early, when the cancer was still localized. Although they undergo treatment—usually the best modern medicine has to offer: surgery, radiotherapy, sometimes chemotherapy—the disease recurs. In other words, 75 percent of deaths from breast cancer occur in women who had caught it early on, only to have a fatal recurrence.

Since the days of Halsted, cancer recurrence has baffled generations of researchers and physicians. Why does it occur so often, even when the disease is caught early and removed, and treatment is administered to kill any residual cells that may be lingering at distant sites? The timing offers a provocative clue. When you look at a graph of recurrence over time, it appears counterintuitive. Instead of the smooth arc you would expect to see, there is a massive upward spike in recurrences at about one year after surgery—and then the line levels back down into the expected smooth arc. "What does that mean?" asked Vikas Sukhatme, dean of the School of Medicine at Emory University and founder and chief executive officer of GlobalCures, a nonprofit dedicated to drug repurposing. "It suggests there are events that occur at the time of surgery. Perhaps the act of taking out the tumor itself. Perhaps it's the wound that's created and the events that follow," suggests Sukhatme.[16]

Pause for a moment to consider this. Think about the massive wound created during surgery and the wound-healing process that follows. "The surgery creates a wound and nature responds in a fairly stereotyped and well-defined manner," says Sukhatme. When a wound is created, the natural sequence of events is as follows: Platelets arrive at the scene to stop the bleeding, but they also release an arsenal of compounds that serve to stoke inflammation, attract immune cells, and sterilize the wound. Next, responding to growth factors, epithelial cells begin to divide and repair the wound. This is a natural and beneficial process, but, in the context of cancer, the effect of the released factors is akin to pouring fuel on a fire. Indeed, the inflammatory and growth factors might "wake up" any remaining cancer cells that had spread beyond the surgical excision and incite them to start multiplying. This process offers a powerful explanation for the as-yet unexplained spike in recurrence at the one-year mark.

An animal experiment performed in 1959 by two brothers at the University of Pittsburgh gives haunting evidence that this is indeed the case. The brothers were inspired to measure the effect of the wound-healing process on cancer growth. To do this, they devised a clever experiment. First, they injected a tiny number of cancer cells, approximately fifty, into the portal veins of a number of rats. (The portal vein drains blood from the gastrointestinal tract directly into the liver.) They then waited five months, sacrificed the animals, and removed their livers. Surprisingly, the rat's livers were healthy, and there was no evidence of tumor growth. The injected cells were unable to take up residence and multiply. The brothers then modified the experiment. They repeated the injection of fifty cells into the rats' portal veins, but this time, starting at the three-month mark, they made incisions across the bellies of the rats. They repeated the incisions every few weeks. The incisions had no other purpose than to test the effect of the factors that were released from the wound-healing process on distant cancer cells. This time, when they looked at the rats' livers after five months they had exploded with visible tumors. And the tumors were not confined to just a few animals—100 percent of the incision-receiving animals had developed tumors.[17]

This research inspired a young Belgian graduate student to ask an interesting question: Is there anything that might be done, any type of intervention during the preoperative period, that might target the inflammatory and growth factors that cascade outward from the surgical wound and help prevent recurrence and change the outcome for women with breast cancer? He turned to the records of women who had undergone mastectomies for breast cancer. His work required nothing more than a database search. What he found was stunning. "In those patients who pre-incisionally [in other words, before the operation started] got one dose of a non-steroidal anti-inflammatory drug, a cousin of aspirin called ketorolac, given intravenously, the recurrence rate was down by about 70 percent," said Sukhatme. (Ketorolac is a drug that is sometimes given in an attempt to mitigate morphine use after surgery.) When the student plotted the outcomes of only the patients given ketorolac, the massive spike in recurrences at one year had vanished. The anti-inflammatory drug had done something remarkable. "When you do the math, over ten thousand lives would be saved annually in the United States if this were to be true in a prospective study," said Sukhatme. And this opportunity is not confined to just breast cancer. The same spike in recurrence rates occurs in lung cancer and some other cancers. "Believe it or not, the data is actually fairly recent," adds Sukhatme. "There is also data in lung cancer showing that in those patients who got ketorolac, or one of its cousins, prior to surgery, there is also a reduced rate of recurrence."

Given this data, why aren't all cancer patients given this $10 shot before surgery? "If you were to go to a hospital today and ask your cancer surgeon for ketorolac, he or she would probably say, 99 percent of the time at the major academic medical centers, a flat-out no. But why? Why has this not become standard of care?" asked Sukhatme. One problem, he speculates, is that the data are retrospective (looking back at the literature) rather than prospective (from a deliberately designed trial going forward, the gold standard for measuring interventions).

There are also some minor risks involved. There is a small risk of more bleeding. But the biggest problem, states Sukhatme, is financial. Critically, the pharmaceutical industry—the companies that do these sorts of trials to win approval from the FDA—have no interest. "They have to look for a return on investment. . . . If they don't have patent protection [ketorolac is off-patent] for a drug they generally will not be interested." Consequently, this simple, safe, and dirt-cheap intervention, which could potentially save tens of thousands of lives and billions of dollars per year, just sits, while more people die. "These are clearly untapped opportunities," says Sukhatme.

It is not only in the treatment of cancer that gains are to be made from repurposing existing drugs. Existing drugs have shown promise in treating common conditions—autoimmune, neurodegenerative, and cardiovascular diseases, for example—as well as uncommon ones, such as retinitis pigmentosa, a rare genetic disease that can lead to blindness. Ketamine, a drug first synthesized in 1962 and approved by the FDA for use as an anesthetic in 1970, has recently been reborn as an off-label "wonder drug" for depression. Ketamine acts remarkably fast, as quickly as 24 hours in some cases. The practitioners who routinely use it off label tout its remarkable ability to reverse depression in patients for whom other drugs have failed. "I had patients who it's basically taken them from being suicidal to living a very full and complete life," said one neuropsychiatrist. "[Some] return on a periodic basis and some of them have just stopped coming in [because they've been cured]."[18]

Metformin alone has shown the potential to treat a range of diseases, from lung fibrosis to depression, polycystic ovary syndrome, neurodegenerative diseases like Alzheimer's, and cardiovascular disease. Because of its strange potential ability to aid in the treatment of such a vast and diverse range of disease, there is a hint at the tantalizing possibility that metformin may be impinging on a much more fundamental mechanism—aging itself. Indeed, because of metformin's "wonder drug" reputation, and the fact that it has already demonstrated the ability to extend the life-span of mice, the FDA has recently approved a monumental clinical trial called the TAME (Targeting Aging with Metformin) trial. Now, however, the issue becomes funding. Because metformin is off patent and there is no "pot of gold" at the end of the trial, Big Pharma has no interest. If Big Pharma doesn't stand to gain from the TAME trial, then who does? The answer is simple: society at large.

To even slightly attenuate the aging process would reap massive benefits for society. A 2013 economic analysis showed that slowing age-related diseases by only 20 percent would save more than $7 trillion in health care costs in the United States alone over the next half century. And the cost to potentially realize this windfall in savings is trivial. "The TAME Trial would cost 96 percent less than the cost to develop and win market approval for a single drug: $69 million vs. $2.4 billion, as estimated in a 2014 Tufts University Study," wrote Nir Barzilai, director of the Institute for Aging Research at Albert Einstein College of Medicine. With so much to gain from testing the ability of a nickel-a-pill drug to slow the aging process, one would like to think that this is where government would step in. Yet the trial remains unfunded.

No One Seems to Give a Shit

Indeed, there are many other tantalizing opportunities that remain untapped. A small but growing body of evidence suggests that a period of simple water-only fasting immediately before the administration of chemotherapy or radiation can significantly mitigate side effects and potentially increase the efficacy of other standard therapies. Yet because fasting is free, who will fund additional trials to prove it? Ironically, precisely because it *is* free, it's hard to imagine how something like a 24- to 48-hour water fast before chemotherapy would ever become part of standard of care. Same with a dietary protocol known as the "ketogenic" diet. The ketogenic diet, standard of care for childhood epilepsy in the 1920s, was an incredibly effective treatment that all but disappeared once antiseizure medications came on the market in the 1940s. Recent data suggest that the diet's therapeutic effect might extend to a range of other diseases, from certain cancers to neurodegenerative conditions.

We have a unique opportunity—with creative regulatory reform and the creative use of technology—to realize the potential of these opportunities sitting in plain sight. In a 2017 *New England Journal of Medicine* review article titled "Evidence for Health Decision Making—Beyond Randomized, Controlled Trials," the author makes the point that "Current evidence-grading systems are biased toward RCTs, which may lead to inadequate consideration of non-RCT data."[19] The author goes on to point out the value of different sources of data, and then concludes the article with this impactful summary: "There will always be an argument for more research and for better data, but waiting for more data is often an implicit decision not to act or to act on the basis of past practice rather than best available evidence. The goal must be actionable data—data that are sufficient for clinical and public health action that have been derived openly and objectively and that enable us to say, 'Here's what we recommend and why.'" It is this remarkably simple statement, "Here's what we recommend and why," calculated after analyzing *all available* evidence, that should be medicine's new guiding mantra.

What other simple interventions, like fecal transplants and "financial orphan" drugs, have fallen through the cracks? Interventions that if broadly implemented could make a huge impact in people's lives? One is basic hand-washing. It doesn't get any lower tech or cost effective. Most studies show that medical staff are compliant with standard handwashing protocols only around 80 percent of the time. The result of this seemingly innocent lapse is dramatic. "Two million people come into hospitals and pick up infections they didn't have because someone failed to practice basic hygiene," said Gawande, again, talking from the TED stage. Of these two million, 90,000 will die from infections they didn't have to get.

Another way to combat serious hospital-acquired infections is merely timing the administration of presurgical antibiotics so that the maximum dose hits the bloodstream at the moment the surgeon's knife makes the first incision. Proper antibiotic timing has been shown to cut the postsurgical infection rate in half. Many simple measures such as this are all-too-often forgotten before surgery. To address this lapse, Gawande, working with WHO, created a nineteen-item checklist for surgical staff, consisting of the modest but critically important procedures that must be performed before, during, and after surgery. The checklist wasn't overly burdensome; it took on average two minutes to fill out. They then implemented the checklist in eight hospitals around the world, from rural hospitals in Tanzania and the Philippines to more urban ones in London and Seattle. "The complication rates fell 35 percent," said Gawande. "It fell in every hospital it went into. The death rates fell 47 percent. This was bigger than a drug." One would imagine that with such evidence of success this lifesaving checklist would be adopted everywhere. "It has been slow to spread. It is not yet the norm," says Gawande. There are few who doubt that the United States has the best-trained doctors in the world. Yet common mistakes, the type such checklists could avoid, kill nearly 200,000 Americans every year.[20]

Surprisingly, the idea of using checklists to avoid simple mistakes is not new; nor is the compelling evidence that they directly translate into a surprising number of lives saved. Peter Pronovost, at Johns Hopkins University, knew that up to 30,000 people die every year from infections coming from intravenous lines, so he developed a checklist consisting of five simple steps that doctors should take before they place such a line. After the checklist was adopted at over 100 hospitals, the infection rates at these hospitals dropped to almost zero. The results were published in the *New England Journal of Medicine* in 2006, yet even today Pronovost's checklist is often ignored.

What inconceivable combination of cognitive biases could allow thousands of people to die every year due to *inaction*—the health care system's inability to recognize and implement simple, low-cost drugs and procedures? Granted, checklists, going backward to research new potential in old drugs, handwashing, diets, fasting, ten-dollar shots to prevent recurrence, and fecal transplants are not very glamorous. What are glamorous are the next-generation medications, the targeted drugs and immunotherapies that cost half a million dollars per treatment, the latest surgical techniques, lasers, proton beams, and 3-D printed joint replacements. These are the treatments that generate excitement, headlines, and—perhaps most importantly—money. Five cent pills, $10 shots, checklists, not eating, handwashing, and enemas made from poop do not. And herein lies the problem: underestimating the power of incentives, first on Charlie Munger's list of cognitive biases from his 1995 Harvard talk "The Psychology of Human Misjudgment." Even though the data supporting these interventions are right there for anyone to look up, there is little interest. Collectively, these simple procedures and medications have the potential to save millions of lives and billions of dollars per year. Health consortiums like the Berkshire-Amazon-JPMorgan venture stand to gain enormously by wholeheartedly adopting this low-hanging fruit. But, for now, it is frustrating how few others seem to give a shit.

CHAPTER 4

The Way Forward

"From Worst to First"

In October 2008 the three Major League Baseball teams with the highest budgets—the New York Yankees, the Detroit Tigers, and the New York Mets—were sullenly watching from the sidelines while the Tampa Bay Rays, the franchise with the second-lowest payroll in the league, were playing in the World Series and glorified on televisions across America. The difference between the teams, besides payroll, was that Tampa was the only one using a data-driven approach. The Oakland A's had a mediocre 2008 season, finishing third in their division, but the data-driven approach that Billy Beane had pioneered was once again proving its merit.

On October 24, a day off between games two and three, a curious op-ed appeared in the *New York Times*. You would have been forgiven if, after reading the authors' names, you thought it was a prank. The co-authors were Newt Gingrich, a far-right Republican; John Kerry, a far-left Democrat; and Billy Beane, the general manager of the Oakland Athletics. The subject that was able to unite this strange trio was health care. The title of the op-ed was "How to Take American Health Care from Worst to First." In summary, it was a recognition of the enormity of the problem and a plea to do better. "In the past decade, baseball has experienced a data-driven information revolution. Number-crunchers now routinely use statistics to put better teams on the field for less money.

Our overpriced, underperforming health care system needs a similar revolution," they wrote.[1]

The problems with health care are easy to spot, they wrote, consisting of everything we've examined so far—overtreatment, inconsistent treatment, procedures backed by slim evidence, bad incentives—and a failure to broadly adopt basic things such as handwashing, checklists, and repurposed drugs. And these problems, noted the authors, always circle back to a single issue: a lack of guiding data. "Remarkably, a doctor today can get more data on the starting third baseman on his fantasy baseball team than on the effectiveness of life-and-death medical procedures. Studies have shown that most health care is not based on clinical studies of what works best and what does not—be it a test, treatment, drug or technology. Instead, most care is based on informed opinion, personal observation or tradition," they wrote. They went on: "America's health care system behaves like a hidebound, tradition-based ball club that chases after aging sluggers and plays by the old rules: We pay too much and get too little in return. To deliver better health care, we should learn from the successful teams that have adopted baseball's new evidence-based methods. The best way to start improving quality and lowering costs is to study the stats."

But the op-ed didn't just point out the problems with America's health care system. The trio offered a solution. They proposed the formation of a data-driven institute with the sole purpose of providing this critical guiding data. "Working closely with doctors, the federal government and the private sector should create a new institute for evidence-based medicine. This institute would conduct new studies and systematically review the existing medical literature to help inform our nation's over-stretched medical providers." And the institute, they were careful to point out, would not overly encroach on the autonomy of physicians. "Evidence-based health care would not strip doctors of their decision-making authority nor replace their expertise. Instead, data and evidence should complement a lifetime of experience, so that doctors can deliver the best quality care at the lowest possible cost." They also offered up success stories. Health care systems that were incorporating evidence-based measures to provide care that was not only better but at a fraction of the traditional cost.

One such system mentioned in the op-ed was an organization called Intermountain Healthcare. What makes Intermountain Healthcare so special? One name comes up: Brent James.

The Billy Beane of Health Care

Make no mistake: medicine must now begin a revolutionary transformation to transition from a central ethos based on physician self-sufficiency to one that cleverly constructs a data-derived boundary around cognitive bias–induced mistakes while still allowing the best parts of a physician's intuition to flourish. Human intuition is an extraordinary, almost indescribable force. In medicine, intuition can be magical—an unconscious tapestry of connections percolating through to a conscious epiphany. The examples are everywhere: Eiseman's "gut feeling" that antibiotics were causing dysentery and that feces might be the cure. The intuition that whispered to Crile that the radical mastectomy might be unnecessary. My favorite example is from the movie *Lorenzo's Oil*. It's the true story of a child with a rare inherited metabolic disorder that typically follows a tragic course, attacking the brain and central nervous system and causing blindness, deafness, paralysis, and then death at an early age. There was no treatment. In fact, the experts had yet to elucidate the precise metabolic pathway underpinning the disease. The parents, with no medical background, refused to give up. They immersed themselves in the endeavor to understand the core pathway behind the disease, reading countless textbooks, journals, and papers, day and night, until the exact metabolic pathology—and the cure—came to the father in a dream. The story is a profound metaphor for the mystical dimensions of human intuition.

Without question, this transformation in medicine is sure to be bumpy as we grapple for the right balance between a physician's autonomy and data-based guidelines—an equilibrium that strives to mitigate flawed decision-making while still retaining, even enhancing, the profound power of human intuition. As this delicate balance is sought, the transformation is sure to be rocky. During the tumultuous transition the Oakland A's went through after Billy Beane fired his talent scouts and committed to analytics the initial backlash was fierce. This transformation will have shades of the battle that Fisher fought to dethrone the radical mastectomy. He, too, faced fierce backlash, some colleagues even calling him a "murderer." Indeed, this fundamental restructuring of the way medicine is practiced recalls an antiquated debate, a debate that has smoldered since the Greeks: intuition versus imperialism—the value of human judgment versus pure data. The clinical trial was the first incursion into a purely intuition-driven system. But it won't be the last.

Since the arrival of the first clinical trial in 1947, the explosion of clinical trials sponsored by the pharmaceutical industry has saturated medicine with a mindboggling amount of data on individual medications, procedures, and surgeries. But, ironically, this data tsunami has also created new gaps in knowledge. The spectrum of five treatments available for someone with newly diagnosed early prostate cancer, referenced in an example given earlier, exemplifies this problem. No one knows which treatment is better because no trial has been done to directly compare one to another. Doctors face decisions like this daily—decisions they must make in a haze of uncertainty. And it's right there—at the fuzzy interface where doctors must make decisions with limited data—where, behavior science shows, humans don't perform well.

The consequences are easy to measure: massive variations in health care from one hospital to the next, from one clinic to the next, and from one physician to the next. Clearly all of the extremes in treatment can't be right at the same time. There have to be "best practices" that lead to the best outcomes somewhere in the spectrum. But to search for the "best practice" is to encroach on the cowboy culture of medicine. Inevitably, some will view adherence to best practices as imposing limits on physicians—restricting their autonomy, devaluing their intuition, and valuing apathetic numbers over empathetic people. This is the frontline in the transition of the practice of medicine into a more evidence-based system.

Now, if there is one hero navigating this transition with the logic of Aristotle and the diplomacy of Kofi Annan, it is Brent James. But some heroes are more conspicuous than others. The archetypal hero is the fireman rushing into a burning building, the quarterback throwing the game-winning pass, the soldier that dies selflessly for his comrades. Brent James is not a household name. He is a different kind of hero, one who is not immediately obvious—except to the few who are paying attention. But if heroism were scaled in terms of human lives and money saved, Brent James would rise to the very top. James's heroism has saved thousands upon thousands of lives, prevented an untold amount of suffering, and conserved billions and billions of dollars.

For over thirty years, sixty-seven-year-old Brent James served as the executive director of the Institute for Health Care Delivery Research and vice president of medical research and continuing medical education for Intermountain Healthcare, a not-for-profit health system based in Salt Lake City, Utah. With 22 hospitals, more than 185 clinics, and 37,000 employees, it is the largest health system in the region. James entered medical school more out of practicality than passion. His first love was math. As the eldest of six kids growing up on a cattle ranch in Blackfoot Idaho, James often read a calculus book for fun. "I'm one of the relatively rare subset of people that finds math fun. Just thinking about it is fun. It's how my brain is wired." It became apparent to James, however, that it might be difficult to make a living with a math degree, and so he turned to medicine. But James never lost his love of numbers. After completing a residence in surgery, he again felt the seduction of numbers. Heeding his impulse, James took a job at the American College of Surgeons, where he employed statistics to study the variation that occurs among oncologists when they attempt to determine cancer stages. Soon after, James took a faculty position at Harvard's T.H. Chan School of Public Health.

While in Boston a rattling divorce left him with a desire to be closer to his family out west. He seized the opportunity to take a position at Intermountain Healthcare in Salt Lake City. James arrived at Intermountain in 1986, on the heels of finishing his training in advanced statistics. His timing was perfect. Intermountain was one of the first adopters of an electronic medical records (EMR) system. For a statistician interested in improving health care, an EMR system represented unlimited possibility—it was the equivalent of a scalpel for a surgeon. James immediately recognized the opportunity. He would be able to use his knowledge of statistics to address one of the most vexing problems in health care: treatment variation.

When James took a look at the records he was astonished. The EMR revealed massive variation in treatment within even the single hospital system. "We started to follow up on the variations. We couldn't determine who was right and who was wrong, but we could sure show that they were different," said James. As disturbing as it was, it was also an opportunity to do better. James called a meeting with the physicians at Intermountain. He showed them the massive differences in treatment for patients with the same diagnosis. "We provoked a firestorm, frankly, a discussion about the best clinical practice within our medical staff." James forced the doctors at Intermountain to confront a question: What treatment is *best*? This led first to constructive discussions and eventually to a consensus agreement on the best treatment for many conditions. James again turned to the medical record system. "We demonstrated a fairly massive narrowing in the variation that seemed to arise from those professional discussions, and it was associated with big improvements in clinical outcomes and at the same time significant drops in cost of care delivery."[2] By themselves, the doctors could not see beyond their own exam room walls. They couldn't track the patient outcomes; they had no way of knowing what the best care was in every scenario. But armed with the EMR, James could.

The die was cast. In James's view there was now unlimited opportunity to improve health care at Intermountain. His unique approach divided health care into two parts: the doctor and the system. Typically the system is intended to be passive, considered as little more than a shell within which the doctors operate, an infrastructure designed to be invisible. But James saw it differently. He boldly imagined how the system could help, becoming a dynamic *partner* with the doctors. James viewed his job as providing the data for doctors to do better, as working *with* them. "Ninety-five percent of our opportunity to improve outcomes is at the level of making it easier to do it right. . . . The trouble is when you mix complex systems with earnest hardworking, smart people, they will fail. . . . As a leader most of the time it's you, not them, it's the system and the context and environment that you create for them. My job is to make it easy to do it right."[3]

James created teams that scoured through the medical records looking for opportunities to improve. When studies clearly provided optimal treatment guidelines, the Intermountain EMR allowed James to see whether or not the doctors were following the guidelines. Electively (meaning optionally) induced labor was one such example. Both doctors and patients often decide to induce labor for various nonmedical reasons, discomfort and convenience being the most cited reasons. In 1999 a recommendation was made by the American College of Obstetricians and Gynecologists, that, for the baby's health, labor should not be electively induced before the 39th week of pregnancy. But doctors across the country didn't seem to heed the advice. Either they missed the recommendation, or they simply had no incentive to follow it. This failure came with consequences. To induce a labor early increased the risk that the baby would be born with respiratory problems. When James and his team looked through Intermountain's records they noticed that the doctors there were doing elective inductions before the 39th week at the same rate as the national average: roughly 30 percent of the time. James immediately sent out a protocol to the hospital's gynecologists urging them to adhere to the recommended guidelines: no elective inductions before the 39th week. The gynecologists took notice, and the rate of elective inductions at Intermountain is now less than 2 percent. Coincident with this reduction, the number of C-sections and babies born with respiratory problems has also fallen. The total savings: $50 million per year.

James and his team went further. When data didn't exist to establish optimal treatment guidelines for a given procedure, James and his doctors designed and executed the necessary studies there at Intermountain. For example, they thoughtfully considered the antibiotics given to patients to prevent surgical infection. A previous RCT had established that antibiotics were effective in preventing surgical-wound infections. The study, however, didn't establish the optimal *time* to take the antibiotics. When James and his team examined Intermountain's surgical records they noticed enormous variation in when the patients received the antibiotics. Some were getting the antibiotics 24 hours before surgery; others, an hour before surgery; and still others, 24 hours after surgery. The timing was all over the map. James reasoned that there had to be an optimal time to deliver the antibiotics that would result in the least surgical infections. To determine the best timing, James and his team convened four groups of surgeons. They asked one group to give the antibiotics within a 2-to-24-hour window prior to surgery, one group to give them within 2 hours prior to the surgery, one group to give them within 3 hours after the surgery, and the last group to give them in a 3-to-24-hour window after surgery.

After analyzing the data obtained from 2,847 patients, the result was clear: There was a massive reduction in infections in the group given the antibiotics 2 hours before the first incision. "Today of course it's a no-brainer," said James. "At the time it was amazingly counterintuitive." James initiated the procedural change among his surgical staff at Intermountain. From now on, across the board, antibiotics were to be given 2 hours before surgery. That year, 1987, the cost savings from reduced surgical infections was a million dollars. Since then, that seemingly simple change has saved thousands of lives and hundreds of millions of dollars.

James and his team then tackled a condition called acute respiratory distress syndrome, usually a complication of the flu, in the same methodical way. In the late 1980s a ventilator was introduced at Intermountain as a possible treatment for respiratory distress syndrome. But the new machine came with a caveat: No one knew the optimal ventilator settings. James and his team soon noticed that the ventilator settings varied wildly from one physician to the next, each one convinced that their settings made the most sense. "I thought there wasn't anybody better in the world at twiddling the knobs than I was," confessed one doctor. But James had a plan: have the doctors decide on consistent settings as a starting point. "Guys, it's more important that you do it the same way than what you think is the right way," James pleaded. When the doctors began twisting the knobs to the agreed-upon settings, James's EMR could then isolate and capture the data. Next, they adjusted the settings and again measured the outcome. In this methodical way, they eventually arrived at the optimal settings. Once these were established, the survival rate quadrupled, from approximately 10 percent before the optimization, to 40 percent.

The list of James's victories at Intermountain goes on and on. Through a series of system tweaks, adverse drug events were reduced by half. Death rates from bypass surgery were also halved—from the national average of 3 percent to 1.5 percent. They standardized lung care for premature babies and cut the number that required ventilator support by 75 percent. They tackled cholecystectomies (removal of the gallbladder), hip replacements, and pacemaker implants. To date, James and his team have optimized hundreds of medical procedures, and the results are measured in human lives. "I can document more than 1,000 [patients] per year in Utah that a few years ago would have died, but today they don't because of that approach," James said.[4]

None of this was easy for Brent James. Once he had established a best-practice protocol at Intermountain he then faced the daunting task of getting the doctors across Intermountain's 22 hospitals and 185 clinics to adopt it. There was the inevitable clash with the cowboy culture of health care. But James was prepared. He knew that once he established irrefutable data showing the best way to treat a patient with a certain condition, getting the doctors at Intermountain to implement it would take finesse and statesmanship.

Robert Watcher, chief of hospital medicine at the University of California, San Francisco, appreciated the delicate situation James was in. He told a *New*

York Times reporter, "He knows that the minute he says, 'I'm right, and you must do this,' he loses everybody but the true believers."[5] But this isn't what James did. And here lies his next display of artistry: inspired diplomacy. James did not see what he was doing as a direct challenge to the most important and coveted qualities of the physician: autonomy, intuition, and self-governance. In fact, he made it clear he had no intention of encroaching in a way that limited a doctor's intuition. James acknowledged that every patient is different. Even with an established, evidence-based protocol, there will be patients that won't bene-fit—and these patients need the skill and intuition of the individual doctor. "And this idea of a cookbook, a straitjacket, it just doesn't fit reality. So we established an evidence-based best practice protocol fully realizing that you could not write a protocol that perfectly fit any patient in the vast majority of circumstances. There are a few narrow circumstances where you can," says James.

Appreciating the touchy nature of the problem, Brent James's deep under-standing of psychology helped. Again, he turned to Intermountain's medical records system. Once the data had established the optimal practice for a given treatment, James used the system to find the doctors who had consis-tently adopted the protocol. He would then track their outcomes. Once it was apparent that they were getting better outcomes than their colleagues, he would become their champion. "Then my main role, believe it or not, was to trumpet their success. So everyplace I went, if you saw me coming down the hall, you could count on me buttonholing you and telling you about the last couple of projects and who did them."

What happened then was a sort of bandwagon effect—one doctor tells another, who tells another . . . Essentially, James, through positive reinforce-ment, co-opted the power of peer pressure. He created a self-perpetuating mechanism of peer-to-peer engagement to push uniform adoption. "Next thing you know, you've got somebody else on board and then you've got a few more on board, and the next thing you know, you're well past the tipping-point." James admits, "They were never going to respond to Intermountain. It's when their colleagues within the profession started to lean on them."

Ultimately, what James was trying to do, he says, was make it easier for doctors to practice medicine. To use data to look out beyond the walls of the hospital or clinic, to sidestep cognitive bias by giving them guidance in moments of uncertainty so that they could focus on what matters the most:

the patient. To him, it's not a battle at all, but an opportunity for the system to be better. "The key question for a leader is: How do we make it easy for them [the doctors] to do it right?" asks James. He masterfully frames the evidence-based system not as a fight, but as a collaboration that allows the intuition of the doctor to be less distracted and more focused. A system that is akin to a guardrail—a background safety buffer that allows doctors to direct their focus and intuition wherever it is most needed.

Another contributor to Intermountain's massive savings—since implemented by other high-quality providers, including the Mayo and Cleveland clinics—is doing away with the main incentive to overtreatment: the fee-for-service payment system, a construct that behavior scientists have been pounding the table about for some time, calling it out as the most obvious and corrosive conflict of interest in all of medicine. It's no coincidence that the best health care providers in the country pay their doctors a salary. "Fee-for-service payments have adverse consequences that dwarf those of the payments from pharmaceutical companies and device manufacturers that have received the lion's share of attention in the conflict of interest literature," said Professor George Loewenstein, a leading expert on conflicts of interest at Carnegie Mellon University.[6] Recognizing the power of incentives, Intermountain takes it a step further. In addition to taking away the incentive to overtreat, Intermountain gives bonuses to the doctors with the best outcomes.

Because the system changes at Intermountain are preventative by nature and also realign incentives, the results may be tallied in both lives *and* dollars saved. By preventing surgical infections, adverse drug interactions, newborn respiratory problems, and on down the list, thousands and thousands of lives are saved every year. As are hundreds of millions of dollars. As Utah's largest health care provider, Intermountain's efficiency is immediately obvious. When the Kaiser Family Foundation, a nonprofit agency for health policy analysis, tallied Utah's per capita spending on health care, they found it to be an astonishing 44 percent below the national average. And according to a 2008 report written by researchers at Dartmouth, if all providers across the country were to achieve Intermountain's level of efficiency, the nation could reduce health care spending on acute and chronic illnesses by as much as 40 percent.[7] In 2009, as the health care debate raged in Washington, DC, President Obama singled out Intermountain as a model of how to do better.

"We have long known that some places, like Intermountain Healthcare in Utah, offer high-quality care at cost below average."[8]

Of course, those who are ultimately paying the bill for health care can't help but notice the successes of well-managed health care systems such as Intermountain's. Insurance companies have begun to adopt some of the same evidence-based, best-practice protocols to rein in the massive variations in treatment and spiraling costs. They, too, are using payment incentives, awarding bonuses to physicians who follow these protocols. And given Charlie Munger's emphasis on proper incentives, the Berkshire-Amazon-JPMorgan health care venture is almost certain to engineer a similarly creative incentive structure.

Variation in treatment has caused health care costs to soar along a dizzying trajectory. In reaction, many insurance companies have adopted "clinical pathways" as a tool to rein in costs. A clinical pathway is a suggested flowchart of treatment for a given condition. There now exist clinical pathways for most broad categories of medicine: cardiovascular disease, cancer, mental illness, and acute care, to name a few. The idea is to standardize treatment using the same formula as Intermountain—pinning down treatment protocols that offer the best outcome for the least cost. For example, when comparing chemotherapies, if two drugs show similar efficacy and have similar toxicity profiles, the insurance company will suggest the lower-cost drug in the clinical pathway. Incorporating the lower-cost drug results in an immediate cost benefit without diminishing a patient's chances for survival. One study that looked at non-small cell lung cancer showed that treating patients "on-pathway" versus "off-pathway" resulted in a 35 percent decrease in cost—$18,042 versus $27,737—with no difference in overall survival.

Owing to the obvious benefits provided by clinical pathways, their use is growing. Today, roughly sixty individual insurance plans across the county, covering more than 170 million Americans, have implemented treatment pathways in oncology. Still, however, physician compliance is not guaranteed. Just as Brent James did, insurance companies have found they must incentivize physicians to follow the pathways. To do this, they typically dangle a carrot in the form of bonuses for those who follow the pathways.

With other hospitals beginning to adopt James's managed-care strategy, and insurance companies steering more and more doctors toward clinical pathways, the noose is slowly tightening around the doctor's long-standing

autonomy. For better or worse, top-down oversight of their day-to-day practice has begun. As has the inevitable backlash. Some doctors are pushing back
against what they call "cookbook medicine"—medicine that they say comes
at the cost of treating each patient as an individual, the cost of restricting a
doctor's vaunted intuition. "It's terrifying," said a physician friend of mine
who interviewed for a position at the Kaiser Permanente health system—an
evidence-based managed-care system very similar to Intermountain—before
starting his own private practice. "You feel like someone is always looking
over your shoulder and watching your every move."

"When we are patients, we want our doctors to make recommendations
that are in our best interests as individuals. As physicians, we strive to do the
same for our patients," said Jerome Groopman, Dina and Raphael Recanati
Chair of Medicine at Harvard Medical School and best-selling author. "But
financial forces largely hidden from the public are beginning to corrupt care
and undermine the bond of trust between doctors and patients." Groopman is fueling the inevitable debate between a physician's independence
and groups like Intermountain and the insurance companies, who, in his
view, have gone too far in directing doctors how to treat their patients.
"Contracts for medical care that incorporate 'pay for performance' direct
physicians to meet strict metrics for testing and treatment. These metrics are
population-based and generic, and do not take into account the individual
characteristics and preferences of the patient or differing expert opinions on
optimal practice," says Groopman.[9]

The problem, claims Groopman, comes down to the occasional patient
who might benefit from going "off pathway." The patient's doctor is then
forced to face a moral dilemma: Do what he or she thinks is best for that
patient and suffer financially or conform to the suggested pathway and get
the bonus. "Margaret Tempero of the National Comprehensive Cancer Network observed that every day oncologists saw patients for whom deviation
from treatment guidelines made sense: 'Will oncologists be reluctant to
make these decisions because of adverse effects on payment?'" asks Groopman. Groopman sees the incursion of best practices and clinical pathways as
a blanket that smothers the ability of doctors to remain autonomous, to rely
on intuition, and ultimately, to make the best decisions for their patients. "In
truth, the power belongs to the insurers and regulators that control payment.

There is now a new paternalism, largely invisible to the public, diminishing the autonomy of both doctor and patient," Groopman wrote in 2014.[10]

Does Groopman's argument hold water? Fundamentally, the question is whether or not the "new paternalism" is better for patients than holding on to the old culture that allows physicians to have all of the control when treating patients. When confronted with this age-old question, James falls back on the data. In fact, it's hard to argue with the results: pneumonia mortality rates cut by 40 percent, surgical infection rates cut by over half, quadrupling the survival rate of acute respiratory distress syndrome. And a 40 percent reduction in overall cost. It's impossible to ignore these results. On one side of the argument, it really is about numbers. "Don't argue philosophy, show me your mortality rates, and then I'll believe you," says James. The numbers don't lie. Reducing the amount of variation in treatment toward an evidence-based protocol saves lives. Period.

But Groopman argues that this comes at an invisible cost. The statistical approach used by James and, increasingly, by insurance companies turns doctors into a type of automaton, putting them on autopilot. He believes that this will inevitably engender a new physician-patient relationship in which doctors will rely too heavily on management. They won't fully consider the person in front of them, digging deep into their personal history and making the intuitive connections that only the wisdom of years of experience will provide. Their intuition will inevitably diminish, and once-sharp instincts will dull. "Medical care is not just another marketplace commodity," says Groopman. "Physicians should never have an incentive to override the best interests of their patients." It's easy to see his point. Anyone who has ever been sick knows the deep desire for intimate, one-on-one interaction with a provider. Patients want empathy, intuition, and to be treated as an individual. As a species, we *desperately* crave the human side of medicine—to be heard.

But Brent James doesn't see it as a zero-sum game where one or the other must prevail. When data can narrow treatment and guide doctors, it should; but, James admits, it will never be able to solve *all* the problems in health care. There will always be situations in which we *must* rely on a doctor's intuition. The way James sees it, best-practice guidelines do not diminish the role of the doctor. They serve merely as a signpost—a data-powered spotlight to help illuminate a small area of the darkness in which medicine is often practiced. Providing best-practice protocols narrows the vast uncertainty and allows doctors to better focus on the patient, says James. However, in the situations where data are not yet conclusive—the many cases where a best-practice protocol does not yet exist—patients *need* a doctor and his or her intuition. "To our physicians I say, 'ladies and gentlemen, it's not just that we allow or even encourage that you adjust this to the needs of your individual patients, we *demand* it,'" says James.

In the end, this debate circles back to Daniel Kahneman and Amos Tversky's groundbreaking work. Brent James's success at Intermountain is empirical proof that in many circumstances doctors don't make optimal decisions. Intuition is often deceptive. This is not an admonishment, but rather simple recognition of what it is to be a human being. Individually, doctors can't look out and track outcomes to guide treatment. But clinical trials and James's EMR can. The history of medicine—examples like the radical mastectomy—offer a poignant narrative of the mistakes of the past. We have a health care system that is still thrashing and heaving, still grappling with the age-old debate between intuition and culture and empirical data and statistics.

But reforms like Brent James's at Intermountain are offering a solution, an awakening, a truce between the two opposing sides and a path to work together moving forward. "Brent is the future. But how long are you willing to wait? It may take a hundred years," said Lucian Leap, a former surgeon and professor of public health at Harvard.[11] What is James's response? "We have not yet begun to understand how good we can be."

The Fresh Food Farmacy

Brent James isn't the only "moneyball" type of health care reformer. There are others, too, who have embraced creative, evidence-based solutions to improving health care. While stumping for health care reform in 2009, Barack Obama mentioned a few other such innovators. "We have to ask why places like the Geisinger Health system in rural Pennsylvania, Intermountain Health in Salt Lake City or communities like Green Bay can offer high-quality care at costs well below average, but other places in America can't," Obama said to an overflowing gymnasium at Green Bay Southwest High School. "We need to identify the best practices across the country, learn from the success and replicate that success elsewhere," he continued. "And we should change the warped incentives that reward doctors and hospitals based on how many tests or procedures they prescribe, even if those tests or procedures aren't necessary or result from medical mistakes. Doctors across this country did not get into the medical profession to be bean counters or paper pushers, to be lawyers or business executives. They became doctors to heal people. And that's what we must free them to do."[12]

One of the health systems Obama mentioned, Geisinger Health—a group of a dozen hospitals and clinics in rural Northeastern and central Pennsylvania—looked for a creative solution to tackle the already massive and growing problem of type 2 diabetes. Like checklists, handwashing, and the repurposing of five-cent, generic drugs, Geisinger's idea seemed, on the surface, like an extraordinarily simple solution centered on treating the cause, rather than the symptoms, of type 2 diabetes. Their solution consisted of a single prescription: eat fresh, healthy food.

Globally, type 2 diabetes is a slow-moving health crisis. The majority of adults in the United States (52.3 percent), have either type 2 diabetes (14.3 percent) or prediabetes (38 percent), a category that is just a hop and a skip away from a diagnosis of full-blown type 2 diabetes. And the cost of treating type 2 diabetes in the United States is staggering—it currently exceeds $240 billion per year—and rising at a dizzying pace.

At its core, diabetes is the inability to process blood sugar due to a condition called "insulin resistance." When we eat a carbohydrate-rich meal, the carbs are broken down through digestion into glucose (sugar). The pancreas, sensing the rise in blood glucose, then releases the hormone insulin. Insulin then facilitates the transport of glucose into cells, where it can be burned as fuel or processed into fat. As we age, however, this finely tuned process can become dysregulated. Our cells begin to lose the ability to respond to insulin; they become resistant to the hormone. The result of this phenomenon is excessive glucose lingering in our blood, elevating our blood sugar to dangerous levels. Glucose, a very rigid molecule, can easily cause physical damage to tissues it comes in contact with. This is why diabetics can experience such a wide range of problems, from nerve damage and cardiovascular disease to kidney disease, blindness, impotence, weight gain, brain fog, and a poorly functioning immune system.

The underlying cause behind the meteoric rise of type 2 diabetes in the world is a function of two lifestyle factors: diet and exercise. Exercise bypasses the need for the pancreas to secret insulin. Even mild movement like walking or doing household chores, for example, will cause muscles to act like sponges, soaking up glucose from the blood—sparing the need for the pancreas to secrete insulin. Additionally, avoiding eating too many carbohydrates also reduces the reliance on the pancreas to secret insulin. However, the combination of a sedentary lifestyle and the overconsumption of carbohydrates is increasing across the globe. Over time, this pernicious combination leads to insulin resistance. Insulin's ability to funnel blood glucose into cells becomes worn out, leading first to prediabetes and then to type 2 diabetes.

The traditional way a doctor will treat diabetes is to do two things: First, prescribe one of the many drugs for type 2 diabetes; and, second, coach the patient on changing lifestyle factors. The problem is that most patients will try changing their lifestyle for a while, but then inevitably slip back into their old routine and become reliant on the drug alone. "I always try to motivate overweight, prediabetic, or type 2 patients on lifestyle changes. I'm not sure it makes any difference," said my family practitioner. "It's like the surge in gym memberships after people make all their New Year's resolutions. The initial enthusiasm eventually fades."

Aware of the futility of the standard approach, Geisinger set out to do better. Their idea: "The Fresh Food Farmacy"—a prescription for free, healthy food and continuous support. The pilot program, which kicked off in 2016, first screened for individuals who would benefit the most: low-income individuals with type 2 diabetes. (Being in a low-income bracket translates into a two- to three-times higher risk for developing type 2 diabetes.) The screening identified 95 individuals who matched the criteria. The doctors at Geisinger then wrote a prescription for free food from the Farmacy, a Geisinger-owned grocery store stocked with healthy, fresh food. The patients were provided with enough free food for two meals a day, along with a suggested weekly menu and recipes. Here, however, the team at Geisinger encountered a pitfall: It would be difficult for an individual to maintain the diet unless the whole family was on board. "The way we behave is really influenced by others around us." Engaging the whole family could "make the program a lot more sticky and more likely to succeed," said Mitesh Patel, a physician and assistant professor of health care management at the Wharton School at the University of Pennsylvania.[13]

Along with the prescription came support. Each patient was required to attend 15 hours of group counseling where they were taught the basics of diabetes—the role of insulin, what blood sugar is, and why too much sugar in the blood is bad, for example. The counselors also dove into topics thoughtfully designed to achieve *sustainable* lifestyle improvements: healthy eating habits, goal setting, exercise, and mindfulness. The patients were given access to a vast support network along the way, including a nurse, a primary care physician, a registered dietitian, a pharmacist, a health coach, a community health assistant, and administrative support personnel—all there to make sure the patient didn't "fall off the wagon." The team offered a range of help, including direct medication-management assistance; nutrition counseling; health coaching; and ongoing case management to address transportation, family care, and any other challenge that might derail a patient. The upshot of this immersive support was striking: patients became engaged. They began to ask about exercise, how to stop smoking, and other health-related concerns.

They also stayed compliant. The lifestyle changes stuck. And the results were dramatic. The blood marker hemoglobin A1C (or simply A1C) is a measurement that reflects the average level of glucose in a person's blood over the previous three months. An A1C level below 5.7 percent is considered normal. An A1C between 5.7 and 6.4 percent signals prediabetes. And type 2 diabetes is usually diagnosed when the A1C is over 6.5 percent. The goal for any diabetes treatment is to lower A1C to a more normal level. After 18 months, the Fresh Food Farmacy program lowered the participants' A1C an average of 2.1 percentage points. This result is remarkable when compared to medication, which lowers A1C by only 0.5 to 1.2 percentage points on average. Each percentage point decrease in A1C is estimated to save $8,000 per year in overall health care costs for the patient, insurance company, or government depending on the situation. But the calculated savings from the pilot program, so far, have proven even more incredible: "Because many of the participants are insured by Geisinger Health Plan, health care spending data are available for 37 of our patients. Thus far, claims data shows costs for our pilot patients dropped by 80 percent, from an average of $240,000 per member per year, to $48,000 per member per year," according to David Feinberg, president and chief executive officer of Geisinger Health System.[14]

With these kinds of savings, it's easy to see how the program will pay for itself rapidly. "It's life-changing," says Feinberg about the results so far. "It's mind-blowing." Because Geisinger has been able to supply the majority of the food from local food banks, with the remaining 40 percent of fresh vegetables, fruits, and fish coming from retail grocery stores, the operational cost per patient is only $2,400 per year—about $6 per week per patient. "If a new diabetes drug became available that could double the effectiveness of glucose control, it would likely be priced considerably higher than $6 per week (and if it wasn't, the pharmaceutical firm's stockholders would be in revolt)," wrote Feinberg.

Moreover, the effects on the patients are immediate. As Feinberg says, "[They] won't go blind; [they] won't have kidney disease, amputations. The list goes on and on." But the ancillary effects are where a program like this gets really interesting. Because of the dramatic lifestyle changes, extending to the entire family in some cases, the Fresh Food Farmacy is shifting how the kids growing up in low-income households perceive the relationship between food and health. "It's always a challenge to get people to maintain lifestyle changes over the long term. If you get the entire family to change the way they eat, you're much more likely to improve health," says Patel. "In health care we spend an awful lot on drugs and devices because it's business," notes Feinberg. "But we spend a very small amount on preventive medicine. . . . It's sort of like we're upside down and backward." Geisinger's Fresh Food Farmacy is a striking example of health care at its best.

CHAPTER 5

Nature or Nurture

What Really Matters?

So far we have examined how cognitive biases have created a range of inefficiencies across the institution of health care. And how recognizing the biases
and confronting them through the use of clinical trials, careful statistical
analysis, repurposed drugs, checklists, and other simple techniques can result
in dramatically improved outcomes at a fraction of the cost. But what about
the individual? How do cognitive biases creep into and affect our individual
health on a personal level? In other words: What do data reveal regarding our
health and well-being that *really matters* when compared to our own potentially biased viewpoint? We all have internal thoughts and intuitions regarding
our health, but how biased are they? Do they serve us well? In the same way
that evidence-based analysis can identify the best practice for a given medical
procedure, could it also identify which lifestyle factors—diet, exercise, and
stress, for example—are most important to our health and well-being?

As we will see, our individual cognitive biases tend to arise out of the same
predicaments that afflict doctors when they treat us as patients: the necessity
of making day-to-day decisions based on little or flawed knowledge. And,
much like statistics have the power to steer doctors away from their flawed
decisions, they can guide us, too, directing us toward the things that really
matter and away from those that do not. Knowledge *is* power—the power
to transcend our internally hardwired biases and focus on the variables that

truly matter in our lives. Furthermore, maintaining our individual health allows us to circumvent the health care system, to bypass the risks of over-treatment, the diagnostic and therapeutic disparities, and the massive costs. Indeed, with regard to our own health, we can be a culture of one. A culture within. A culture that strives to identify and live by the lifestyle variables that will keep us out of the health care system. And, as we will also see, our internal biology is much more flexible and dynamic than scientists have previously appreciated. In other words, recent science has revealed that we have much more control over our own destiny than imagined.

Although we may all define health slightly differently, in general most peo-ple define it as the "state of being free of illness or injury." And anyone who has dealt with illness knows how easy it can be to take health for granted. As seventeenth-century English historian Thomas Fuller wrote, "Health is not valued till sickness comes."[1] Until then, it feels like a right granted to us, our default state. It is all many of us have ever known. When sickness does come, only then do most of us fully appreciate the importance of our health. "It is health that is real wealth and not pieces of gold and silver," said Gandhi.[2]

So how do we stay healthy? How do we ward off disease and live happy, productive lives until a ripe old age? One place to look for the answer is from our planet's oldest residents. As we know, certain cultures revere their old more than others. In many cultures the elderly are treasures, enshrined as the most prized of citizens. In these cultures the old have a wisdom attainable only through experience. They are the threads that weave the culture's past to its present. Even in America's youth-obsessed culture, we are fascinated by centurions, but more for the secrets they must surely hold. Secrets about preserving the precious state of youth for as long as possible, yes, but also secrets about how to live happily in the face of all the misfortune and pain pervading our world. This is a select group, to be sure. Simply to make it into the exclusive club of centurions is a remarkable feat. In the industrialized world only 1 out of every 6,000 people will live to age 100. People who live to be older than 110—or supercentenarians as they are called—are extremely rare, with only 1 in 7 million reaching this category. What did they do to keep disease at bay? Indeed, the same question gets posed to this select group in every interview: "What is the secret to a long and happy life?" Here are some of their answers.

In 2015, 104-year-old Elizabeth Sullivan of Texas, claimed that the secret to her longevity was Dr Pepper; she had consumed three cans of it a day for the past forty years. In contrast, that same year Misao Okawa (117 years)—at the time believed to be the world's oldest living person—said her secret was eating sushi and getting a good night's sleep. In 2013, Jeralean Talley, a 115-year-old American, said it was hog's head cheese that had kept her healthy for so long. Earth's purported oldest resident in 2016, Emma Morano-Martinuzzi of Verbania, Italy (117), said the secret was eating raw eggs and cookies. Richard Overton, America's oldest veteran of the Second World War at 112, swore by 12 cigars a day and a nip of whiskey in his morning coffee. And 111-year-old Grace Jones of England agreed; she claimed a nightly sip of whiskey and a "worry-free mentality" were key. Then there was Japan's former oldest living resident, Jiroemon Kimura, who said he lived to be 116 thanks to sunbathing, while Jessie Gallan (109) from Scotland said her longevity was due to "staying away from men" and eating porridge.

On the other hand, 115-year-old Ana Maria Vela Rubio of Spain claimed it was a positive attitude. Koku Istambulova from Chechnya, however, currently believed the oldest person ever at age 129 (not officially verified) disagreed: She said she had not had a single happy day in her entire life and had no idea how she had managed to live so long. She said her long life had been a "punishment from God." When asked for her secret to a long life, she responded, "It was God's will. I did nothing to make it happen. I see people going in for sports, eating something special, keeping themselves fit, but I have no idea how I lived until now." She continued, "Looking back at my unhappy life, I wish I had died when I was young. I worked all my life." She said that she "did not have time for rest or entertainment." She did confess, however, that she avoided meat and liked a "fermented milk drink." And in 2016 the oldest known person in the United States, Adele Dunlap (113), swore by oatmeal. Both she and her son admitted to being befuddled by her extreme longevity. "She never went out jogging or anything like that. She smoked, and when my father had his first heart attack, they both stopped. I think she ate anything she wanted," said her son.

So what is the secret? Is it raw eggs, oatmeal, Dr Pepper, or fermented milk? Or could it perhaps be plenty of sleep, a positive (or negative) attitude, being worry-free, drinking whiskey, or eating hog's head cheese? The massive variation in these answers should come as no surprise. As individuals, we are incapable of knowing; cognitive biases seduce us into believing something has an effect when it most likely does not. Only statistical analysis can approach this question—teasing out the variables that matter from those that do not.

The human mind intrinsically wants to make things simple. It yearns to reduce what keeps us healthy down to as few variables as possible: raw eggs, exercise, or a good night's sleep, for example. Unfortunately, maintaining our health cannot be reduced this easily. But when epidemiologists analyze the variables that impact longevity, a consistent pattern does emerge, and the pattern forces us to reckon with biological mechanisms that are more complex—and fascinating—than many of us ever imagined.

One question has always lingered at the center of biology: What determines our fate? Is it nature or nurture? The nature side of the question is now well described by the science of genetics—the combined effect of the 23 chromosomes we inherit from our mother and the 23 we inherit from our father. The nurture side of the question, however, has been much harder to pin down. In the past, nurture has typically been described in philosophical or psychological dimensions rather than concrete biological mechanisms.

Only a few decades ago, the vast majority of biologists would have claimed an individual's fate lay in the genes inherited from his or her mother and father. But recent studies have shown that the genes we inherit play the lesser role in our destiny. Only approximately 20 percent of our life-span is hardwired into us by heritable genetics alone (nature). Conversely, this means that roughly 80 percent of our longevity is determined by lifestyle and chance events (nurture).

So how do such intangible variables of nurture as the experiences of victory, elation, nurturing friends and family—or, by the same token, pain, loss, trauma, and loneliness—become etched into our biology? The answer lies in an exploding new branch of molecular biology called *epigenetics*. Simply put, epigenetics is the study of why and how individual genes get turned on and off and the resultant effects on our health. Imagine your genes are like a piano. A piano cannot do anything by itself; it takes a pianist to play the piano to create music. Your genes are the same. By themselves, they don't do anything. But through the process of epigenetics, the functionality of our genes is brought to life. Epigenetics is the music of our genomes. Another way to look at epigenetics: If the genome is the hardware, then the epigenome is the software. "I can load Windows, if I want, on my Mac," says Joseph Ecker, PhD, a Salk Institute biologist. "You're going to have the same chip in there, the same genome, but different software."[3]

"Genes Are Not Our Destiny"

The biological importance of the signals, switches, signposts, and levers that turn on certain genes and turn off others in every human cell—all 40 trillion of them—was first recognized by the English geneticist Conrad Waddington in the early twentieth century, when the gene was still only a dim abstraction. In the winter of 1943, ten years before the structure of DNA was discovered by the Anglo-American duo Watson and Crick, the Nobel prize–winning quantum physicist Erwin Schrödinger gave the first of three public lectures at Trinity College, Dublin. His topic was a strange one for a physicist: "What Is Life?" In the lecture Schrödinger imagined life, *all* life, to be reduced to a kind of "code script." Waddington's imagination extended even further. He understood that certain traits like eye color or height might be determined by Schrödinger's "code script" (later determined to be DNA), but he imagined other traits to be more complex, the result of communication among genes, or, put another way, the signals that turn genes on and off. To describe this imagined process Waddington coined the word *epigenetics*. "Epi" is Greek for "above" or "on." As Waddington envisioned it—and could only describe metaphorically—epigenetics is the cellular functionality that exists "above" traditional genetics.

History would eventually show that Waddington was far ahead of his time. When Watson and Crick walked into the Eagle Pub on February 28, 1953, and Crick shouted "We've discovered the secret of life"—after the two had elucidated the structure of DNA—the double helix was planted in the center of the biological universe. This was Schrödinger's illusory molecule finally brought to life. The irregular pattern of the paired molecules down the center of the helix suggested the "code script" that Schrödinger predicted. Few discoveries have captivated the imagination like the discovery of DNA's structure. At no time before or since has science revealed a material structure so utterly overflowing with implications—so enormously suggestive.

Yet while the rest of the world was captivated by Watson and Crick's discovery, Waddington remained unimpressed. "The actual 'creative process' by which the 1953 'breakthrough' was achieved does not, however, in my opinion, rank very high as scientific creation goes," wrote Waddington. "The major discoveries in science consist in finding new ways of looking at a whole group of phenomena. Why did anyone ever come to feel that the structure of DNA was the secret of life? It was the result of a long battle. . . . Solving a puzzle like this demands a very high intelligence . . . but this is not the sort of operation that was involved in such major scientific advances as Darwin's theory of evolution, Einstein's relativity or Plank's quantum theory."[4] And while the world was intensely focused on the newly discovered gene, Waddington was already looking beyond it. "DNA plays a role in life rather like that played by the telephone directory in the social life of London: you can't do anything much without it, but, having it, you need a lot of other things—telephones, wires and so on—as well," wrote Waddington. Nevertheless, once the article announcing the discovery of DNA was circulated, a new "gene-centric" era of molecular biology was born. Surely, it was widely believed, all the mysteries of our biology would be found in the genetic code. Watson and Crick won the Nobel Prize, and Waddington's epigenetics was all but forgotten.

But it would not be forgotten for long. At 10:19 a.m. on June 26, 2000, President Bill Clinton approached the podium in the East Room of the White House to announce that a rough draft of the human genome was finished. The inexorable sweep of technology had culminated in the Human Genome Project, a massive effort to read our autobiography, spelling out all 3.42 billion letters in our genome. "We are here to celebrate the completion of the first survey of the entire human genome. Without a doubt this is the most important map, most wondrous map ever produced by human kind," said Clinton. Sitting three rows back and slightly to the right of the podium, in a white suit, was James Watson. Three minutes into the speech Clinton looked directly at Watson. "It was not even fifty years ago that a young Englishman named Crick and a brash, even younger American named Watson, first discovered the elegant structure of our genetic code. Dr. Watson, the way you announced your discovery in the journal *Nature* was one of the great understatements of all time. 'This structure has novel features which are of considerable biological interest.'" As laughter erupted from the audience, Clinton bowed to

Watson, and said, "Thank you, sir!" The laughter turned to applause. This map, Clinton went on, was sure to usher in a revolution in "the diagnosis, prevention, and treatment of most, if not all, human diseases."[5]

This is where molecular biology took an interesting turn—a turn that mimicked the shift in perception forced upon astronomy when Copernicus displaced the earth as the center of the universe. The gene, once the center of the biological universe, would also be forced to reckon with a new reality—a reality that would redeem Conrad Waddington. When Clinton announced the rough draft of the human genome, it was believed, as he said, that individual genes were behind "most, if not all human disease." But as the twenty-first century progressed, a new realization would surface— that there is astonishing little variation in our genomes. In other words, one person's genes are not that different from the next, certainly not enough to account for "most, if not all human disease."

"Our DNA is overwhelmingly identical. Indeed, all the beautiful permutations of the human form—the differences between the tallest and shortest, the brown-eyed and the green-eyed—are explained by just a tiny fraction of those base pairs," wrote science reporter Brian Resnick. And, "finding the genetic differences that make one person taller or shorter than another is like looking for needles in a haystack."[6] For example, when Clinton made his announcement, Francis Collins, director of the NIH, predicted that there would be a dozen genes involved in diabetes, "and that all of them will be discovered in the next two years." In the end, it was discovered that *hundreds* of genes are involved in diabetes, each with a tiny contribution to its development—making the prediction of who will and who won't acquire the disease wickedly complex. "We're going to hit a ceiling really quickly," said Cecile Janssens, an epidemiologist at Emory, about the predictive power of genetic variation. "All the SNPs [genetic variations] that we are discovering now have such a tiny effect," said Janssens.

If twentieth-century molecular biology was defined by genetics, then twenty-first-century molecular biology was shaping up to be defined by epigenetics. The twenty-first century ushered in the realization that epigenetics, the volume-control dials on each of the 22,000 genes in the human genome—and not genetic variation permanently inscribed into our DNA— is what really accounts for most of human disease. "Epigeneticists, once a subcaste of biologist nudged to the far peripheries of the discipline, now find themselves firmly at its epicenter," wrote Pulitzer Prize–winning author Siddhartha Mukherjee.[7]

"Genes are not our destiny," said Tim Spector, professor of genetics and director of the TwinsUK registry at King's College London. Spector, perhaps more than anyone, has a unique insight into the role individual genes play in determining our health. When he founded TwinsUK in 1992, Spector appreciated that with identical twins nature had provided the perfect experimental system to help untangle the role individual genes play in complex diseases and traits. Identical twins share the same genetic code in every cell of their bodies. They are genetic clones of each other. Spector realized if he created a registry he would be able to follow thousands of pairs of twins over their lifetime and determine which diseases are 100 percent genetic, and which ones are more complex—an amalgam of genetic and environmental influences.

Pairs of identical twins serve as a proxy for the degree that genetics (inherited DNA) influences a disease process. If a disease is purely genetic—Huntington's disease, for example—both twins will get it 100 percent of the time. Therefore, Huntington's has what's called a *concordance rate* of 100 percent; it is an exclusively genetic disease. Very few diseases fall into this category, however. Most diseases are a blend of genetic and environmental influences, like schizophrenia. If one twin develops schizophrenia, the other twin has a coin's-flip chance of developing it. Its concordance rate is 50 percent. Therefore, schizophrenia is revealed to have equal genetic and environmental components. Overall, twin studies have led to estimates that inherited genes determine only 20 percent of our longevity. In other words, your genes hold a minority stake in how long you will live. "Most people when they read the sort of headlines describing twins that have died within hours of each other think this is very much the norm," said Spector. "But nothing could be further from the truth. The fact is most twins die not within hours, not within months, often not within years. And they do not die of the same diseases. In fact, they don't even get the same disease usually, even if those diseases are very strongly genetic and very common like diabetes, heart disease, arthritis, etc."[8]

With the realization that much of our health is determined more by nurture than nature, researchers naturally asked, but how? What possible biological mechanisms could record something as effervescent and intangible as nurture? How could things like trauma, triumph, isolation, and love, for example, be unpacked into a biological stamp on our health? When a pair of twins, perfect genetic clones of each other, raised in similar environments for much of their lives, experience a divergence in their health—one develops diabetes, or heart disease, or cancer, for example, and the other does not—what is the cellular mechanism lurking behind the two drastically different outcomes? What cellular process nudged one twin onto a dramatically different course? This is where the science of epigenetics has made a spectacular return. Researchers like Spector have revealed that epigenetics provides a mechanistic explanation for the 80 percent of disease that our genes alone cannot account for. To fully appreciate the majesty of epigenetics, it is critical to understand how it operates at a cellular level.

Epigenetics

Here's where we stop for a brief refresher in molecular biology. Watson and Crick's discovery of the structure of DNA answered an ancient query that went back as far as Hippocrates: Where were the instructions to build and run a living organism? But the closing of that door with Watson and Crick's discovery immediately flung open another: How is the information contained within DNA translated into action? Crick soon worked out the details, a beautifully orchestrated decoding system that transformed the information contained within a segment of DNA (a gene) by way of an intermediate messenger molecule called *messenger RNA* (mRNA) into a protein. Proteins are the workhorse molecules of the cell. They provide structure, catalyze thousands of chemical reactions to generate cellular energy, act as signaling molecules (hormones), and form the receptors for other hormones to attach to. They function like intricate circuit boards within the cell, relaying signals from outside the cell and eliciting the designated biological response. Proteins carry out the day-to-day cellular operations. This is how biological information is transferred. This information flow—from gene to mRNA to protein—is the central process of life. Crick famously called this process the "central dogma of biology."

In essence, epigenetics describes the cellular mechanisms that have the ability to change the rate of this information flow within the cell, the rate at which genes are expressed into their protein products. To manufacture more or less of a protein changes cellular functionality. For example, the epigenetic downregulation in production of a protein that forms insulin receptors reduces the cell's ability to respond to circulating insulin, potentially leading to the development of type 2 diabetes. Conversely, the epigenetic upregulation of the same protein can increase the cell's ability to respond to insulin.

Epigenetic modifications comprise a range of unique operations, from stable, long-lasting mechanisms to those that are either more transient and intermediate or extremely dynamic and moment-to-moment. The stable, long-lasting epigenetic mechanism is responsible for the different cell types that make up our tissues and organs. While each of our 40 trillion cells contains the same complement of DNA within its nucleus—23 chromosomes apiece from each of parent—differing cell types express dramatically different sets of genes. For example, a nerve cell has the genes responsible for producing stomach acid turned off, while the cells lining the stomach have these genes turned on. Skin cells will have the gene for melanin (the protein that makes you tan) turned on, and liver cells will have it turned off—both cells contain the same chip, but have different software installed. The epigenetic mechanism that "locks in" the functioning of a particular cell type, as in the examples just given, is a very stable modification called *methylation*. Methylation is the direct attachment of a *methyl group* molecule (one carbon atom and three hydrogen atoms) to specific nucleotides within a gene on a strand of DNA. The attached methyl group physically blocks RNA polymerase from transcribing the gene into mRNA, thus preventing the expression of that gene. The gene is permanently turned off.

However, most epigenetic mechanisms are not as stable and long-lived as direct methylation. Others are more adjustable, acting like volume-control dials that allow for the fine-tuning of a gene's expression. In the late eighteenth century a German biochemist named Albrecht Kossel discovered that *chromatin* (all the material found in a cell's nucleus, DNA and protein material) contains an interesting repeating protein that is attached to DNA. Kossel called the individual protein subunit a *histone*. In the decades following their discovery, the function of histones puzzled biologists. The biochemists showed that chromosomes were *saturated* with histones from end to end, but their purpose remained elusive.

By the middle of the twentieth century the purpose of histones was finally understood: They solved a molecular packaging problem. The human genome consists of about three billion nucleotides. Stretched end to end, the 46 chromosomes inside the nucleus reach over three meters in length. Clearly evolution had to come up with a solution to package our chromosomes into the incommodious volume of the nucleus, a compartment measuring only one millionth of an inch across. The solution was the evolution of histones. Histones are globular, ball-shaped proteins with a long protein tail that protrudes outward. Eight histones will naturally combine to form a structure that looks like eight table tennis balls stuck together in two layers, four on top and four directly under them. Like thread on a spool, DNA neatly wraps twice around each histone octamer to create a structure called a *nucleosome*. Nucleosomes then condense into a fiber that coils in upon itself again and again to form "supercoiled" loops (imagine a twisted telephone cord repeatedly coiling in on itself). In this manner over three meters of DNA can be neatly wound into a hyper-condensed state that is able to fit inside a nucleus.

For a time, despite their intimate association with DNA, histones appeared to be little more than a molecular organizer, a biological hose reel. They were "the biochemical equivalent of nuts, bolts, and bungee cords to keep the all-important genetic molecule in its proper dimensions," with all the charm, as one researcher put it, "of a brick wall."[9] But a flurry of papers in 1996 by a biochemist named David Allis at Rockefeller University in New York, would shatter for good the mundane view of histones—transforming them from "a brick wall" to dynamic regulators of genetic expression.

Working with a single-cell protozoon (pond scum) Allis noticed something curious: Corresponding with the protozoa ramping up protein production was the attachment of a specific molecule called an *acetyl group* to the tails of histones. Conversely, when ramping down genetic expression the acetyl groups were missing from the histones' tails. Inspired that he might have discovered a new epigenetic mechanism, Allis began a frenzied search for the control knobs—the enzymes responsible for attaching and detaching the acetyl groups from the histone tails. He soon discovered the protein responsible for the attaching, called a *histone acetyltransferase*, or HAT for short, and the one responsible for the detaching, called *histone deacetylase*, or HDAC for short. Together the two proteins could easily be imagined to function as the adjustment dials. HATs penciled in the instructions to turn up the expression of genes, and HDACs served as the erasers, turning down expression. "It couldn't have been a more wonderful one-two punch. I am not sure the chromatin field has been the same since," said Allis. "It wasn't rocket science to figure out this enzyme pair of reactions might function as an on-off switch. . . . You couldn't turn your back on what these findings were saying. Most people thought chromatin [histones] was just a passive platform that wraps DNA. But those two papers made people think about a more active process in which chromatin truly participates."[10]

By the mid-1990s researchers were waking up to the importance of epigenetics. The recognition that there were mechanisms lurking within our genomes that acted "upon" our genes had unveiled a new image of the genome. The flat, binary, two-dimensional image of our genes was morphing into that of a rich, three-dimensional, dynamic, and flexible genome. Direct methylation, the stable, long-lived epigenetic modification, installed the operating code that imparted the unique functionality of different cell types. Histone acetylation provided a more flexible mechanism; it was a fine-tuning epigenetic modification that permitted more variability in the expression of our genes. And finally, a class of epigenetic modulators called *transcription factors* would reveal the genome to be an extraordinarily dynamic mosh pit of activity.

Indeed, in terms of life's dynamic, day-to-day genetic operations, transcription factors play the lead role. "Transcription factors occupy the top of the hierarchy of epigenetic information," as one researcher put it. The importance of transcription factors is revealed in their sheer quantity. Our genomes are *littered* with transcription factors. Of the 22,000 genes within the human genome, approximately 2,000, or 10 percent, encode transcription factors.

In our adult bodies, the epigenetic chatter of transcription factors that occurs every day, hour, even second, is staggering. Receptors on the cell surface are constantly assessing the internal physiological environment and can respond to subtle changes via transcription factors. An individual's routine activities—taking a walk, eating, or experiencing an emotion—can elicit a complex epigenetic response. And epigenetic responses are far from mutually exclusive; each affects the other in a network of overlapping functionality.

To illustrate the epigenetic signaling from transcription factors real time, imagine two individuals having lunch. One eats a meal of steak from a feedlot (grain-fed) cow and French fries, and then chooses to watch TV. The other has wild salmon and fresh vegetables and then decides to go for a walk on a sunny day. Our first subject has now melted into the couch and is taking in intermittent segments of a show as he drifts in and out of sleep. The chains of carbohydrate (starch) in the French fries have been broken down into glucose in his small intestine, and the concentration of glucose is rising rapidly in his bloodstream. This triggers the release of insulin from his pancreatic beta cells. The combination of rising blood sugar and insulin release activates three important transcription factors: *liver X receptor* (LXR), *sterol regulatory element-binding protein 1c* (SREBP-1c), and *carbohydrate response element-binding protein* (ChREBP).

From a purely mechanistic standpoint, transcription factors are epigenetic modulators in the most real sense, literally exerting their effect "on top of" DNA, as Waddington had prophetically imagined it. The three transcription factors bind to designated sites within the DNA called *regulatory regions*, each factor docking onto a precisely matching *regulatory site*, where the nucleotides within the grooves of DNA's helical structure fit the molecular architecture of the transcription factor's surface like a lock and key. Now, each bound to its designated regulatory site within the genome, the three exert their effect. The regulatory sites, as their name implies, are concentrated in the "promoter" regions of the genes that produce the proteins responsible for setting in motion a series of metabolic processes required to turn the excess blood sugar into fat. The process, termed *lipogenesis*, takes the excess glucose and, through a series of steps, converts it into four fatty acids: palmitate, stearate, palmitoleate, and oleate. These fatty acids are then incorporated into triglycerides for transport. The triglycerides are then further packaged into fatty particles called *very low-density lipoproteins* (VLDL) and secreted into the bloodstream. Once in the capillaries of adipose tissue (fat tissue) and muscle tissue, the VLDL particles are broken down and can be used in two ways. If our subject was active, the broken-down fat would be taken up preferentially by the muscle tissue and burned for energy in a process called *beta oxidation*. However, because he's not active, the majority of the VLDL particles are broken down and repackaged into triglycerides within the adipose cells for long-term energy storage (fat).

Conversely, consider our subject who ate salmon and vegetables for lunch. After lunch she notices it's a nice day and decides to go for a walk. The sun begins to warm her skin. Some of the photons penetrate past the skin's outer layers and mingle with a cholesterol-based provitamin circulating in her blood. The energy from the photon converts the provitamin to vitamin D_3. The vitamin is then quickly converted to its active form in the liver and kidneys. Once active, the vitamin diffuses into the nuclei of cells and binds with its receptor. The pair then binds to another protein, the *retinoic X receptor*. The entire complex now acts as a transcription factor and will bind to small sequences of DNA called *vitamin D response elements* (VDREs), thousands of which have been identified throughout the genome.

As our subject walks, enjoying the warmth of the sun on her skin, hundreds of genes flicker to life, some affecting a range of biological processes that are not immediately obvious: increased calcium absorption, bone development, immune system modulation, and resistance to certain infectious disease, for example. Invigorated by the warmth of the sun and the fresh air, she walks faster. Her muscles began to strain. The proteins from the salmon are digested into individual amino acids. Her straining muscles need fuel, so they absorb glucose and a certain class of amino acid called *branched-chain amino acids*. The selective displacement of branched-chain amino acids from her bloodstream results in a higher circulating proportion of the amino acid tryptophan. This is significant because only one type of transport protein is capable of shuttling tryptophan through the blood-brain-barrier, and branched-chain amino acids strongly outcompete tryptophan for access to that carrier—like thousands of cars trying to cross a single-lane bridge at the same time. But, because she is rapidly burning the branched-chain amino acids, tryptophan is able to diffuse freely into her brain.

She has walked for 10 minutes, and with the sun still spilling onto her skin she's made 20,000 IUs of vitamin D. Her liver has converted much of it to the active form of vitamin D. The activated vitamin D has then gone on to form transcription factors within the nuclei of cells that possess a vitamin D receptor, or vitamin D *competent* cells, in the words of Waddington. Ricocheting within the nucleus the transcription factors eventually bind to VDREs, finally eliciting the upregulation of a vast spectrum of genes.

One of the genes that is turned on codes for the enzyme *tryptophan hydroxylase 2* (TPH2). TPH2 initiates the conversion of the tryptophan now flooding our subject's brain into the neurotransmitter *serotonin*, and the concentration of serotonin begins to build within her presynaptic neurons.

Whether serotonin will be released into the neural synapse, where it exerts its effect, is influenced by several factors. One is the proportion of certain fatty acids in the bloodstream: Its release is inhibited by the presence in the bloodstream of specific omega-6 fatty acids and facilitated by the presence of marine omega-3 fatty acid *eicosapentaenoic acid* (EPA). Recall, our subject dined on salmon, which is rich in EPA. Another factor is the fluidity of the neural membrane, which determines the mobility of the serotonin receptors that span the neural membrane, floating unanchored like inner tubes on the surface of a lake. *Docosahexaenoic acid* (DHA), another omega-3 fatty acid, is crucial to neural membrane fluidity; the more DHA in a membrane, the more fluid the membrane is. It is the most abundant fatty acid in the brain, making up 30 percent of the fatty acid content. Serotonin receptors in DHA-rich membranes are supple, less rigid, and bind serotonin more easily—much like a well-oiled and pliable baseball glove is able to catch a ball more easily. Salmon also contains DHA.

Between the sunlight, exercise, and the composition of her lunch, an epigenetic chain reaction is set in motion: Sunlight triggers vitamin D synthesis, resulting in the transcription of the serotonin-synthesizing enzyme THP2; exercise promotes tryptophan from the digested salmon to enter the brain; and the fatty acids in the salmon help facilitate the release and uptake of the newly manufactured serotonin.

The edges of her thoughts soften. The anxious, subconscious shadows brighten. She feels a certain weightlessness. The singing of birds and the colors seem more vivid. Without her even realizing it, she thinks happier, more optimistic thoughts. Numerous studies have linked positive emotions to serotonin levels. Serotonin concentrates in the discrete brain regions known to regulate social cognition and decision-making. Collectively, these regions of the brain are called "the social brain." The importance of serotonin's effect on the social brain can be demonstrated by a simple experiment in which subjects are given boluses of branched-chain amino acids. The extremely high concentrations of branched-chain amino acids completely saturate the blood-brain-barrier transport protein, preventing tryptophan from entering the brain, and the subjects' brain serotonin levels plummet. The behavior changes are immediate and obvious. The subjects become more impulsive, aggressive, and experience impaired learning and memory. They have an inability to resist short-term gratification and show difficulty in long-term planning. The results are thought-provoking, especially when considering approximately 70 percent of the world's population has inadequate levels of vitamin D and equally inadequate intake of marine omega-3 fatty acids. On a graver scale, insufficient levels of vitamin D, EPA, or DHA, in combination with certain genetic factors, leads to dysfunctional serotonin activation at key developmental stages in growing children. This confluence of circumstances very likely contributes to serious neuropsychiatric disorders and depression.

Serotonin's ability to flush out negative thoughts, encourage positive ones, and trigger a general sense of well-being triggers a cascade of physiological responses that improve one's overall health. Cast over a lifetime, negative emotions can exert a powerful effect on longevity. Serotonin's influence goes beyond the occasional good mood. In a classic study, autobiographies written by 22-year-olds were ranked from high to low for positive emotional content. The authors whose autobiographies ranked in the lowest quartile for positive emotions died on average 10 years earlier than those in the highest quartile.[11]

It is apparent that seemingly minor decisions, what to eat, how to interact with our environment, even how we choose to perceive the world—all the thoughts and memories that swarm through our minds—have profound effects on our epigenomes through the activation of transcription factors. The inputs are calculated every day. Genes are turned on and turned off moment to moment. The output of this vast and fluctuating algorithm influences our moods, colors our thinking, and governs the innermost workings of our bodies on a molecular level. It influences how active we are, how compulsive, thoughtful, enthusiastic, rational, reclusive, and creative. It affects our abilities, our health and vitality, our susceptibility to specific diseases and disorders, and how we interpret and respond to the world. "Nature," wrote Conrad Waddington, "is more like an artist than an engineer." Indeed, our bodies are unlike any machine. Engineers match form to function, but nature does the same in a way that is so artful in its flexibility, so staggering in its complexity, that it defies the imagination.

———————

This brings us back to where we left off. First, with our new appreciation of epigenetics, let's return to the question left unanswered: Why do identical twins, perfect genetic clones, usually die at different times from different diseases? The answer is because most of our health, approximately 80 percent, is dictated by the events in our lives that fall into the murky category of nurture, from random events like trauma and heartbreak to the more tangible—diet, social life, and exercise. Only around 20 percent of our health is predetermined by our inherited genes.

In the case of identical twins, the divergence in health due to random events, astonishingly, begins in utero. Monozygotic twins begin life the product of perfect symmetry: a single egg splitting into two identical halves. But soon after, the random messiness of life begins. When the placenta emerges to feed the growing identical twins, it can take two forms: a single placenta that feeds both twins, or two separate placentas, one for each twin. If a single placenta forms an asymmetry can be introduced, with one twin receiving a slightly better exchange of blood and, by extension, a better delivery of nutrients: vitamins, minerals, amino acids, fats, and growth factors, for example.

This asymmetry of nutrient delivery can have consequences. When life begins a sperm fertilizes an egg to form a single-cell zygote. At that point a group of specialized enzymes wipes our operating system (software) clean by removing *all* the methyl groups from the newly formed zygote's DNA (remarkably, this process also rewinds the biological age of the zygote to age zero). The cell-by-cell installation of the new epigenetic operating system then occurs as the embryo develops. Each new cell establishes the proper methylation pattern so that the right genes are expressed to impart the critical functionality of whatever tissue the cell is forming—liver cells express liver-associated genes, muscle cells express muscle-associated genes, and so on. It is easy to imagine the effect of varying nutritional input on this critically important process. When researchers use extremely sensitive assays to measure the methylation patterns of cells from identical twins sharing a placenta, they can detect a difference. This difference is most likely due to the asymmetrical distribution of nutrients. Not yet born, the twins' health has already begun to diverge—with each twin expressing their array of identical genes slightly differently.

Once set in motion, the epigenetic divergence of the erstwhile perfectly identical twins accelerates. When researchers track the methylation patterns of twins throughout their lives, a clear pattern emerges: The longer they are apart—leading different lives and collecting different experiences—the wider the divergence in their epigenomes. The "nurture" of their separate lives is sculpted directly "onto" their DNA. How does this divergence then manifest into disease propensity? Let's look at an example.

Imagine the tragic scenario where one identical twin develops childhood leukemia and the other does not. When researchers analyze both twins' genomes, they find a striking difference: the infamous *BRCA1* gene is hypermethylated in the twin with leukemia and appears normal in the twin that is healthy. When we hear of *BRCA1* it is usually associated with breast or ovarian cancer, and it is the inherited, mutated version of *BRCA1*. Angelina Jolie brought attention to *BRCA1* in her *New York Times* article "My Medical Choice," which highlighted her decision to have a preventive double mastectomy to change the odds handed to her by having inherited the *BRCA1* gene mutation from her mother.[12]

However, in some cases of childhood leukemia and thyroid cancer, the individual who develops cancer did not inherit a mutated version of the gene, as Jolie had; rather, for unknown reasons, the gene has been epigenetically silenced by direct methylation. Functionally, the turning off of the inherited gene by direct methylation is essentially the same thing as inheriting a mutated version—in both cases, the BRCA1 protein (the product of the *BRCA1* gene) cannot perform its designated biological task (BRCA1 helps to repair DNA damage and is involved in mitochondrial biogenesis). To date, researchers have found many divergent epigenetic modifications that are involved in a wide spectrum of diseases, including Alzheimer's, autism, bipolar disorder, autoimmune diseases, mental illness, and a variety of cancers.

Although the conditions, events, or behaviors that lead to the hypermethylation of the *BRCA1* gene in some children and not others remain a mystery, researchers have been able to link certain variables on the nurture side of the equation that are responsible for epigenetic changes that can dramatically affect our health. What are these important "nurture variables"? The answer may surprise you.

If you were to stand on a street corner and ask passersby the question posed at the beginning of this chapter: What "nurture variables," or lifestyle factors, determine how long someone will live? You would likely get the same wide-ranging answers that the supercentenarians gave, everything from whiskey to hog's head cheese. But if you ask enough people, a consistent set of common answers will emerge: genetics, diet, exercise, habits (smoking versus not smoking, for instance), and stress. I know because I've done this. Again thanks to twin studies, we know that the variables outside of genetics (nurture) account for 80 percent of our longevity. How much do these lifestyle factors matter? Recent research has shown that, although all the usual suspects—diet, exercise, smoking, and stress—do matter, there is another, perhaps underappreciated, factor that vastly eclipses the others in importance: your social life.

Social Genomics

Julianne Holt-Lunstad, a professor of psychology at Brigham Young University, Utah, has asked the exact same question: Which lifestyle factors matter the most to our longevity? To establish the answer, she and her colleagues measured the effects of a variety of lifestyle factors in over four million people. The study revealed something remarkable about our biology. The top two factors for reducing the likelihood someone will die early are two features of their social life: strong connections, or close friends, and a factor called *social integration*—the amount of social interaction one has as one moves through the day: chatting with the neighbor walking by or people at the gym, or belonging to a club, for example. According to the study, having close personal friends and strong social integration are by far the most consistent and powerful predictors for how long someone will live.

Indeed, Holt-Lunstad's research is clear, perceived loneliness is extraordinarily corrosive to our health—negatively impacting one's health more than smoking over 15 cigarettes a day. Being lonely translates to a 50 percent greater risk of early death compared to those with a robust social life. By comparison, being obese raises the chance of dying before the age of 70 by around 30 percent. And, Holt-Lunstad's research shows, moving through life with a rich social network is twice as important as exercise and diet.

Similar studies have shown the astonishingly tight connection between our social lives and our health with equally dramatic results. A 2006 University of California study tracked almost 3,000 women with breast cancer to see if there was a correlation between the richness of their social networks and their survival. The result was dramatic. The study showed that the women with fewer friends were *four times* as likely to die from the disease compared to women with more robust social connections.[13] Other studies affirmed the association. For example, a study performed by psychologist Martha McClintock at the University of Chicago dramatically illustrated the connection between loneliness and cancer development in rats. McClintock isolated one group of 20 rats by putting each rat in a cage by itself. McClintock divided a second group of 20 rats into four cages, each containing five rats. All 40 rats were genetically prone to mammary cancer. The isolated rats, however, exhibited a 135 percent increase in the number of tumors over the grouped rats, and an 8,391 percent increase in the size of tumors. They exhibited anxious, nervous behavior and ultimately died sooner than the grouped rats. The impact of chronic loneliness on our health measured in terms of longevity is profound: People with more robust networks of friends are likely to live an average of fifteen years longer than lonely people.

But how does loneliness so drastically affect our health? How can something intangible, like social interaction, affect our health more drastically than real, tangible factors such as exercise, diet, air pollution, obesity, or smoking? The answer is a biological loop that knits the neurological inputs generated from interacting with people (perceptions) into a deeply complex cellular response that occurs at the level of the epigenome. The study of this endlessly complex and fascinating looping system has been coined *social genomics*—an emerging field that centers on how human interaction, or the lack thereof, ultimately affects our health by changing the expression of certain genes.

In the past researchers have tried to understand behavior primarily from the inside out—linking hormones, stress factors, and neurotransmitters to behavioral patterns. Perhaps, says McClintock, this has been the problem all along, "If you look at the journals in my field, 90 percent of the articles look at the effects of physiological, neural, and hormonal systems on behavior, and 10 percent look at the effects of behavior on hormones and the nervous system," she said. "I don't think a balance of 90–10 is an accurate reflection of how nature works."[14] Maybe, as McClintock suggests, researchers have gotten it backward. Maybe the more interesting and dramatic effects on our bodies come from the fuzzy interface of our own perception—face-to-face interactions stimulating the brain to result in effects that cascade through neural networks and penetrate to the level of our DNA through epigenetics.

One of the first studies to show how loneliness penetrates to our core biology came in 2007. The researcher analyzed genes in the white blood cells (immune cells) of healthy older adults who reported different levels of social connectedness. Among the 22,283 genes assayed, 209 showed a different level of expression in the cells of people who reported feeling lonely and distant compared to the cells of those who reported feeling less lonely consistently over the course of four years. When the researchers analyzed the specific genes that were expressed differently, a striking pattern emerged. "These effects did not involve a random smattering of all human genes, but focally impacted three specific groups of genes. Genes supporting the early 'accelerator' phase of the immune response—inflammation—were selectively upregulated. However, two groups of genes involved in the subsequent 'steering' of immune responses were down-regulated: genes involved in responses to viral infections, and genes involved in the production of antibodies by B lymphocytes." In other words, the lonely subjects' immune systems were more prone to deleterious inflammatory responses and less able to mount a targeted response to infection. The authors of the study went on, "These results provided a molecular framework for understanding why socially isolated individuals show heightened vulnerability to inflammation-driven cardiovascular diseases (i.e., excessive non-specific immune activity) and impaired responses to viral infections and vaccines (i.e., insufficient immune responses to specific pathogens). A major clue about the psychological pathways mediating these effects came from the observation that differential gene expression profiles were most strongly linked to a person's subjective sense of isolation, rather than their objective number of social contacts."[15]

That last sentence deserves examining—the "person's *subjective* sense of isolation, rather than their *objective* number of social contacts." In other words, loneliness isn't an absolute condition. Rather, it is defined by an individual's need. As with sleep or caloric requirements, individuals have different social requirements, too. One person might feel well-rested after six hours of sleep, for example, while another person needs nine hours. It is the same with loneliness. Introverts need fewer friends and social interactions throughout the day to feel "not-lonely," whereas extroverts may require much more interaction.

At the very least, the importance of our social lives to our individual health is vastly underappreciated. "There is robust evidence that social isolation and loneliness significantly increase risk for premature mortality, and the magnitude of the risk exceeds that of many leading health indicators," wrote Holt-Lunstad.[16] Loneliness is a health crisis. Obesity, especially in America, tends to get stamped as public health enemy number one. But the results of Holt-Lunstad's research are clear: As a health risk, loneliness eclipses obesity. "Being connected to others socially is widely considered a fundamental human need—crucial to both well-being and survival. Extreme examples show infants in custodial care who lack human contact fail to thrive and often die, and indeed, social isolation or solitary confinement has been used as a form of punishment. Yet an increasing portion of the US population now experiences isolation regularly."

According to a study conducted by the AARP Foundation, approximately 47.8 million adults over age 45 in the United States are estimated to be suffering from chronic loneliness.[17] The most recent US census data show that more than half of the population is unmarried and more than a quarter of the population now lives alone. And the trend continues. Marriage rates and the number of children per household have continued to decline. "With an increasing aging population, the effect on public health is only anticipated to increase. Indeed, many nations around the world now suggest we are facing a 'loneliness epidemic.' The challenge we face now is what can be done about it," said Holt-Lunstad.

There are places, however, where there is no "loneliness epidemic." Where societies are structured around human interaction. When epidemiologists look at the so-called blue zones, regions where the residents live far longer than average, statistical analysis and observation revel a consistent pattern of social cohesion. Sardinia, a remote, mountainous Italian island in the Mediterranean, is one such place. Six times as many centenarians live on Sardinia than on the Italian mainland, ten times as many as compared to North America. And, strangely, the Sardinian men live as long as the women. (In contrast to the rest of the industrialized world, where women live on average seven years longer than men.) Susan Pinker, author of *The Village Effect*, visited this region to see what made it unique. "Architectural beauty is not its main virtue; density is. Tightly spaced houses, interwoven alleys and streets, it means that the villagers' lives constantly intersect," wrote Pinker. "Wherever I went to interview these centenarians I found a kitchen party. I quickly discovered by being there in this 'blue zone' that as people age, and across their life-spans, they are always surrounded—by extended family, by friends, by neighbors, the priest, the barkeeper, the grocer. People are always there or dropping by; they are never left to live solitary lives."[18]

Perhaps the best way to close this section is by looking at the person with the longest life-span ever recorded: Jeanne Louise Calment, of France. Calment was born in 1875, three years before Halsted arrived in Vienna for his European tour, and a year before Alexander Graham Bell patented the telephone. She died in 1997 at the age of 122. One might imagine that to live that long—far longer than most gerontologists thought was even possible—Calment must have had "perfect" genetics coupled to a "perfect" lifestyle. Yet nothing about her family could predict Calment's extreme longevity. Members of her immediate family did live longer than average, but not extraordinarily so: Her brother lived to the age of 97, her father lived to 93, and her mother to 86.

At the age of 21 Calment married her second cousin, a wealthy shop owner, and consequently Calment never had to work. She and her husband lived a life of active leisure. She enjoyed fencing, mountaineering, bicycling, roller-skating, playing the piano, painting, attending the opera, tennis, swimming, and even tagged along on her husband's hunting parties. "I had fun; I am having fun," said Calment, looking back on her life. Calment's husband introduced her to smoking after dinner when she was twenty-one. She smoked one or two cigarettes a day until she was 117. She enjoyed port wine, of which she usually had a glass or two per day. And she also enjoyed sweets, especially chocolate, of which she reportedly ate two pounds per week. According to those who knew Calment, her most distinguishing feature seemed to have been her steadiness. She never appeared stressed about anything. "I think she was someone who, constitutionally and biologically speaking, was immune to stress," said a friend. "If you can't do anything about it, don't worry about it," she once quipped. When Calment turned 100 she rode her bike from house to house in her hometown of Arles, France, to thank everyone who had congratulated her on her birthday. She reluctantly entered a nursing home at the age of 110. Calment claimed she didn't care for socializing much. "I didn't enjoy visiting, I didn't like the fashionable world, but I loved being out in the fresh air." But those observing her in the nursing home suggested otherwise. There she befriended one of the nurses who smoked a French brand of cigarette that was dark and particularly strong. She reportedly switched to the nurse's brand and often joined her new friend in the evening for a smoke. One evening Calment fell on the stairs going up to the nurse's room and broke her hip. After undergoing an operation to repair her hip she was warned that, due to her age, she might not be able to walk again. "I'll wait, I've got plenty of time," she replied. Within a few days she was able to get out of bed and even stand. However, the injury left her mostly dependent on a wheelchair. Most days, after an afternoon nap, Calment enjoyed going to other rooms and talking with the other residents about the current events she had learned about that day. She remained witty to the end, often sparring and joking with the reporters who interviewed her. "I've never had but one wrinkle, and I'm sitting on it," she liked to joke. In every article I could find about Calment, I couldn't find one where she confessed to being lonely. Although it seems she didn't have a voracious requirement for social connections, she had more than enough throughout her life. She expressed mostly gratitude for her long life. At the age of 120 she said, "I dream, I think, I go over my life. I never get bored."

All told, there is certainly nothing remarkable about Calment's lifestyle. She smoked sparingly, drank a little bit, enjoyed good food, and ate desserts. She didn't worry much. She was active and social, never professing to feeling lonely. Perhaps the way she lived her life is a good lesson for us all. Her life reflects the science behind longevity. Genetics, clean air, exercise, diet, and avoiding bad habits do matter, but perhaps not to the extent that many of us believe. What matters the most is being connected, fulfilled, and engaged in the world. It's beautiful, in a way, that the science of health and longevity also serves as a guidepost for a rich and meaningful life. Don't worry so much. Have an occasional dessert or drink if you want to. Be active. Play. Be moderate. Engage with the world and the people around you. Not only will you live longer, but you will live better.

Cognitive Traps and the Pursuit of Happiness

By the 1980s Tversky and Kahneman's work began to receive a lot of attention. The implications of prospect theory infiltrated nearly every institution, corporation, and academic field in the United States and beyond, and people were noticing. But the growing attention was lopsided. In 1984 Tversky received a phone call notifying him that he had won a MacArthur "genius" grant, an award that came with a quarter of a million dollars. "He was pissed," said a friend of Tversky. "What are these people thinking? How can they give a prize to just one of a winning pair? Do they not realize they are dealing the collaboration a death blow?" And it wasn't just the MacArthur grant, it was an open spigot of praise and prizes directed at Tversky alone, as if Kahneman hadn't existed. Soon after, Tversky received a Guggenheim Fellowship, an invitation to the American Academy of Arts and Sciences, honorary degrees from Yale and many other universities, and too many speaking invitations to count. The praise for their work was so one-sided that Kahneman couldn't help but feel slighted. Predictably, it put a strain on their relationship.

In the winter of 1996 Tversky received terrible news: he had melanoma. And it had spread. The doctors told him he didn't have much time. Tversky didn't tell many people the news, but he told Kahneman. He and Kahneman spoke almost every day until the day he died. Kahneman was the person that he wanted to end his life talking to, and the conversations were at times painful. Tversky told him he was the person that caused him the most pain in his life. "Ditto," said Kahneman. The intensity of their relationship coupled with the intensity of the fame that followed was bound to create some bad feelings. However, in the end, they loved each other as much as ever. Tversky died on June 2, 1996, at the age of 59.

After Tversky's death the attention from their work slowly shifted to Kahneman. In 2001 Kahneman received a phone call inviting him to Stockholm to speak at a conference where members of the Nobel committee would be in the audience. It was clear Kahneman was under consideration for the Nobel Prize, and the prize he was being considering for was for the work he did with Tversky on prospect theory. The speech that he prepared, however, had nothing to do with the theory. In fact, many were befuddled by Kahneman's choice to a present a different topic entirely. It was a topic that had swept Kahneman away for the last few years, a topic he found completely fascinating: happiness.

We often hear people refer to health and happiness interchangeably: "Wishing you and yours health and happiness," or, "May you have a long, happy, healthy life." Health may be required to live, but happiness is what makes life worth living. But what *is* happiness? This simple question had begun to consume Kahneman. In many ways Kahneman's genius lay in asking the right questions. Prospect theory had been born of the simple question: How do people make decisions? Now, before the Nobel committee members, Kahneman was asking them to consider another simple, yet deeply profound question: What is happiness? What really matters regarding our individual happiness and well-being compared to what we think matters? Or, put another way: How do cognitive biases sabotage our ability to achieve happiness? Can we parse out what really *does* matter to our sense of well-being and happiness from what we *think* matters? The definition of happiness is, as Kahneman said, the state of being happy. But think about that—the *state* of being happy. This definition implies an element of time, being happy *in the moment*. In another moment you might not be happy; you might even be miserable. The temporal component of happiness intrigued Kahneman. When he read through previous studies of happiness he noticed something others had failed to detect. They all measured the happiness of the subjects involved by asking them: "Are you happy?" This question automatically impels the respondent to reflect back on his or her life to tap into a narrative of memories to answer the question. This was very different, reasoned Kahneman, than the *state* of being happy, or being happy in this very moment in time. Being happy right now was radically different than reflecting back and tallying up a lifetime of experiences.

Here Kahneman found it helpful to divide a human being into two distinct selves: the experiencing self and the remembering self. These two selves, reasoned Kahneman, were actually very different people. "I think of it in terms of two selves," said Kahneman, "There is an experiencing self, that's the one that's doing the living moment to moment. And then there is a remembering, evaluating self. That's the one that answers questions like, How was it? How was the experience? How was your vacation? How's your life these days? This is a very different person that we're asking, they are not necessarily the same." He also describes the two selves this way, "One is being happy in your life and the other is being happy *about* your life."[19]

The experiencing self is living through a continuum—a stretched-out plane of existence that is experienced seamlessly moment to moment and eliciting an ever-varying spectrum of emotions depending on our intrinsic neurochemistry and what is occurring at the time. The experiencing self is innocent and pure, capable only of existing and feeling at each fleeting moment in time. One moment we might feel the gut-wrenching pain of loss, while later we might feel the elation and laughter of being surrounded by friends and family at a holiday party. The existence of the experiencing self is transitory; once a moment in time is experienced it is gone forever. In comparison, the remembering self has permanence. The remembering self selects a finite series of moments to record as memories. These memories are then put into a mental photo album that becomes an ongoing narrative of our lives. The remembering self is a storyteller. When someone asks if you are happy, the remembering self is called into action. You will recall the ongoing story of your life, and *perceived* happiness begins to color your answer. Perhaps you think of the college degree you didn't get, a failed marriage, or a low-paying job, and view your life as unhappy. While another may think of the professional degree, the successful marriage, or their high-paying job, and report their life as happy. According to Kahneman, there is a problem: In a way, the remembering self is devious, manipulative, and does not have the experiencing self's best interest at heart.

In order to reveal the divergence between the remembering self and the experiencing self, Kahneman first needed a way to measure the happiness of the experiencing self. It is easy to measure the happiness of an individual's remembering self, you just ask the person, "Are you happy?" Or, "Are you satisfied with your life?" But to measure the level of moment-to-moment happiness of the experiencing self was more challenging. Ultimately Kahneman and his colleagues found a way. They could do this by simply asking people, "Are you happy right now, in this moment?" In addition, they gave each of their subjects a beeper that would go off at various times throughout the day, prompting them to rate their level of happiness at that moment in time. In this way they could measure the happiness of their subjects' experiencing selves as they moved through their lives.

Kahneman's research revealed that the relationship between the remembering self and the experiencing self is boundlessly complex and fascinating. Kahneman offered an example from a report a student had given of listening to a recording of symphony music. The music, recalled the student, was absolutely glorious, and he had a wonderful experience listening to it. However, at the end of the recording there was a terrible screeching sound. "This ruined the entire experience for me," reported the student, very emotionally. Kahneman thought this was crazy. Clearly the experience was wonderful. Sure, the screeching noise was a fleeting moment of displeasure, but this shouldn't negate the 20 minutes of enjoyment the beautiful music had given the student. Yet the remembering self recorded a purely negative conception of the entire experience.

Kahneman performed another experiment that further exposed this divergence between the two selves. He had subjects put one hand in painfully cold water for 60 seconds and had them record the experience as they remembered it. He then repeated the experiment with the other hand, except this time at the end of the 60 seconds a valve was opened, allowing enough warm water to enter to raise the temperature by a degree. The water was still painfully cold, just slightly less so. The subjects had to keep the second hand in the slightly warmer water for an additional 30 seconds and then record the memory of the experience. The result was strange, even counterintuitive. Even though the subjects who experienced the slight raise in temperature experienced more total pain, 90 seconds versus 60 seconds, they remembered the experience as less painful. When told they had to repeat one of the two experiments, the majority chose to repeat the 90-second one. "This is direct conflict between the experiencing self and the remembering self," says Kahneman. "What defines a story are changes, significant moments, and endings. Endings are very, very important." If the experience or "story" ends at the peak moment of pain, we remember the entire event much more negatively. The same goes for the story of the student listening to the symphony; the ending defined how he remembered the entire experience. "Choices people make are guided by their memory, they are not guided by the reality of the experience."[20]

According to Kahneman, the distorted perception of time represents another departure between the experiencing self and the remembering self. "The biggest difference between them is in the handling of time. From the point of view of the experiencing self, if you have a vacation, and the second week is just as good as the first then the two-week vacation is twice as good as the one-week vacation. That's not the way it works at all for the remembering self. For the remembering self the two-week vacation is barely better than the one-week vacation. Because there are no new memories added, you have not changed the story."[21]

The value of material items between the two selves is also vastly divergent. For example, when you ask people how much happiness their car brings them, the answer correlates pretty well to the blue book value of the car. In other words, people with expensive cars report that their car makes them happier. Yet, when you ask people how their commute to work was, the correlation to the price of the car is zero. People with expensive cars hate their commute as much as people with cheaper cars. "When you stop to think about it when do you get pleasure from your car? And the answer is when you're *thinking* about your car," says Kahneman. The same goes for a house. An expensive house brings pleasure only when the owner *thinks* about it. The moment-by-moment life of the experiencing self is not changed by the value of the house, it is dictated by what is happening inside the house—the difference between a house full of friends and family celebrating a birthday and a house where people seldom visit, for example. The divergence between the two selves is especially poignant when it comes to the amount of money someone makes. The remembering self is convinced that more money will equate to increased happiness, yet the data strongly suggest otherwise. Research shows that people's day-to-day happiness level is strongly affected when they make less than $60,000 a year, but it suddenly flatlines at $60,000. In other words, making more than $60,000 per year does not result in increased happiness. "We looked at how feelings vary with income. It turns out that below an income of $60,000 a year, for Americans . . . people are unhappy, and they get progressively unhappier the poorer they get. Above that we get an absolutely flat line. I mean, I've rarely seen lines so flat. Clearly what is happening, money does not buy you experiencing happiness, but lack of money certainly buys you misery, and we can measure that misery very, very clearly. In terms of the remembering self you get a very different story. The more money you earn the more satisfied you are. That does not hold for emotions," says Kahneman.[22]

The clear message from Kahneman's research is that the experiencing self—a vulnerable, exposed being, only capable of feeling in the moment—is at the mercy of the remembering self. The experiencing self has no voice.

The remembering self is making all the decisions in our lives, and the experiencing self is dragged along without a say, often to places that aren't in his or her best interest. "We don't think of our future as experiences, we think of our future as anticipated memories," says Kahneman. As such, our remembering self often guides our lives toward a future of anticipated memories that are important only to the remembering self: material objects, higher-paying jobs, and bucket-list vacations, for example. The data clearly show that the experiencing self doesn't care about these things.

To illustrate this dichotomy between the two selves, Kahneman has us perform a thought experiment. Pretend you get an offer to take a vacation anywhere you want to go in the world. But there is a condition. Once the vacation is over, all the photos and social-media posts will be destroyed, and you will be given a drug that wipes away the memory of the vacation. "Now, would you choose the same vacation?" asks Kahneman. "And if you would choose a different vacation there is a conflict between your two selves and you need to think about how to adjudicate that conflict."

His research on happiness has, at times, perplexed Kahneman. The blurry interface between the two selves can be contradictory and counterintuitive. Early on Kahneman thought the often-neglected experiencing self mattered the most. After all, this is the version of ourselves doing most of the feeling. But the data have forced him to change his mind. The satisfaction or pain someone feels as they reel back though their life's narrative turns out to be very important to us as human beings. And even when we are not directly thinking about our own life story it is always idling somewhere in the background, somehow bleeding over into the experiencing self and coloring our moment-by-moment feelings. "When I was young and foolish, and by that, I mean about eight years ago, I thought that really what matters is the experiencing self. Who cares about the remembering self, it's just a story that we're telling, and I thought we can neglect that. If we really succeed in studying the experiencing self, then we'll have the real answer to people's well-being," said Kahneman. Yet, for Kahneman, this is where the subject of happiness—the hazy relationship between the two selves—becomes impossible to untangle. The scorecard of the remembering self, he discovered, matters more to people than he had anticipated. Even though the remembering self, the ultimate decision-maker in our lives, is laden with demonstrable cognitive biases—inaccurate memories of pleasure and pain, a flawed emphasis on material wealth, and an irrational preference for anticipated memories over experience, for example. Even so, says Kahneman, the importance of the remembering self's version of our lives appears to be a critical variable in our overall happiness. "People just don't go along with the idea that the experiencing self is really the end-all and be-all. It turns out that people have a narrative of their life, they have a story of their life, they care a great deal about that story. They make decisions for that story, they make choices to keep that story good or improve it. People care a great deal and take actions based on anticipated memories and on evaluations." In the end, Kahneman leaves the question of which matters more, the experiencing self or the remembering self, up to each one of us. "I do not answer the philosophical question of which matters more."[23]

And who is to say who is happier? We can imagine a person who seems very happy in the moment, someone who smiles and laughs a lot yet, in thinking back on life, sees only failure: perhaps no college degree, a low-paying job, or missed goals. Conversely, we can imagine someone who doesn't smile or laugh much, who doesn't seem happy moment to moment, yet is very satisfied with his or her life's story, has achieved their goals, and fulfilled what they set out to do. Who is happier? No one can know.

Kahneman found another series of data on the happiness of the experiencing self quite puzzling: the effect of one's country of origin on the experiencing self's level of happiness. "Let me tell you the results and I find them stunning and I don't understand where they come from. The Danes, the Swiss, the Dutch, 3 or 4 percent of the people report being depressed the day before. The Americans, the Greeks, the Indians report about 14 percent. The Palestinians report 30 percent and the Armenians report close to 50 percent. There are enormous differences. National circumstances has a big effect on people's lives," says Kahneman. The degree to which it matters is remarkable—why would the Dutch, Swiss, and Danes be over three times happier than the Americans? Yet the data speak clearly: Our national circumstances are critical to our level of happiness.

While Kahneman's work on happiness, like his prospect theory, is beginning to influence public policy, it also has the capacity to have a profound impact on an individual level. Learning about the research on happiness allows one to confront and examine the two selves within. Have you favored one at the expense of the other? Has the remembering self, with all of its cognitive traps, held a tyrannical reign over your life? Have you relentlessly pursued the improvement of your life's "story" to the detriment of experience? Chased money, materialism, and recognition over the things that the experiencing self craves—intimate relationships, friendships, and experiences? Or perhaps your life is tilted the other way. Perhaps you've invested in experience over the things that the remembering self prizes and missed out on achieving goals, resulting in a dissatisfying life story. Or is it possible that you have struck a perfect balance, answering both of their needs? In the end, we each have to answer these questions alone.

In writing this section I couldn't help but reflect on how Kahneman's happiness research applies to the next generation's relationship with social media. For myself, I remember a childhood largely in service of the experiencing self. My brother and our friends spent most of our free time outside. We often played in the woods, lost in our imaginations, saturated in the moment. My kids and their friends today, however, have had very different childhoods, often defined by small screens and their interactions on social media. I imagine that for many these new influences are shifting the realm of childhood from being dominated by the experiencing self to being dominated by the remembering self. Most social media is nothing if not a running narrative of the remembering self's life. One platform even calls this running narrative of posts a "story." Now when one observes people on vacation it can seem as though the vacation was intended more to fuel a social media feed than for any actual enjoyment of the occasion.

The outcome of this experiment is as yet unknown. One thing is clear, however: Suicide rates among this generation have risen dramatically—especially for girls and women (across all age ranges) for whom the rate increased by 50 percent from 2006 to 2016, compared to a rise of 21 percent for all ages of boys and men during the same time period. The social media portrayal of young people's lives is subject to the judgment of others every day, as if their self-worth is continually on trial. And this goes for adults as well. Rigorous research bears this out. One recent study designed to obtain a clearer picture of the relationship between social media use and well-being, used three waves of data from 5,208 adult Facebook users. The results were definitive. "Overall, our results showed that, while real-world social networks were positively associated with overall well-being, the use of Facebook was negatively associated with overall well-being. These results were particularly strong for mental health; most measures of Facebook use in one year predicted a decrease in mental health in a later year. We found consistently that both liking others' content and clicking links significantly predicted a subsequent reduction in self-reported physical health, mental health, and life satisfaction."[24]

In 2013, after studying happiness for two decades, Kahneman suddenly stopped. "I gradually became convinced that people don't want to be happy. They want to be satisfied with their life," he said. The reason he abandoned happiness research, as he explains it, seems to reflect an acquired cynicism for humanity's pursuit of happiness. "People don't want to be happy the way I've defined the term—what I experience here and now. In my view, it's much more important for them to be satisfied, to experience life satisfaction, from the perspective of 'What I remember,' of the story they tell about their lives. I furthered the development of tools for understanding and advancing an asset that I think is important but most people aren't interested in."[25]

What you decide to do with this knowledge is of course up to you. For me, Kahneman's study of happiness aided the realization that the remembering self—the evaluating, decision-making version of ourselves; the version that is in charge of steering our lives—is rife with cognitive biases. This version of ourself is not particularly good at recalling past incidents of pain and pleasure and using these to make future decisions about pain and pleasure. As Kahneman put it, "Choices people make are guided by their memory, they are not guided by the reality of the experience." This version of ourself often chooses materialism and money over the things our experiencing self cherishes the most, such as intimacy, conversation, and friendship. This version of ourself is more concerned with the memory of a vacation than the experience of it. This version of ourself is always comparing ourself to others. "Life satisfaction is connected to a large degree to social yardsticks—achieving goals, meeting expectations. It's based on comparisons with other people," says Kahneman.[26] Charlie Munger likes to point out that envy is the only one of the seven deadly sins with zero upside: "Combine gluttony and lust and you can have a helluva weekend . . . but with envy, you only feel bad."[27] In the end, Kahneman offers this very simple advice: "One way to improve life is simply by tilting the balance toward more affectively good activities, such as spending more time with friends or reducing commuting time."

Kahneman's ultimate realization that most people are more concerned with the remembering self's version of happiness—or "life satisfaction," as Kahneman calls it—over the experiencing self's happiness, may be a cultural phenomenon that is more tightly woven into the fabric of certain societies than others. But there is an important connection to be made here: the relationship between the two selves and health. We've already learned that attending to our experiencing self's needs for friendship, socialization, and intimacy can profoundly affect our epigenome in a way that promotes health and longevity. And this is indeed found to be the case in blue zones, where social cohesiveness binds generations of families and friends and society is built around these connections. There is no denying that we crave intimacy and acceptance all the way to the level of our genome. Our immune system simply doesn't care what car we have in the garage.

It is pretty clear that Kahneman himself seems to be more empathetic to the needs of the experiencing self than the remembering self. Perhaps it is simply a function of his own ego: He is truly not concerned with awards, attention, and approval. Or perhaps it is because he has already achieved a life to his remembering self's overwhelming satisfaction. Certainly, the life Kahneman appears to value more, the life of the experiencing self, is the life that both epidemiological data and genomics data strongly suggest is the better version for your health.

But it is not that simple. Few things in biology ever are. One intriguing study has revealed an interesting connection between the remembering self and longevity. This 2001 study looked at the difference in longevity between nominees and winners of Academy Awards compared to a control group of actors who were never nominated. The researchers identified 762 actors who were at one time nominated for an Academy Award in a leading or a supporting role. The researchers then matched each nominee with at least one other cast member of the same sex who was in the same film and born in the same era to serve as the control group. The results were telling. Within the group of 762 Academy Award nominees, 235 had won one or more Oscars. The 235 winners lived almost four years longer on average than the non-nominated, control group of actors. Further, actors who had won multiple Oscars lived up to six years longer on average than the control group of actors. "It suggests that an internal sense of self-esteem is an important aspect to health and health care," said the lead author of the study.[28]

Kahneman's two versions of ourselves, the remembering self and the experiencing self, may serve as a good models to help us better mentally categorize and think about happiness, yet this bifurcated model may not entirely reflect the true complexity of our biology. The two versions of ourselves are not standing in separate corners ignoring each other. They are bound together, continuously interacting, arguing, agreeing, bickering, and supporting each other. Our mind is constantly engaged in an intricate, internal dance of which our life is the choreographer.

A New Culture

In the summer of 2009 Atul Gawande received a surprise in the mail. It was a check for $20,000 sent unannounced by a man named Charlie Munger. Admittedly, Gawande was confused. He had never met Munger or even ever corresponded with him. Gawande, then 43, was best known for his writing. He had penned two best-selling books, *Complications* and *Better*, and was a staff writer for the *New Yorker*, which had just published his article "The Cost Conundrum." The article, which I touched on earlier, was a deep-dive into the massive cost variations to be found among local health care markets across the United States. The piece focused specifically on McAllen, Texas, one of the most expensive markets in the country. Gawande had traveled there personally and uncovered the cause: a local culture of competitive entrepreneurship among the doctors that had manifested in "across-the-board overuse of medicine." The McAllen doctors had been acting less and less like doctors and more and more like businessmen.

It was this article that had caught Munger's attention and inspired him to impulsively write out a check for twenty grand and mail it to the article's author. Gawande was given no explanation for the check other than that Munger had deemed his article "so socially useful." Flattered, yet still confused by the spontaneous gift, Gawande mailed it back to Munger. "He sent it back to me again and said, 'Do with it what you want.'" Gawande finally relented and donated the money to Brigham and Women's Center for

Surgery and Public Health, where he worked as a surgeon. The money was used to help supply oxygen monitors to low-income countries.

With this odd exchange behind him, and the money put to good use, Gawande settled back into his busy routine of operating, teaching at Harvard, writing, and lecturing. In 2010 *Time* magazine name Gawande one of the world's most influential thinkers. In 2012 he published another *New York Times* best-seller, *The Checklist Manifesto*, and helped found Ariadne Labs, named for the Greek goddess who showed Theseus the way out of the Minotaur's maze using a simple thread. Ariadne Labs served as a testing ground for high-impact "guiding threads" like surgical checklists—a bridge between Gawande and his staff's innovative ideas about improving health care and their real-world implementation. Gawande penned more award-winning articles for the *New Yorker* in the years that followed, and in 2014 he presented the BBC's distinguished Reith Lectures, delivering a series of four talks in London, Boston, Edinburgh, and Delhi, entitled "The Future of Medicine." Then, in 2018, Gawande again heard from Munger.

The true architect behind the Berkshire-Amazon-JPMorgan health care consortium is a man named Todd Combs, one of two investment lieutenants handpicked by Buffett and Munger to succeed them. It was Combs who, in the winter of 2018, had a flash of insight. Like a parasite, America's health care crisis had infected Berkshire and was relentlessly siphoning away resources and productivity. But perhaps Berkshire didn't have to passively allow the broken health care system to exploit their organization, reasoned Combs. Perhaps they could address it internally—fix it from the inside out.

Combs is cut from the same cloth as Buffett and Munger, his recruitment by the pair reflecting the self-sustaining culture that Berkshire has cultivated its entire existence. Like Buffett and Munger, he is in a perpetual state of learning. "I read about 12 hours a day," Combs once reported in a rare interview. Like Buffett and Munger, Combs is a student of human nature. "He [is] fascinated by psychology and the sorts of biases that drive decision-making. Books such as *Talent Is Overrated* and *The Checklist Manifesto* have become staples in the hedge fund world, where money managers are constantly looking for an edge. But Combs was interested in those ideas well before they became trendy," said a colleague.[29] Steeped in Berkshire's culture, Combs knew that his first steps in tackling a problem as complex as health care were to learn as much as he could, and, vitally, to pick the right person to lead the new venture.

This meant talking to hundreds of people and researching their patterns of thought and their track records. Gawande doesn't recall exactly when Combs began considering him to head the consortium that he had been quietly putting together for months. But the leadership at Berkshire had noticed something extraordinary in him, and he had climbed to the top of their internal list. And then, in the summer of 2018, he received a call offering him a job. They asked him to be the chief executive officer of the Berkshire, Amazon, and JPMorgan health care company. He accepted.

It's easy to see why he was picked. Gawande fits perfectly into the Berkshire culture. Like Munger, Buffett, and Combs, Gawande is often described as humble yet brilliant, and he's a voracious learner. "I can't think of anybody who'd be better. I don't know of anybody who'd be better," said Arnold Epstein of Harvard's T.H. Chan School of Public Health. "He's excited. He's nervous. And he's also incredibly humble," said another colleague. But the fledgling company, with its ambitious goals, does have its naysayers. "Just because you know an industry is underperforming and you have a lot of money doesn't mean you have a successful strategy," said Leemore Dafny, a professor at Harvard Business School.[30] And Zack Cooper, Yale School of Public Health, tweeted: "I do hope Amazon, JPMorgan, and Berkshire succeed. Health care is wildly inefficient. However, it's a bit like Mayo Clinic, Cleveland Clinic, and Partners in Health coming out and saying they don't like their computers so they're going to form a new IT company."[31]

But the consortium is under no illusions about the difficulties that they face. And while others may see Gawande's relative lack of experience as a negative, Bezos sees it as a strength. "We said at the outset that the degree of difficulty is high and success is going to require an expert's knowledge, a beginner's mind, and a long-term orientation. Atul embodies all three, and we're starting strong as we move forward in this challenging and worthwhile endeavor," said Bezos.[32]

For now, Gawande is tasked with delivering better and more efficient care for the venture's 1.2 million employees. But the vision for the venture is much grander, and extends much further. If he can implement scalable improvements, then who knows? Other health systems may also adopt them.

Politicians might even stand to learn from what Gawande and his team will do. Indeed, for three corporate giants, the goal of the venture is strangely altruistic. It will be set up as a nonprofit organization and serve as an incubator for ideas that, they hope, will be adopted around the world. "This work will take time but must be done," said Gawande. "The system is broken, and better is possible."[33]

————————

Now the question becomes: *How* is better possible? What needs to be done? Indeed, just Atul Gawande being himself has proven to have incredible value. Six years after his *New Yorker* article about McAllen was published, Gawande looked back to see what, if anything, had changed there. What he discovered was striking: Between 2009 and 2012, costs in McAllen had dropped by almost $3,000 per Medicare recipient. Total savings to taxpayers were projected to have reached almost half a billion dollars by the end of 2014. After the article was published, journalists from Texas newspapers and television crews had swarmed the city. The shit hit the fan in McAllen.

"The reaction here was fierce, just a tremendous amount of finger-pointing and yelling and screaming," said one of the whistleblowers in Gawande's article. "We hated you," another doctor told Gawande. "The story put us in a spotlight, in a bad way, but, in a good way at the same time." Beyond the yelling and screaming and finger-pointing, the dustup from Gawande's article had painfully real consequences. "Several federal prosecutions cracked down on outright fraud. Seven doctors agreed to a $28 million settlement for taking illegal kickbacks when they referred their patients to specialty medical services. An ambulance-company owner was indicted for reporting 621 ambulance rides that allegedly never happened. Four clinic operators were sent to jail for billing more than 13,000 visits and procedures under the name of a physician with dementia," wrote Gawande. The prosecutions had a knock-on effect. One doctor told Gawande it caused the McAllen doctors to say, "Hey, we're under the magnifying glass. We need to make sure we're doing things strictly by the book."

The changes that occurred in McAllen happened because Gawande shined a spotlight on what was going on. The pen can still be mightier than the sword. When what has always been invisible is suddenly made visible, the light can have a sterilizing effect. This is what happened in McAllen. Charlie Munger has often said that exposing fraud is one of the best things a person can do for a capitalistic society. For society to work, we all have to play fairly. They were not playing fairly, or honorably, in McAllen, and Gawande called them out.

Atul Gawande knows what he has to do. First, he recognizes precisely where we are in the sweep of history. In previous generations medicine had made massive leaps forward with the discovery of a single new therapy—penicillin, for example. We are beyond that. This is the age of the system. "We are going from the century of the molecule to the century of the system," said one of Gawande's colleagues. "DNA, genes, energy, future. It's how the genes connect together that actually determine what diseases do. It's how the neurons connect together and form networks that create consciousness and behavior. And it's how the drugs and the devices and specialists all work together that create the care that we want," said Gawande in one of his BBC lectures.

Nature provides a good example. Over three billion years ago life began as a self-replicating molecule. This evolved into a self-replicating cell, which in turn evolved into a multicellular organism, with individual cells now performing a certain task for a given system. Multicellular life is a collective, if you will, an economy of divided labor. Evolution is a march up the ladder of functionality; molecules to cells to multicellular organisms. Nature repeats patterns. Societal organization, including medicine, is marching up the same ladder of complexity. We have gone from caves, to cities, to the industrial revolution, and up and up. Medicine is following the same path, becoming a multicellular organism, in a sense, a system of divided specialties.

Looking down from 30,000 feet, Gawande knows that America's biggest problems in health care come from the wild variations in care that have been highlighted in previous chapters. Period. "In 2010, the Institute of Medicine issued a report stating that waste accounted for 30 percent of health-care spending, or some $750 billion dollars a year, which was more than our nation's entire budget for K–12 education. The report found that higher prices, administrative expenses, and fraud accounted for almost half of this waste. Bigger than any of those, however, was the amount spent on unnecessary health care services," wrote Gawande. "Millions of people are receiving drugs that aren't helping them, operations that aren't going to make them better, and scans and tests that do nothing beneficial for them, and often cause harm."[34] Really, the needle doesn't have to move much to see an improvement. The Commonwealth Fund report, a survey that ranks the quality of health care in ten developed nations, has ranked the United States the worst of the lot for five years running.

And here is the way forward. Just as Fisher's clinical trial provided the statistical data to halt the radical mastectomy in its tracks, statistics of a new kind will guide reformers like Gawande—providing the means to identify, and cull out, the waste. Capitalistic markets find a way of rewarding those that do things better and cheaper. For example, Walmart has initiated a program for employees who require spine, heart, and transplant procedures—procedures that account for the lion's share of the costs associated with unnecessary overtreatment. The program covers all expenses if the employee will go to one of six centers, places like Mayo and Cleveland Clinic where doctors are incentivized to not overtreat by being paid a salary. Here, if patients don't need an operation, they won't get one. The result: less suffering and less wasteful spending.

Humans have a tendency to overcomplicate things. In fact, there is a name for this propensity: the *complexity bias*. Complexity bias is a logical fallacy that leads us to give unjustified credence to complex concepts preferentially over more simple ones. Occam's razor, the problem-solving principle that contends that simpler solutions are more likely to be correct than complex ones, might perhaps seem intuitively obvious. Yet somehow, as a civilization, it is here that we seem so often to fail. For example, there is a simple solution to our nation's health care crisis that is dangling right in front of us: change our physicians' payment incentive from fee-for-service to salary. If this was enacted as a regulatory law, the vast majority of physicians in the country would become completely different doctors overnight. Freed from worrying about which procedures might cause them to lose money, freed from having to think like businesspeople, they could finally focus on the thing that matters: delivering the best care to the patient in front of them. At a recent dinner party, where the wine was flowing freely, I overheard a doctor say that his practice had fired a doctor for "not being productive." When I asked him what he meant he explained, "He wasn't billing out enough." This has to end. For humans, incentives are incredibly powerful. Charlie Munger knows this.

Merely making better use of EMR systems—like Brent James did at Intermountain—can result in massive improvements in health care. Early on James realized the power of data and exploited it to guide physicians' decision-making, reducing the massive variation in treatment by allowing data to reveal the "best practice" for a given problem. Since then, a unique company named Flatiron Health—launched in 2012 when a cousin of one of the founders was diagnosed with leukemia—has developed an EMR system with a variety of unusual features. But Flatiron doesn't simply market an EMR system. They are able to sift through records accumulated from multiple practices to extract and analyze meaningful "real-world data" that can better guide cancer treatment. Like James and his team at Intermountain, Flatiron Health is more than just an EMR, it is a comprehensive, top-down managed system. This type of system—coupled with artificial intelligence (AI)—is the future: a system that is constantly capturing data and learning the best way to treat patients.[35]

We are not entirely rational creatures. Psychologists like Kahneman and Tversky have defined our illogical circuits. The evidence-based systems like Intermountain, Geisinger, and Flatiron Health are attempting to "childproof" the environment for us—padding the corners and plugging the outlets. They save us from ourselves. And the outcomes of these systems speak for themselves. Simply put, systems make health care better. They funnel the wild variations in treatment down into a single "best practice." And any argument that this funneling process is limiting a doctor's ability to treat each patient individually doesn't hold water. The data are very clear. To reduce variation by establishing a best practice improves outcomes. The funnel is not constraining physicians; it is narrowing their margin of error and permitting them to focus on the patient with more acuity. At its best, technology delivers us from the drudgery of life. It frees our hands and our attention. Over a hundred years ago traveling from one city to another by horse and buggy would consume all of someone's effort and attention. When the automobile arrived, traveling became easier. Soon driverless cars will allow someone to focus on completely other things while traveling from one city to the next—to read, listen, or notice things that would not otherwise be noticed. Best practices are the driverless cars that free a physician to attend entirely to the patient's needs. Best practices are not a straitjacket;

they are the emancipators of intuition. The biggest danger now is that we won't moneyball health care fast enough.

The incursion of big data and AI into medicine will only increase from here. In October of 2018 Google announced the development of a deep-learning tool called Lymph Node Assistant, or LYNA. This AI system is capable of telling the difference between cancerous and noncancerous biopsy slides 99 percent of the time. The system is capable of much greater accuracy than pathologists. When pathologists incorporate the system into their practice they find that it reduces the rate of missed micrometastases by a factor of two and cuts inspection time in half.

The inevitable backlash against the incursion of evidence-based systems and technology into medicine is sure to intensify. New technologies always encounter resistance before they are adopted. The automated push-button elevator was invented in 1900, yet it wasn't until the 1950s that it was accepted. Even though the new elevators were safer, people had a hard time trusting an elevator without a human operator. Before Westinghouse invented the airbrake for trains in the mid-1800s, a "brakeman" would have to climb to the top of the train to manually crank a wheel to stop the train. It was a terribly dangerous job that had to be performed in all kinds of weather, and every year many brakemen were injured or killed. Still, the idea of automated brakes powered by air was resisted. The brakemen's union even published newspaper ads to drum up public outrage: "Are you going to trust your life to air?" Driverless cars are sure to follow the same predictable pattern. And the same is true for flying: While it is considered very safe, 50 percent of all air travel accidents today are due to human error. But the continuous process of identifying these human errors and developing automated systems to correct them has made air travel safer and safer.

Another example is Russian chess grandmaster Gary Kasparov, considered by many to be the greatest player of all time, who has experienced a uniquely intimate incursion of technology into his profession over the span of his career. For Kasparov, it began with what's known as a "simultaneous exhibition" match in the summer of 1985 in Hamburg, Germany. Kasparov's opponents that summer day consisted of 32 personal computers programmed by four companies to play chess. Kasparov would walk from one board to the next, and the faceless computer would make its move the moment

Kasparov arrived. Although one of the 32 games was uncomfortably close, in the end the human brain prevailed, and Kasparov won all 32 games in a clean sweep. Twelve years later, Kasparov again found himself sitting across from a computer. This time it was a single game against a $10 million IBM supercomputer named Deep Blue. The match received no lack of attention from the media. The *Guardian* proclaimed it was Kasparov's job to "defend humankind from the inexorable advance of artificial intelligence." *Newsweek*'s headline called it "The Brain's Last Stand." But that day in New York City Kasparov lost to Deep Blue—the first defeat of a reigning world chess champion by a computer under tournament conditions. When Kasparov lost to Deep Blue the world changed, and so did Kasparov. Kasparov was forced to grapple with the existential meaning of the loss and the rapidly evolving relationship between humans and machines. And there was a distinction. The relationship Kasparov was contending with was not simple; it didn't exist merely on the physical plane, like replacing a brakeman with an automatic air brake. Rather, it was machines transcending into something uniquely human. The game of chess is a game of logical analysis, but it is also a game of subtle intuition—a nexus between reason and instinct. For a machine to beat the best human chess player alive was unsettling. Up until that day in New York, machines had woven their way into our lives from the bottom up by replacing simple tasks, those we believed "beneath" us. Now, however, a machine had proven better than humans at the very capabilities that define us, the abilities that set us apart from the rest of the animal kingdom: logic and intuition. It was almost as if the earth was no longer the center of the universe. Could a machine be programmed with creativity and the intuition of a human being? As he grappled with the meaning, what Kasparov did next was not to further the rivalry but to facilitate a truce of sorts. He developed something called "advanced chess," which allows each player to pick a computer program to play with them—a person versus person game with each player assisted by a computer. The idea was to merge the best qualities of both—the nanosecond number-crunching ability of the computer alongside the subtle instincts that are thought to be uniquely human. And this is exactly what happened. Advanced chess brought the level of chess to heights unattainable by man or machine alone; it became a beautiful hybrid of cognitive strengths. And why should there be a distinction? Why are we naturally inclined to frame chess as "human versus machine" or "human alongside machine"? After all, machines are developed and programmed by humans, so advanced chess is really just humankind at its best. Kasparov's advanced chess offers a powerful example of how health care might be transformed.

How the inevitable incursion of data into medicine is framed will be critical. As reformers like James and Gawande and technology like Google's LYNA impinge on physicians' autonomy—and perhaps their sense of self-worth—the cries of fear and resistance will be heard, just as happens with every new technology. As the infinite borders of a physician's autonomy are drawn tighter by data-driven systems, the complaints of "cookbook medicine" and data "straitjackets" will become louder. But it would serve all of us well if we skipped the instinctual, knee-jerk reaction to medicine's technological transformation. Perhaps it can be framed differently. Kasparov's advanced chess should be held up as a beacon, a perfect metaphor for the merger of technology and medicine—*advanced medicine*—in the pursuit of a new and better culture. Combining the analytic strengths of evidence-based medicine and AI with human intuition will transport the practice of medicine to heights unattainable by humans alone. Technology will serve to liberate physicians' intuition and enhance their capacity to make the imaginative leaps of insight that remain uniquely human. After all, Spock and Kirk were better together.

———————

This transformation will free physicians to focus on something else: the human side of medicine. Sick people need empathy. Programs like Geisinger's innovative Fresh Food Farmacy would not be successful without the human component. This fundamental human need is not some superficial nicety, we now know it penetrates deep into our core biology. Human interaction, including the empathetic support we receive from our health care providers, changes the expression of genes in our immune systems in a way we have not appreciated until recently. And this beneficial shift in immune function can drastically change our health outcomes for the better. Human-human interaction is part of healing, and it is something that technology will never replace.

On a societal level we need to do better. The current trend is disturbing: The citizens of western civilizations are feeling more and more isolated and lonely. A nationwide survey by the health insurer Cigna found that loneliness is widespread in America, with nearly 50 percent of respondents reporting that they felt alone or left out "always" or "sometimes." More than half of survey respondents said that they "always" or "sometimes" feel that no one knew them well. Fifty-six percent reported they "sometimes" or "always" felt like the people around them "are not necessarily with them." And two in five felt they lacked companionship, their relationships weren't meaningful, and that they were isolated from others. Surprisingly, the survey revealed that younger generations are more strongly affected by loneliness. The survey used a scale range from 20 to 80, with people scoring 43 and above considered lonely and with higher scores suggesting a greater level of loneliness and social isolation. The 2018 survey revealed that "members of Generation Z, born between the mid-1990s and the early 2000s, had an overall loneliness score of 48.3. Millennials, just a little bit older, scored 45.3. By comparison, baby boomers scored 42.4. The Greatest Generation, people ages 72 and above, had a score of 38.6 on the loneliness scale."[36]

The nuances revealed from the survey show that it's difficult to pin the cause on social media alone, or American's obsessive consumerism and overworking. For example, it's not simply the existence of social media but how it's used that matters. Just passively scrolling through feeds is associated with negative feelings, but actively reaching out to people in a way that facilitates meeting face to face, is associated with positive feelings. Likewise, working too much is associated with loneliness, but working too little, or not at all, is also associated with loneliness. Like most things in life, it's the subtleties that matter. The balance.

One simple way to dramatically lower health care costs is through prevention. Benjamin Franklin's quip that "an ounce of prevention is worth a pound of cure" is as true today as when he coined it hundreds of years ago. Yet our health care system is heavily weighted toward the procedures, devices, and medications aimed at treating problems once they have already occurred, with too little attention paid to preventing them from occurring in the first place. What is the way forward here? How do we effectively prevent health problems on a societal level? The science of social genomics presented in this book hints at a creative way to approach the problem. The data is becoming more and more convincing that human connections are dramatically important to our health and happiness. Our sense of well-being and our actual physical well-being—our innermost biology—are tangled together in a way that can't be undone, they are forever quilted together—we need both to be healthy and happy. But there is no need to wait for society to change. We are all empowered to act. Examine your own life. Find the right balance between your remembering self and your experiencing self. Don't get caught up in the American penchant for envy and comparison. Remember Kahneman's research that clearly shows that happiness levels off at $60,000 a year. Warren Buffet once told a PBS reporter that his $77 billion worth of shares in Berkshire stock has, "no utility to me. They can't do anything to make me happier. I'm already happy," remarked Buffett. "If I could spend $100 million on a house that would make me a lot happier, I would do it." But he is wise enough to know that it wouldn't. Buffett has lived in the same house that he purchased for $31,500 in 1958. "For me, that's the happiest house in the world. And it's because it's got memories, and people come back, and all that sort of thing."

To be sure, the arc of history is a continuum of societal change. Societies can change from aggressive to passive. They can be inclusive or exclusive, welcoming or xenophobic—build walls or open their borders. Styles, trends, values, ethics, and norms change. Societies evolve, shift, and adapt. They live and breathe like the people that comprise them. Perhaps policy-makers will consider this happiness metric someday. In the U.K. they already do, with policy decisions aimed at maximizing their citizens' happiness. Societies could be guided to be more like the blue zones. Every downtick in loneliness that we achieve translates directly into improved health—better cardiovascular health, improved immune function, and reduced "all-cause mortality." And this effect appears to be even more amplified with younger people. Lonely, directionless young people are a tinderbox for any society.

Perhaps our policy-makers would do well to follow the advice of Thomas Jefferson, who said, "The care of human life and happiness, and not their destruction, is the first and only legitimate object of good government."[37] And again, as individuals possessing free will, we don't have to wait for society to change. If you take nothing else from this book, I hope you take home the examples of the power of relationships. Indeed, Kahneman would not be Kahneman without Tversky, and vice versa. Buffet would not be Buffett without Munger, and vice versa. The sum of the two made up the whole. We are better, healthier, and happier together.

The Future of Medicine

So, what is the future of medicine? How good *can* we get? To begin with, the low-hanging fruit must be picked. Eliminating payment systems that incentivize physicians to overtreat is obvious. Reducing the massive variation in treatment that occurs daily across the country by adopting evidence-based systems to establish best practices is another obvious need. Making full use of our pool of existing drugs can happen now by forming a panel of experts from government and the private sector to comb through the massive amount of data supporting the use of drugs like metformin in cancer, or ketamine for drug-resistant depression, for example. Their potential benefit versus their risk can then be rationally calculated and best practices established for their use. Common mistakes—adverse drug interactions, hospital-acquired infections, and so on—will be eliminated by fail-proof systems. Looking far into the future, the antiquated "magic bullet" approach to pharmacology will be replaced by combinations of drugs for complex diseases such as cancer and autoimmunity. Drugs will be given in elaborate combinations, timed precisely to inhibit an exact cellular pathway at exactly the right moment, rewriting the epigenetic tags responsible for the disease and reversing it at its source. Doctors' office visits will routinely include a gut biome readout; missing species of good bacteria will be added back in, bad ones eliminated. Genes that result in pointless suffering will be edited out using CRISPR (clustered regularly interspaced short palindromic repeats), an otherworldly technology that allows scientists to rewrite our genomes at will.

Technologies will reverse the damage of aging—aggregated proteins will be dissolved, senescent cells eliminated, stem cells replaced. Whole organs will be regenerated in the lab from our own tissue and replaced as needed. Degenerative disease will slowly be eliminated altogether. Mental illness will be solved though targeted drugs and cognitive exercises that rewire or reestablish missing or errant neural connections. And these changes will march alongside societal changes that make a life worth living. Loneliness will be eliminated though social programs that bring people together and provide purpose. People won't be allowed to fall through the cracks anymore. Communities will be planned and built more like the blue zones—the markets, streets, shops, and town centers all strategically designed around human connection.

Is this utopian vision realistic? I believe it is. Think of what we have accomplished in a single person's lifetime. Jeanne Louise Calment, once the oldest living person known, witnessed the transformation of medicine from something barbaric into something almost angelic. Technology builds on technology, and the pace is exponential. Even with all the problems we have today, the vector of progress is always headed in the right direction. With creative reformers like Brent James and Atul Gawande, coupled with improving medicines, devices, and AI systems, it is a time for hope. The possibilities are limitless. Perhaps Brent James said it best: "We have not yet begun to understand how good we can be."

Acknowledgments

A book like this is, by definition, a synthesis of many other people's hard work. To that end, I am deeply grateful to Michael Lewis for bringing to life the story of the 2002 Oakland A's in *Moneyball* and Daniel Kahneman and Amos Tversky's work in *The Undoing Project*. Many other writers and journalists did the heavy lifting from which I benefited—they conducted the original interviews and fleshed out great stories. In particular, I owe a debt of gratitude to the many wonderful reporters at the *New York Times* and NPR, as well as the writers Robert Pearl, Sherwin B. Nuland, Alice Schroeder, Janet Lowe, Daniel Kahneman, and Atul Gawande.

And, of course, thank you to the outstanding editors who did the polishing: Makenna Goodman, my brother, Brady Christofferson, and Jennifer Lipfert.

Notes

Introduction: Is Health Care Fixable?

1. Health Clinics Limited, "Study of the Safety, Tolerability and Efficacy of Metabolic Combination Treatments on Cancer (METRICS)," https://clinical trials.gov/ct2/show/NCT02201381?term=metformin+mebendazole&cond=cancer&rank=1.

Chapter 1: A New System

1. Lewis, *The Undoing Project*, chap. 1.
2. Viera, "For Lin, Erasing a History of Being Overlooked."
3. Lewis, *The Undoing Project*, chap. 1.
4. Lewis, chap. 3.
5. Lewis, chap. 5.
6. Michael Lewis, "How Two Trailblazing Psychologists Turned the World of Decision Science Upside Down," *Vanity Fair* (Hive), November 14, 2016, https://www.vanityfair.com/news/2016/11/decision-science-daniel-kahneman-amos-tversky.
7. Daniel Kahneman, "Intuition and Rationality, a Conversation with Daniel Kahneman," by Harry Kreisler, UC Berkley, Conversations with History Series, 2007, http://globetrotter.berkeley.edu/people7/Kahneman/kahneman-con3.html.
8. Amos Tversky and Daniel Kahneman, "Judgment under Uncertainty: Heuristics and Biases," *Science*, New Series 185, no. 4157 (September 1974), 1124–1131.
9. Vedantam, "Daniel Kahneman on Misery, Memory, and Our Understanding of the Mind."
10. Amos Tversky and Daniel Kahneman, "On the Psychology of Prediction," *Psychological Review* 80, no. 4 (1973), 237–251.
11. Lewis, *The Undoing Project*, chap. 7.
12. Tversky and Kahneman, "The Framing of Decisions and the Psychology of Choice."
13. Barry Ritholtz, "Danny Kahneman on Heuristics, Biases, and Cognition," *Masters in Business*, April 9, 2016, podcast, https://ritholtz.com/2016/08/mib-kahneman-heuristics-biases-cognition/.

14. Amos Tversky and Daniel Kahneman, "Prospect Theory: An Analysis of Decision under Risk," *Econometrica* 47, no. 2 (March 1979), 263–292.

15. Daniel Kahnaman, *Thinking, Fast and Slow*, (New York: Farrar, Straus and Giroux, 2013), 271.

16. Lewis, *The Undoing Project*.

17. Eugene F. Fama, Chicago Booth Convocation Address, speech, June 15, 2013, quote found at https://www.ifa.com/quotes/eugene_fama/.

18. Michael C. Jensen, "Some Anomalous Evidence Regarding Market Efficiency," *Journal of Financial Economics*, no. 2–3, (June–September 1978), 95–101, https://doi.org/10.1016/0304-405X(78)90025-9.

19. Lowe, *Damn Right*, chap. 3.

20. Munger, "Charlie Munger Commencement Address–USC."

21. Lowe, *Damn Right*, chap. 3.

22. Lowe, chap. 4.

23. Lowe, chap. 4.

24. Lowe, chap. 4.

25. Lowe, chap. 4.

26. Lowe, chap. 4.

27. Lowe, chap. 4.

28. Kahneman, *Thinking, Fast and Slow*, 256.

29. Munger, "Charlie Munger Commencement Address–USC."

30. Schroeder, *The Snowball*, 215.

31. Roger Lowenstein, *Buffett: The Making of an American Capitalist* (New York: Random House, 1995), 75.

32. Daniel Sparks, "Warren Buffett's Advice for a Stock Market Crash," *The Motely Fool*, April 18, 2018, https://www.fool.com/slideshow/warren-buffetts-advice-stock-market-crash/?slide=3.

33. Lowe, *Damn Right*, chap. 20.

34. Brett D. Fromson, "How Do You Think Big?" *Washington Post*, January 9, 1994, pg. HI.

35. Charlie Munger, Wesco Financial Corporation Annual Report, 1989. https://rememberingtheobvious.files.wordpress.com/2012/08/wesco-charlie-munger-letters-1983-2009-collection.pdf.

36. Munger, "The Psychology of Human Misjudgment."

37. Munger, "The Psychology of Human Misjudgment."

38. Charles Munger, "A Lesson on Elementary, Worldly Wisdom as it Relates to Investment Management and Business," 1994, speech, USC Business School, transcript, https://ritholtz.com/2012/02/a-lesson-on-elementary-worldly-wisdom-as-it-relates-to-investment-management-business/.

39. Charles D. Ellis, "The Loser's Game," *Financial Analysts Journal* 31, no. 4 (July/August 1975), 19–26.

40. Buffett and Berkshire Hathaway, Inc., Letter to the Shareholders.

41. Martin, "Warren Buffett and Tony Robbins Agree on the Best Way to Invest Your Money."

42. Buffett and Berkshire Hathaway, Inc., Letter to the Shareholders.

43. Gawande, "How Do We Heal Medicine?"

Chapter 2: How Health Care Became a "Culture of Inefficiency"

1. Nuland, *Doctors: The Biography of Medicine*, 389.

2. Imber, "Re-Examining The Father Of Modern Surgery."

3. Rutkow, *Seeking a Cure: A History of Medicine in America*, 127.

4. Mukherjee, *The Emperor of All Maladies*, chap. 1.

5. Mukherjee, *The Emperor of All Maladies*, chap. 8.

6. H. L. Menken, *A New Dictionary of Quotations on Historical Principles from Ancient and Modern Sources* (New York: Alfred A. Knopf, 1942); Hippocrates, *Of the Epidemics*.

7. Nardi, "Petrarch, Physicians, and Controlled Trials," 141.

8. Modjarrad, "A Changing Paradigm for Medical Research."

9. Marcus White, "James Lind: The Man Who Helped to Cure Scurvy with Lemons," *BBC News*, October 2016, https://www.bbc.com/news/uk-england-37320399.

10. Graham Sutton, "James Lind Aboard Salisbury," *JLL Bulletin: Commentaries on the History of Treatment Evaluation* (2004), http://www.jameslindlibrary.org/articles/james-lind-aboard-salisbury/.

11. James Lind, "Treatise on Scurvy," (Edinburgh, 1753), quoted in Iain Milne, "Who Was James Lind, and What Exactly Did He Achieve?" *Journal of the Royal Society of Medicine* 105, no. 12 (December 2012), https://doi.org/10.1258/jrsm.2012.12k090.

12. William Bechtel and Robert C. Richardson, "Vitalism," *Routledge Encyclopedia of Philosophy*, ed. E. Craig (Routledge 1998). https://mechanism.ucsd.edu/teaching/philbio/vitalism.htm.

13. Claude Bernard, *An Introduction to the Study of Experimental Medicine* (New York: Schuman, 1949).

14. Bernard, *An Introduction to the Study of Experimental Medicine*.

15. Paul D. Ellis, *The Essential Guide to Effect Sizes: Statistical Power, Meta-Analysis, and the Interpretation of Research Results* (Cambridge University Press, 2010).

16. Hróbjartsson, Gøtzsche, and Gluud, "The Controlled Clinical Trial Turns 100 Years: Fibiger's Trial of Serum Treatment of Diphtheria."

17. Marcus Tullius Cicero, *Pro Ligario* (Section XII), 46 BC, quote found at https://todayinsci.com/C/Cicero_Marcus/CiceroMarcus-Quotations.htm.
18. Mukherjee, *The Emperor of All Maladies*, chap. 8.
19. Doll, "Sir Austin Bradford Hill and the Progress of Medical Science," 1526.
20. Austin Bradford Hill, *Principles of Medical Statistics* (Oxford University Press, 1971).
21. Doll, "Sir Austin Bradford Hill and the Progress of Medical Science," 1522.
22. Doll, 1521.
23. Doll, 1522.
24. Doll et al., "Mortality in Relation to Smoking: 50 Years' Observation on Male British Doctors," *BMJ* 328, no. 7455 (2004),1519.
25. George Crile, *Surgery, Your Choices, Your Alternatives* (Boston: G.K. Hall, 1980).
26. Saxon, "George Crile Jr., 84, Foe of Unneeded Surgery, Dies."
27. Kate Travis, "Bernard Fisher Reflects on a Half-Century's Worth of Breast Cancer Research," *Journal of the National Cancer Institute* 97, no. 22 (November 2005), 1636–37.
28. Susan Okie, "Treating Breast Cancer: Findings Question Need for Removal," *Washington Post*, October 29, 1979, A24.
29. Bernard Fisher et al., "Ten-Year Results of a Randomized Clinical Trial Comparing Radical Mastectomy and Total Mastectomy with or without Radiation," *New England Journal of Medicine* 312, no. 11 (March 1985), 674–81. https://doi.org/10.1056/NEJM198503143121102.
30. Fisher et al., "Twenty-Five-Year Follow-up of a Randomized Trial Comparing Radical Mastectomy, Total Mastectomy, and Total Mastectomy Followed by Irradiation," 567–75.
31. Gawande, "How Do We Heal Medicine?"
32. Richard Harris, "Doctors Scrutinize Overtreatment."
33. Harris, "Doctors Scrutinize Overtreatment."
34. Grady, "Good News for Women With Breast Cancer: Many Don't Need Chemo."
35. O'Connor, "Heart Stents Still Overused, Experts Say."
36. Leonhardt, "Making Health Care Better."
37. Volinn et al., "Small Area Analysis of Surgery for Low-Back Pain," *Spine*, May 17, 1992 (5), 575–81.
38. Reflections on Variation. The Dartmouth Atlas of Health Care. Quote was taken from site accessed on September of 2018.
39. Gawande, "The Cost Conundrum."
40. Gawande, "The Cost Conundrum."
41. Gawande, "The Cost Conundrum."
42. Gawande, "The Cost Conundrum."
43. Susan Perry, "US Physicians Say Up to 30 Percent of Medical Services are Unnecessary," *MinnPost*, September 12, 2017, https://www.minnpost.com

/second-opinion/2017/09/us-physicians-say-30-percent-medical-services-are
-unnecessary/.

44. Dartmouth Atlas, https://www.dartmouthatlas.org/faq/.

45. Voltaire, *Oxford Essential Quotations*, ed. Susan Ratcliff (Oxford University Press, 2012), http://www.oxfordreference.com/view/10.1093/acref/9780191843730 .001.0001/q-oro-ed5-00011218. From the *Oxford Essential Quotations*: "This quote is attributed to Voltaire from the end of the nineteenth century, but it's probably apocryphal; earlier versions are generally anonymous, as in *The Quarterly Journal of Science, Literature, and the Arts* from 1823: 'Physic,' says a foreign writer, 'is the art of amusing.'"

46. Sir William Osler, *Aphorisms from His Bedside Teachings and Writings* (New York: Henry Schuman, 1961), 105.

47. Gilbert Welch, *Overdiagnosed: Making People Sick in the Pursuit of Health* (Boston: Beacon Press, 2012).

48. Horgan, "Cancer Establishment Admits We're Getting Overtested and Overtreated."

49. Horgan, "Cancer Establishment Admits We're Getting Overtested and Overtreated."

50. Gawande, "Overkill."

51. Brody, "When Treating Cancer Is Not an Option."

52. Leonhardt, "Making Health Care Better."

53. Schlosser, "In What Ways Is the US Healthcare System Inefficient?"

54. "Obama's Remarks at the White House Health Care Forum," *New York Times*.

55. "Billionaire Investor Warren Buffett Speaks with CNBC's Becky Quick," May 9, 2017, *Squawk Box*, transcript, CNBC News Releases, https://www.cnbc .com/2017/05/09/full-transcript-billionaire-investor-warren-buffett-speaks-with-cnbc-percent-u2019s-becky-quick-on-percent-u201csquawk-box-percent -u201d.html.

56. Kim, "Warren Buffett: I Was Wrong on Google and Amazon, Jeff Bezos Achieved a Business 'Miracle.'"

57. "Amazon, Berkshire Hathaway and JPMorgan Chase and Co. to Partner on US Employee Healthcare," Business Wire.

Chapter 3: How Simple and Effective Treatments Get Lost

1. Peyton Rous, "Surmise and Fact on the Nature of Cancer," *Nature*, May 16, 1959.

2. B. Eismann et al., "Fecal Enema as an Adjunct in the Treatment of Pseudomembranous Enterocolitis," *Surgery* 44, no. 5 (November 1958), 854–9.

3. Associated Press, "FDA Struggles to Regulate Fecal Transplants."

4. E. Gough, H. Shaikh, and A.R. Manges, "Systematic Review of Intestinal Microbiota Transplantation (Fecal Bacteriotherapy) for Recurrent Clostridium difficile Infection," *Clinical Infectious Diseases* 53, no. 10, (November 2011), 994–1002, https://doi.org/10.1093/cid/cir632.

5. Els van Nood et al., "Duodenal Infusion of Donor Feces for Recurrent *Clostridium difficile*," *New England Journal of Medicine* 368 (2013), 407–415, https://doi.org/10.1056/NEJMoa1205037.

6. Associated Press, "FDA Struggles to Regulate Fecal Transplants."

7. Gawande, "How Do We Heal Medicine?"

8. Linda Geddes, "Too Affordable: How Can We Overcome the Drug Repurposing Paradox?," *Cancerworld*, no. 73–74 (September 12, 2016), 14.

9. "20th WHO Model Lists of Essential Medicines," World Health Organization (March 2017), https://www.who.int/medicines/publications/essential/medicines/en/.

10. Robin Bannister. Interview with the author, October 2018.

11. Apple, "Forget the Blood of Teens. This Pill Promises to Extend Life for a Nickle a Pop."

12. Sam Apple, "An Old Idea, Revived: Starve Cancer to Death," *New York Times Magazine*, May 12, 2016, https://www.nytimes.com/2016/05/15/magazine/warburg-effect-an-old-idea-revived-starve-cancer-to-death.html.

13. Jessica Glenza, "Statins Could Reduce Risk of Breast Cancer Death by 38%, Research Shows," *The Guardian*, June 2, 2017, https://www.theguardian.com/society/2017/jun/02/statins-breast-cancer-death-research.

14. Linda Geddes, "The Cancer Drugs in Your Bathroom Cabinet."

15. Geddes, "The Cancer Drugs in Your Bathroom Cabinet."

16. Vikas P. Sukhatme, "A Simple, One-Time, Inexpensive and Non-Toxic Intervention to Improve Cancer Survival," December 8, 2015, presentation, Massachusetts Institute of Technology, MIT Laboratory for Financial Engineering YouTube, https://www.youtube.com/watch?v=H8zVrYEW8vE; Sukhatme et al., "Reduction of Breast Cancer Relapses with Perioperative Non-Steroidal Anti-Inflammatory Drugs: New Findings and a Review," 4163–176.

17. Sukhatme, "A Simple, One-Time, Inexpensive and Non-Toxic Intervention."

18. Debara, "Why Ketamine Infusions Are the Next Wonder Drug for Depression."

19. Frieden, "Evidence for Health Decision Making—Beyond Randomized, Controlled Trials."

20. Gawande, "How Do We Heal Medicine?"

Chapter 4: The Way Forward

1. Beane, Gingrich, and Kerry, "How to Take American Health Care from Worst to First."

2. James, "In Conversation with . . . Brent C. James, MD, MStat," interview by Robert Wachter.

3. James, "Dr. Brent James Interview," interview by Charles Denham.

4. James, "Dr. Brent James Interview," interview by Charles Denham.

5. Leonhardt, "Making Health Care Better."

6. Ian Larkin and George Loewenstein, "Business Model–Related Conflict of Interests in Medicine," *JAMA* 317, no. 17 (2017), 1745, https://doi.org/10.1001/jama.2017.2275.

7. Rosetta, "Intermountain Healthcare: A Model System?"

8. John Daley, "Obama Singles Out Intermountain Healthcare as Model System," *KSL.com*, September 10, 2009.

9. Hartzband and Groopman, "How Medical Care Is Being Corrupted."

10. Hartzband and Groopman, "How Medical Care Is Being Corrupted."

11. Leonhardt, "Making Health Care Better."

12. Monegain, "Intermountain, Geisinger Get Spotlight in Obama Talk."

13. Aubrey, "Fresh Food by Prescription: This Health Care Firm Is Trimming Costs—and Waistlines."

14. Tirrell and Gralnick, "Diabetes Defeated by Diet: How New Fresh-Food Prescriptions Are Beating Pricey Drugs."

Chapter 5: Nature or Nurture

1. Dr. Thomas Fuller, *Gnomologia*, 1732, quote found at http://www.quotationspage.com/quote/2039.html.

2. Mahatma Gandhi, *Keys to Health* (India: Navjivan Publishing House, 1948), quoted in Akos Somoskovi, "It Is Health that Is Real Wealth, Not Pieces of Gold and Silver," *Indian Journal of Medical Research* 137, no. 3, (March 2013), https://www.ncbi.nlm.nih.gov/pmc/articles/PMC3705649/.

3. Cloud, "Why Your DNA Isn't Your Destiny."

4. James Watson, *The Double Helix* (New York: Scribner, 1998).

5. White House Office of the Press Secretary, "Remarks Made by the President, Prime Minister Tony Blair of England (via satellite), Dr. Francis Collins, Director of the National Human Genome Research Institute, and Dr. Craig Venter, President and Chief Scientific Officer, Celera Genomics Corporation, on the Completion of the First Survey of the Entire Human Genome Project."

6. Resnick, "How Scientists Are Learning to Predict Your Future with Your Genes."

7. Siddhartha Mukherjee, "Same But Different."

8. Spector, "Identically Different."

9. Angier, "DNA's Wrapping Holds Key to Genes at Work."

10. Downey, "Profile of C. David Allis."

11. Deborah D. Danner, David A. Snowdon, and Wallace V. Friesen, "Positive Emotions in Early Life and Longevity: Findings from the Nun Study," *Journal of*

Personality and Social Psychology 80, no. 5 (May 2001), 804–13, https://www
.apa.org/pubs/journals/releases/psp805804.pdf.

12. Angelina Jolie, "My Medical Choice," *New York Times*, May 14, 2013, https://
www.nytimes.com/2013/05/14/opinion/my-medical-choice.html.

13. Kroenke et al., "Social Networks, Social Support, and Survival After Breast
Cancer Diagnosis."

14. Angier, "Scientist at Work: Martha K. McClintock; How Biology Affects
Behavior and Vice Versa."

15. Cole et al., "Social Regulation of Gene Expression in Human Leukocytes."

16. Knapton, "Loneliness Is Deadlier than Obesity, Study Suggests."

17. Anderson and Thayer, "Loneliness and Social Connections: A National Survey
of Adults 45 and Older."

18. Pinker, "The Secret to Living Longer May Be Your Social Life."

19. Kahneman, "The Riddle of Experience vs. Memory."

20. Kahneman, "The Riddle of Experience vs. Memory."

21. Kahneman, "The Riddle of Experience vs. Memory."

22. Kahneman, "The Riddle of Experience vs. Memory."

23. Mandel, "Why Nobel Prize Winner Daniel Kahneman Gave Up on Happiness."

24. Shakya and Christakis, "A New, More Rigorous Study Confirms: The More You
Use Facebook, the Worse You Feel."

25. Mandel, "Why Nobel Prize Winner Daniel Kahneman Gave Up on Happiness."

26. Mandel, "Why Nobel Prize Winner Daniel Kahneman Gave Up on Happiness."

27. Author notes from Berkshire Hathaway annual meeting, May 2007.

28. Redelmeier and Singh, "Survival in Academy Award-Winning Actors and Actresses."

29. Noah Buhayar, "What Do Bezos, Buffett and Dimon Have in Common? Meet
Todd Combs," *Live Mint*, March 27, 2018, https://www.livemint.com
/Companies/P7dlAN76rFl6H6tpyCQaYM/What-do-Bezos-Buffett-and
-Dimon-have-in-common-Meet-Todd-C.html.

30. Sanger-Katz and Abelson, "Can Amazon and Friends Handle Health Care?
There's Reason for Doubt."

31. Megan Thielking, "Amazon, Two Other Giants Are Promising to 'Disrupt' the
Health Care Industry. Health Care Experts Doubt It," *Stat*, January 30, 2018,
https://www.statnews.com/2018/01/30/amazon-health-care-reaction/.

32. Anthony Noto, "JPMorgan, Amazon and Berkshire Name CEO for Healthcare
Venture," *New York Business Journal*, June 20, 2018, https://www.bizjournals
.com/newyork/news/2018/06/20/jpmorgan-amazon-and-berkshire-name
-ceo-for.html.

33. Mike Miliard, "Atul Gawande to Lead Amazon, Berkshire Hathaway and
JPMorgan Chase Venture," *Healthcare IT News*, June 20, 2018, https://www

.healthcareitnews.com/news/atul-gawande-lead-amazon-berkshire-hathaway-and-jpmorgan-chase-venture.

34. Gawande, "Overkill."
35. You can find more information about Flatiron Health at https://flatiron.com/.
36. Rhitu Chatterjee, "Americans Are a Loney Lot, and Young People Bear the Heaviest Burden," *Shots*, NPR, May 2, 2018, https://www.npr.org/sections/health-shots/2018/05/01/606588504/americans-are-a-lonely-lot-and-young-people-bear-the-heaviest-burden.
37. Thomas Jefferson, "Letter to the Republicans of Washington County, Maryland, March 31, 1809," *Founders Onlines*, National Archives, https://founders.archives.gov/documents/Jefferson/03-01-02-0088.

Selected Bibliography

Achenbach, Joel. "In Chess Battle, Only the Human Has His Wits about Him." *Washington Post*, May 10, 1997. http://www.washingtonpost.com/wp-srv/tech /analysis/kasparov/post3.htm?noredirect=on.

Acker, Denise. "Catherine Duff's Story: Surviving C diff. through At-Home Treatment Leads to Policy Change." *Patients' View Institute Blog*, December 12, 2016. https://gopvi.org/blog/.

Adl-Tabatabai, Sean. "Oldest Living Person at 128 Reveals Secret to Longevity Is 'Fermented Milk.'" *News Punch*, May 16, 2018. https://newspunch.com /oldest-person-128-fermented-milk/.

Almendrala, Anna. "C-Diff Kills 15,000 People a Year. Feces Donations May Change That." HuffPost, February 26, 2015. https://www.huffpost.com/entry/c-diff -fecal-transplant_n_6681996.

"Amazon, Berkshire Hathaway and JPMorgan Chase and Co. to Partner on U.S. Employee Healthcare." Business Wire, January 30, 2018, 7:00 a.m. EST. https:// www.businesswire.com/news/home/20180130005676/en/.

Anderson, G. Oscar, and Colette Thayer. "Loneliness and Social Connections: A National Survey of Adults 45 and Older." AARP, "AARP Research: Life and Leisure," September 2018. https://www.aarp.org/research/topics/life/info-2018 /loneliness-social-connections.html.

Angier, Natalie. "DNA's Wrapping Holds Key to Genes at Work." *New York Times*, September 17, 1991. https://www.nytimes.com/1991/09/17/science/dna-s -wrapping-holds-key-to-genes-at-work.html.

———. "Scientist at Work: Martha K. McClintock; How Biology Affects Behavior and Vice Versa." *New York Times*, May 30, 1995. https://www.nytimes.com/1995 /05/30/science/scientist-work-martha-k-mcclintock-biology-affects-behavior -vice-versa.html.

Anspach, Dana. "Why Average Investors Earn Below Average Market Returns." The Balance, January 28, 2019. https://www.thebalance.com/why-average -investors-earn-below-average-market-returns-2388519.

Apple, Sam. "Forget the Blood of Teens. This Pill Promises to Extend Life for a Nickel a Pop." *Wired*, July 1, 2017. https://www.wired.com/story/this-pill -promises-to-extend-life-for-a-nickel-a-pop/.

Arias, Elizabeth, Melonie Heron, and Betzaida Tejada-Vera. "United States Life Tables Eliminating Certain Causes of Death, 1999–2001." *National Vital Statistics Reports* 61, no. 9. May 31, 2013, US Department of Health and Human Services: Centers for Disease Control and Prevention. https://www.cdc.gov/nchs/data/nvsr /nvsr61/nvsr61_09.pdf.

Associated Press. "FDA Struggles to Regulate Fecal Transplants." *CBS News*, June 26, 2014, 5:35 p.m. EST, https://www.cbsnews.com/news/fda-struggles -to-regulate-fecal-transplants/.

Aubrey, Allison. "Fresh Food by Prescription: This Health Care Firm Is Trimming Costs—and Waistlines." NPR, May 8, 2017, 4:43 a.m. EST, https://www.npr.org /sections/thesalt/2017/05/08/526952657/.

Barzilai, Nir. "Metformin and the TAME Trial: Magic Pill or Monumental Tool?" *TEDMED Blog*, August 29, 2017, https://blog.tedmed.com/metformin-tame -trial-magic-pill-monumental-tool/.

Beane, Billy, Newt Gingrich, and John Kerry. "How to Take American Health Care from Worst to First." *New York Times*, October 24, 2008, Opinion, https://www .nytimes.com/2008/10/24/opinion/24beane.html.

"Believed to Be World's Oldest, Woman in France Dies at 122." Supercentenarian.com. August 4, 1997, https://www.supercentenarian.com/oldest/jeanne-calment.html.

Bernhardt Wealth Management. "Dr. Daniel Kahneman." Blog post. September 19, 2016. http://www.bernhardtwealth.com/blog/dr-daniel-kahneman.

Bhatt, Arun. "Evolution of Clinical Research: A History Before and Beyond James Lind." *Perspectives in Clinical Research* 1, no. 1 (January-March 2010): 6–10. https://www.ncbi.nlm.nih.gov/pmc/articles/PMC3149409/.

Bleyer, Archie, and H. Gilbert Welch. "Effect of Three Decades of Screening Mammography on Breast-Cancer Incidence." *New England Journal of Medicine* 367 (November 2012): 1998–2005. http://doi.org/10.1056/NEJMoa1206809.

Boyle, Peter. "Tobacco Smoking and the British Doctors' Cohort." *British Journal of Cancer* 92, no. 3 (February 2005): 419–20. http://doi.org/10.1038/sj.bjc.6602361.

Briggs, Bill. "Patients Treated at Cancer Centers Live Longer: Study." Hutch News. Fred Hutchinson Cancer Research Center. November 6, 2015, https://www.fredhutch .org/en/news/center-news/2015/11/cancer-center-patients-live-longer.html.

Brink, Susan. "Weighing Over-Treatment vs. Ending Treatment: When It Comes to Cancer, Do Last-Ditch Treatment Efforts Do More Harm Than Good?" *U.S. News and World Report*, October 11, 2013, Health, https://health.usnews.com /health-news/hospital-of-tomorrow/articles/2013/10/11/long-term-cancer -patients-struggle-with-over-treatment-vs-ending-treatment.

Brody, Jane E. "When Treating Cancer Is Not an Option." *Well* (blog), *New York Times*, November 19, 2012, https://well.blogs.nytimes.com/2012/11/19/when-treating-cancer-is-not-an-option/.

Buffett, Warren E. Letter to Shareholders. Omaha, NE: Berkshire Hathaway Inc., February 25, 2017. http://www.berkshirehathaway.com/letters/2016ltr.pdf.

Butcher, Lola. "First Published Cost-Effectiveness Study of Evidence-Based Clinical Pathways Documents 35% Lower Costs with No Differences in Survival." *Oncology Times* 32, no. 5 (March 2010): 23–4. http://doi.org/10.1097/01.COT.0000369687.66705.3e.

"Cancer Biology: Tumours Hate Company." *Nature* 462, no. 828 (December 2009). https://doi.org/10.1038/462828d.

Carnegie Mellon University. "Doctors Should Be Paid by Salary, Not Fee-for-Service, Argue Behavioral Economists." ScienceDaily, May 9, 2017. https://www.sciencedaily.com/releases/2017/05/170509121934.htm.

Castillo-Fernandez, Juan E., Tim D. Spector, and Jordana T. Bell. "Epigenetics of Discordant Monozygotic Twins: Implications for Disease." *Genome Medicine* 6, no. 7 (July 2014): 60. https://www.ncbi.nlm.nih.gov/pmc/articles/PMC4254430/.

Clabots, Connie R., Stuart Johnson, Mary M. Olson, Lance R. Peterson, and Dale N. Gerding. "Acquisition of *Clostridium difficile* by Hospitalized Patients: Evidence for Colonized New Admissions as a Source of Infection." *Journal of Infectious Diseases* 166, no. 3 (September 1992): 561–67. http://doi.org/10.1093/infdis/166.3.561.

"Clinical Pathways." American Society of Clinical Oncology. https://www.asco.org/practice-guidelines/cancer-care-initiatives/clinical-pathways.

Cloud, John. "Why Your DNA Isn't Your Destiny." *Time*, January 6, 2010. http://content.time.com/time/subscriber/article/0,33009,1952313-3,00.html.

Cole, Steve W. "Social Regulation of Human Gene Expression." *Current Directions in Psychological Science* 18, no. 3 (June 2009): 132–37. http://doi.org/10.1111/j.1467-8721.2009.01623.x.

Cole, Steve W., Louise C. Hawkley, Jesusa M. Arevalo, Caroline Y. Sung, Robert M. Rose, and John T. Cacioppo. "Social Regulation of Gene Expression in Human Leukocytes." *Genome Biology* 8 (September 2007). https://doi.org/10.1186/gb-2007-8-9-r189.

Collier, Roger. "Legumes, Lemons and Streptomycin: A Short History of the Clinical Trial." *CMAJ* 180, no. 1 (January 2009): 23–4. https://doi.org/10.1503/cmaj.081879.

Crofton, J. "The MRC Randomized Trial of Streptomycin and Its Legacy: A View from the Clinical Front Line." *Journal of the Royal Society of Medicine* 99, no. 10 (October 2006): 531–34. http://doi.org/10.1258/jrsm.99.10.531.

Culpepper, Chuck. "An All-Around Talent, Obscured by His Pedigree." *New York Times*, September 14, 2010, Pro Basketball. https://www.nytimes.com/2010/09/15/sports/basketball/15nba.html?auth=login-email.

Daley, John. "Obama Singles Out Intermountain Healthcare as Model System." KSL.com. September 10, 2009. https://www.ksl.com/article/7873613.

Dartmouth Atlas Project. "Interactive Apps." The Dartmouth Institute for Health Policy and Clinical Practice. http://www.dartmouthatlas.org/keyissues/issue.aspx?con=1338.

Debara, Deanna. "Why Ketamine Infusions Are the Next Wonder Drug for Depression." *Bulletproof* (blog). https://blog.bulletproof.com/ketamine-infusions-depression-treatment/.

"The Demand for Poop." *National Post*, November 5, 2015, Weekend Post. https://nationalpost.com/features/the-demand-for-poop.

Doll, Richard. "Sir Austin Bradford Hill and the Progress of Medical Science." *BMJ* 305 (December 1992): 1521. https://doi.org/10.1136/bmj.305.6868.1521.

Downey, Philip. "Profile of C. David Allis." *Proceedings of the National Academy of Sciences of the United States of America* 103, no. 17 (April 2006): 6425–27. https://www.ncbi.nlm.nih.gov/pmc/articles/PMC1458902/.

Eakin, Emily. "The Excrement Experiment: Treating Disease with Fecal Transplants." *New Yorker*, December 1, 2014. https://www.newyorker.com/magazine/2014/12/01/excrement-experiment.

Feinberg, Andrea T., Allison Hess, Michelle Passaretti, Stacy Coolbaugh, and Thomas H. Lee. "Prescribing Food as a Specialty Drug." NEJM Catalyst, April 10, 2018, Care Redesign. https://catalyst.nejm.org/prescribing-fresh-food-farmacy/.

Filip, Mihaela, Valentina Tzaneva, and Dan L. Dumitrascu. "Fecal Transplantation: Digestive and Extradigestive Clinical Applications." *Medicine and Pharmacy Reports* 91, no. 3 (2018): 259–65. http://dx.doi.org/10.15386/cjmed-946.

Fisher, Bernard, Jong-Hyeon Jeong, Stewart Anderson, John Bryant, Edwin R. Fisher, and Norman Wolmark. "Twenty-Five-Year Follow-up of a Randomized Trial Comparing Radical Mastectomy, Total Mastectomy, and Total Mastectomy Followed by Irradiation." *New England Journal of Medicine* 347, no. 8 (August 2002): 567–75. https://www.nejm.org/doi/pdf/10.1056/NEJMoa020128.

Frankel, Matthew. "The Average American's Investment Returns—and How You Can Do Better." The Motley Fool, November 1, 2015. https://www.fool.com/investing/general/2015/11/01/the-average-americans-investment-returns-and-how-y.aspx.

———. "Here's How Much $10,000 Invested in Berkshire Hathaway Stock in 1964 Is Worth Now." The Motley Fool, July 24, 2017. https://www.fool.com/investing/2017/07/24/heres-how-much-10000-invested-in-berkshire-hathawa.aspx.

Frieden, Thomas R. "Evidence for Health Decision Making—Beyond Randomized, Controlled Trials." *New England Journal of Medicine* 377 (August 2017): 465–75. http://doi.org/10.1056/NEJMra1614394.

Gardner, Martha N., and Allan M. Brandt. "'The Doctors' Choice Is America's Choice.' The Physician in US Cigarette Advertisements, 1930–1953." *American*

Journal of Public Health 96, no. 2 (February 2006): 222–32. http://doi.org
/10.2105/AJPH.2005.066654.

Gawande, Atul. "The Cost Conundrum: What a Texas Town Can Teach Us about
Health Care." *New Yorker*, June 1, 2009, Annals of Medicine. https://www.new
yorker.com/magazine/2009/06/01/the-cost-conundrum.

———. "The Future of Medicine." The Reith Lectures, BBC, 2014. https://www
.bbc.co.uk/programmes/articles/6F2X8TpsxrJpnsq82hggHW/dr-atul-gawande
-2014-reith-lectures.

———. "How Do We Heal Medicine?" Filmed February 2012 in Long Beach, CA.
TED video, 19:12. https://www.ted.com/talks/atul_gawande_how_do_we
_heal_medicine.

———. "Overkill." *New Yorker*, May 11, 2015, Annals of Health Care. https://www
.newyorker.com/magazine/2015/05/11/overkill-atul-gawande.

Geddes, Linda. "The Cancer Drugs in Your Bathroom Cabinet." *Guardian*, June 12,
2016. https://www.theguardian.com/science/2016/jun/12/.

———. "Too Affordable: How Can We Overcome the Drug Repurposing Paradox?"
Cancerworld, September 12, 2016. https://cancerworld.net/wp-content/uploads
/2016/09/CW_73-74_Drug-Watch.pdf.

Giampia, Nick. "Munger on Health Care: It's Wrong to Keep Treating to Make
Money." FOX Business, May 8, 2017, Health Care. https://www.foxbusiness.com
/features/munger-on-health-care-its-wrong-to-keep-treating-to-make-money.

Goldberg, Lewis R. "Simple Models or Simple Process? Some Research on Clinical
Judgments." *American Psychologist* 23, no. 7 (July 1968): 483–96. https://projects
.ori.org/lrg/PDFs_papers/simple.models.68.pdf.

Goodman, Brenda. "The Rise of the Do-It-Yourself Fecal Transplant." WebMD,
December 9, 2015, Digestive Disorders. https://www.webmd.com/digestive
-disorders/news/.

Grady, Denise. "Good News for Women with Breast Cancer: Many Don't Need
Chemo." *New York Times*, June 3, 2018, Health. https://www.nytimes.com
/2018/06/03/health/breast-cancer-chemo.html.

Grossman, Samantha. "This 104-Year-Old Women Says Dr Pepper Is What's
Keeping Her Alive." *Time*, March 20, 2015. http://time.com/3752352/104-year
-old-woman-dr-pepper/.

Hancock, Edith. "These Are the Secrets to Long Life, According to 5 of the Oldest
People in the World." Business Insider, December 8, 2016. https://www.business
insider.com/the-secrets-to-long-life-according-to-the-oldest-people-in-the
-world-2016-12.

Harmon, Katherine. "Fasting Might Boost Chemo's Cancer-Busting Properties."
Scientific American, February 8, 2012, Health. https://www.scientificamerican
.com/article/fasting-might-boost-chemo/.

Harris, Richard. "Doctors Scrutinize Overtreatment, as Cancer Death Rates Decline." NPR, June 5, 2018, Shots: Health News From NPR. https://www.npr.org/sections /health-shots/2018/06/05/617104810/doctors-scrutinize-overtreatment-as-cancer -death-rates-decline.

Hartzband, Pamela, and Jerome Groopman. "How Medical Care Is Being Corrupted." *New York Times*, November 18, 2014, Opinion. https://www.nytimes.com/2014 /11/19/opinion/.

Hayasaki, Erika. "Identical Twins Hint at How Environments Change Gene Expression." *Atlantic*, May 15, 2018, Science. https://www.theatlantic.com /science/archive/2018/05/twin-epigenetics/560189/.

Hellmann, Melissa. "U.S. Health Care Ranked Worst in the Developed World." *Time*, June 17, 2014, Health. http://time.com/2888403/u-s-health-care-ranked -worst-in-the-developed-world/.

Hjelmborg, Jacob vB., Ivan Iachine, Axel Skytthe, James W. Vaupel, Matt McGue, Markku Koskenvuo, Jaakko Kaprio, Nancy L. Pederson, and Kaare Christensen. "Genetic Influence on Human Lifespan and Longevity." *Human Genetics* 119, no. 312 (April 2006). https://doi.org/10.1007/s00439-006-0144-y.

Holt-Lunstad, Julianne, Timothy B. Smith, and J. Bradley Layton. "Social Relation-ships and Mortality Risk: A Meta-Analytic Review." *PLoS Medicine* 7, no. 7 (July 2010): e1000334. http://doi.org/10.1371/journal.pmed.1000316.

Horgan, John. "Cancer Establishment Admits We're Getting Overtested and Overtreated." *Scientific American*, August 5, 2013, *Cross-Check* (blog). https:// blogs.scientificamerican.com/cross-check/.

Hróbjartsson, Asbjørn, Peter C. Gøtzsche, and Christian Gluud. "The Controlled Clinical Trial Turns 100 Years: Fibiger's Trial of Serum Treatment of Diphthe-ria." *BMJ* 317, no. 7167 (October 1998): 1243–45. https://www.ncbi.nlm.nih .gov/pmc/articles/PMC1114170/.

Hulbert, Mark. "This Is How Many Fund Managers Actually Beat Index Funds." Marketwatch, May 13, 2017. https://www.marketwatch.com/story/why-way -fewer-actively-managed-funds-beat-the-sp-than-we-thought-2017-04-24.

Imber, Gerald. "Re-Examining the Father of Modern Surgery." Interview by Terri Gross and Dave Davies. *Fresh Air*, NPR, February 22, 2010. https://www.npr.org /templates/transcript/transcript.php?storyId=123570287.

Jackson, Chris, and Negar Ballard. "Over Half of Americans Report Feeling Like No One Knows Them Well." Ipsos, May 1, 2018. https://www.ipsos.com/en-us /news-polls/us-loneliness-index-report.

Jackson, Jackie. "Jeanne Louise Calment: The Oldest Woman." JAQUO. http:// jaquo.com/jeanne-calment/.

James, Brent C. "In Conversation with . . . Brent C. James, MD, MStat." Interview by Robert Wachter. *Perspectives on Safety*, U.S. Department of Health and

Human Service's Agency for Healthcare Research and Quality, February 1, 2011, Patient Safety Network. https://psnet.ahrq.gov/perspectives/perspective/97/In-Conversation-with-Brent-C-James-MD-MStat.

———. "Dr. Brent James Interview." Interview by Charles Denham, July 8, 2010. TMIT. Video, 29:01, published August 16, 2012. https://www.youtube.com/watch?v=QztwlbRn6wo.

Kahneman, Daniel. "Daniel Kahneman on Misery, Memory, and Our Understanding of the Mind." Interview by Shankar Vedantam. *Hidden Brain*, NPR, March 12, 2018. http://publicradioeast.org/post/daniel-kahneman-misery-memory-and-our-understanding-mind.

———. "The Riddle of Experience vs. Memory." Filmed February 2010. TED video, 20:00. https://www.ted.com/talks/daniel_kahneman_the_riddle_of_experience_vs_memory?language=en.

Kasparov, Garry. *Deep Thinking: Where Machine Intelligence Ends and Human Creativity Begins*. New York: PublicAffairs, 2017.

Khoruts, Alexander. "Fecal Microbiota Transplantation—Early Steps on a Long Journey Ahead." *Gut Microbes* 8, no. 3 (April 2017): 199–204. http://doi.org/10.1080/19490976.2017.1316447.

Kim, Meeri. "You'll Never Believe What Doctors Are Using to Fight Gut Infections: Fecal Transplants." *Washington Post*, January 6, 2014, Health and Science. https://www.washingtonpost.com/national/health-science/.

Kim, Tae. "Warren Buffett: I Was Wrong on Google and Amazon, Jeff Bezos Achieved a Business 'Miracle.'" CNBC, May 7, 2018, 8:43 a.m. EDT. https://www.cnbc.com/2018/05/05/.

Knapton, Sarah. "Loneliness Is Deadlier than Obesity, Study Suggests." *Telegraph*, August 6, 2017, Science. https://www.telegraph.co.uk/science/2017/08/06/loneliness-deadlier-obesity-study-suggests/.

Kremer, William. "The Brave New World of DIY Faecal Transplant." BBC News Magazine, May 27, 2014. https://www.bbc.com/news/magazine-27503660.

Kroenke, Candyce H., Laura D. Kubzansky, Eva S. Schernhammer, Michelle D. Homes, and Ichiro Kawachi. "Social Networks, Social Support, and Survival after Breast Cancer Diagnosis." *Journal of Clinical Oncology* 24, no. 7 (March 2006): 1105–11. http://doi.org/10.1200/JCO.2005.04.2846.

Krueger, Joachim I. "Kahneman in Quotes and Questions." *Psychology Today*, January 16, 2012. https://www.psychologytoday.com/us/blog/one-among-many/201201/kahneman-in-quotes-and-questions.

LaVito, Angelica. "Dr. Atul Gawande to Start as CEO of Buffett, Bezos and Dimon's Health-Care Venture." *Health and Science*, CNBC, Monday, July 9, 2018, 9:26 a.m. EDT. https://www.cnbc.com/2018/07/06/dr-atul-gawande-to-start-as-ceo-buffett-bezos-dimon-health-venture.html.

Leonhardt, David. "In Health Reform, a Cancer Offers an Acid Test." *New York Times*, July 7, 2009, Economic Scene. https://www.nytimes.com/2009/07/08/business/economy/08leonhardt.html.

———. "Making Health Care Better." *New York Times Magazine*, November 3, 2009. https://www.nytimes.com/2009/11/08/magazine/08Healthcare-t.html.

Lerner, Barron H. "How Clinical Trials Saved Women with Breast Cancer from Disfiguring Surgery: Bernard Fisher's Battle Against the Radical Mastectomy." *Atlantic*, August 9, 2013, Health. https://www.theatlantic.com/health/archive/2013/08/how-clinical-trials-saved-women-with-breast-cancer-from-disfiguring-surgery/278531/.

Lewis, Michael. "A Bitter Ending: Daniel Kahneman, Amos Tversky, and the Limits of Collaboration." *Chronicle of Higher Education*, January 29, 2017. https://www.chronicle.com/article/A-Bitter-Ending/238990.

———. *The Undoing Project: A Friendship that Changed Our Minds.* New York: W.W. Norton, 2016.

Lowe, Janet. *Damn Right: Behind the Scenes with Berkshire Hathaway Billionaire Charlie Munger.* Hoboken, NJ: Wiley & Sons, 2000.

Mandel, Amir. "Why Nobel Prize Winner Daniel Kahneman Gave Up on Happiness." Haaretz, October 7, 2018. https://www.haaretz.com/israel-news/.premium.MAGAZINE-why-nobel-prize-winner-daniel-kahneman-gave-up-on-happiness-1.6528513.

Markel, Howard. "The Real Story behind Penicillin." *News Hour*, PBS, September 27, 2013, 2:06 p.m. EDT, Health. https://www.pbs.org/newshour/health/the-real-story-behind-the-worlds-first-antibiotic.

Martin, Emmie. "Warren Buffett and Tony Robbins Agree on the Best Way to Invest Your Money." *Make It*, CNBC. June 28, 2018. https://www.cnbc.com/2018/06/19/warren-buffett-and-tony-robbins-agree-invest-in-index-funds.html.

McCormick, Jinny. "German Soldiers Forced to Eat Poop to Cure Dysentery Outbreak." War History Online, January 15, 2016. https://www.warhistoryonline.com/featured/german-soldiers-eat-poop.html.

Modjarrad, Kayvon. "A Changing Paradigm for Medical Research: The Evolution of the Clinical Trial." *Hektoen International* 5, no. 4 (Fall 2013). http://hekint.org/2017/02/01/a-changing-paradigm-for-medical-research-the-evolution-of-the-clinical-trial/.

Monegain, Bernie. "Intermountain, Geisinger Share the Spotlight in Obama Talk." Healthcare IT News, June 12, 2009. https://www.healthcareitnews.com/news/intermountain-geisinger-share-spotlight-obama-talk.

Morabia, Alfredo. "Claude Bernard, Statistics, and Comparative Trials." The James Lind Library. http://www.jameslindlibrary.org/articles/claude-bernard-statistics-and-comparative-trials/.

Mukherjee, Siddhartha. "Same but Different: How Epigenetics Can Blur the Line
Between Nature and Nurture." *New Yorker,* May 2, 2016, Annals of Science.
https://www.newyorker.com/magazine/2016/05/02/breakthroughs
-in-epigenetics.

——. *The Emperor of All Maladies: A Biography of Cancer.* New York: Scribner, 2010.

Munger, Charlie. Charlie Munger Commencement Address at University of
Southern California, May 13, 2007. Video, 37:04, published March 2, 2017, Value
Investor's Club. https://www.youtube.com/watch?v=5U0TE4oqj24.

——. "The Psychology of Human Misjudgment." Speech given at Harvard
University, 1995. https://jamesclear.com/great-speeches/psychology-of-human
-misjudgment-by-charlie-munger.

Nardi, Olivier. "Petrarch, Physicians, and Controlled Trials." *BMJ* 329, no. 7458
(July 2004): 141. https://doi.org/10.1136/bmj.329.7458.141.

Neubauer, Marcus. "Clinical Pathways Can Lead to Cost Savings, Better Care."
OBR Oncology, October 2014. http://obroncology.com/article/clinical-pathways
-can-lead-to-cost-savings-better-care-2/.

Nuland, Sherwin B. *Doctors: The Biography of Medicine.* New York: Alfred A Knopf, 1988.

"Obama's Remarks at the White House Health Care Forum." *New York Times,*
March 5, 2009, Politics. https://www.nytimes.com/2009/03/05/us/politics
/05obama-text.html.

O'Brien, Jack. "What People Are Saying about Amazon's Bombshell Announcement." Health Leaders, January 30, 2018. https://www.healthleadersmedia.com
/finance/what-people-are-saying-about-amazons-bombshell-announcement.

O'Connor, Anahad. "Heart Stents Still Overused, Experts Say." *Well* (blog). *New
York Times,* August 15, 2013. https://well.blogs.nytimes.com/2013/08/15/heart
-stents-continue-to-be-overused/.

Park, Alex. "Should We Regulate Poop as a Drug?" *Mother Jones,* August 18, 2014.
https://www.motherjones.com/environment/2014/08/fecal-transplant
-fda-openbiome-rebiotix/.

Parker-Pope, Tara. "Overtreatment Is Taking a Harmful Toll." *Well* (blog), *New
York Times,* August 27, 2012. https://well.blogs.nytimes.com/2012/08/27
/overtreatment-is-taking-a-harmful-toll/.

Pearl, Robert. *Mistreated: Why We Think We're Getting Good Health Care—and Why
We're Usually Wrong.* New York: PublicAffairs, 2017.

Perry, Susan. "U.S. Physicians Say up to 30 Percent of Medical Services Are Unnecessary." MinnPost, September 12, 2017. https://www.minnpost.com/second
-opinion/2017/09/us-physicians-say-30-percent-medical-services-are-unnecessary/.

Pinker, Susan. "The Secret to Living Longer May Be Your Social Life." Filmed April
2017. TED video, 16:03. https://www.ted.com/talks/susan_pinker_the_secret
_to_living_longer_may_be_your_social_life?language=en.

Ramsey, Lydia. "The 10 Most Popular Prescription Drugs in the US." Business Insider, December 28, 2017. https://www.businessinsider.com/common-popular-prescription-drugs-us-2017-7.

Redelmeier, Donald A., and Sheldon M. Singh. "Survival in Academy Award–Winning Actors and Actresses." *Annals of Internal Medicine* 134, no. 10 (May 2001): 955–62. http://doi.org/10.7326/0003-4819-134-10-200105150-00009.

Resnick, Brian. "How Scientists Are Learning to Predict Your Future with Your Genes: But What Are the Limits?" Vox, August 25, 2018, 9:35 a.m. EDT, https://www.vox.com/science-and-health/2018/8/23/17527708/.

Retsky, Michael, Romano Demicheli, William J.M. Hrushesky, Patrice Forget, Marc De Kock, Isaac Gukas, Rick A. Rogers, Michael Baum, Vikas Sukhatme, and Jayant S. Vaidya. "Reduction of Breast Cancer Relapses with Perioperative Non-Steroidal Anti-Inflammatory Drugs: New Findings and a Review." *Current Medicinal Chemistry* 20, no. 33 (November 2013): 4163–76. http://doi.org/10.2174/09298673113209990250.

Roach, Mary. *Gulp*. New York: W.W. Norton, 2013.

Robertson, Alexander. "Pensioner Dubbed 'Amazing Grace' Turns 111 as She Reveals a Nightly Dram of Whisky and Not Worrying about Life Are the Secrets of 'Still Feeling 21.'" *Daily Mail*, September 18, 2017, 11:17 EDT. https://www.dailymail.co.uk/news/article-4895606/.

Rosetta, Linda. "Intermountain Healthcare: A Model System?" *Salt Lake Tribune* (UT), August 29, 2009. https://archive.sltrib.com/story.php?ref=/ci_13232387.

Rutkow, Ira. *Seeking a Cure: A History of Medicine in America*. New York: Scribner, 2010.

Salahi, Lara. "Doctors Call to Stop Chemotherapy Overuse, Cut Cancer Costs." ABC News. https://abcnews.go.com/Health/CancerPreventionAndTreatment/doctors-call-stop-chemotherapy-overuse-cut-cancer-costs/story?id=13688585.

Sanger-Katz, Margot, and Reed Abelson. "Can Amazon and Friends Handle Health Care? There's Reason for Doubt." *New York Times*, January 30, 2018, The Upshot. https://www.nytimes.com/2018/01/30/upshot/can-amazon-and-friends-handle-health-care-theres-reason-for-doubt.html.

Saxon, Wolfgang. "Dr. George Crile Jr., 84, Foe of Unneeded Surgery, Dies." *New York Times*. September 12, 1992. https://www.nytimes.com/1992/09/12/us/dr-george-crile-jr-84-foe-of-unneeded-surgery-dies.html.

Schlosser, Mario. "In What Ways Is the US Healthcare System Inefficient?" *Life* (blog). HuffPost, November 8, 2017. https://www.huffpost.com/entry/in-what-ways-is-the-us-he_n_12849148. Originally appeared on Quora, November 2, 2016.

Schnipper, Lowell E., Thomas J. Smith, Derek Raghavan, Douglas W. Blayney, Patricia A. Ganz, Therese Marie Mulvey, and Dana S. Wollins. "American Society of Clinical Oncology Identifies Five Key Opportunities to Improve Care and

Reduce Costs: The Top Five List for Oncology." *Journal of Clinical Oncology* 30, no. 14 (May 2012): 1715–24. http://doi.org/10.1200/JCO.2012.42.8375.

Schroeder, Alice. *The Snowball: Warren Buffett and the Business of Life.* New York: Bantam Books, 2008.

Shakya, Holly B., and Nicholas A. Christakis. "A New, More Rigorous Study Confirms: The More You Use Facebook, the Worse You Feel." *Harvard Business Review*, April 10, 2017, Health. https://hbr.org/2017/04/a-new-more-rigorous -study-confirms-the-more-you-use-facebook-the-worse-you-feel.

Spector, Tim. "Identically Different." Published May 23, 2013. Kings College, London. https://www.youtube.com/watch?v=1W5SeBYERNI.

"The St. Bartholomew's Hospital Reports." *Lancet* 96, no. 2465 (November 1870): 764. http://doi.org/10.1016/s0140-6736(02)60124-2.

Sukhatme, Vikas P. "An Inexpensive, Safe and Easy Intervention to Increase Cancer Survival." December 8, 2015, presentation. Video, 30:34, published January 21, 2016, MIT Laboratory for Financial Engineering. https://www.youtube.com /watch?v=H8zVrYEW8vE.

Szabo, Liz. "So Much Care It Hurts: Unneeded Scans, Therapy, Surgery Only Add to Cancer Patients' Ills." Press-Enterprise, October 24, 2017. https://www .pe.com/2017/10/24/.

———. "Why Many Cancer Patients Don't Have Answers on Life Expectancy." American Association for Physician Leadership. July 25, 2017. https://www. physicianleaders.org/news/why-many-cancer-patients-dont-have-answers-on -life-expectancy.

Tirrell, Meg, and Jodi Gralnick. "Diabetes Defeated by Diet: How New Fresh-Food Prescriptions Are Beating Pricey Drugs." CNBC, June 21, 2018, 9:57 a.m. EST. https://www.cnbc.com/amp/2018/06/20/diabetes-defeated-by-diet-new-fresh -food-prescriptions-beat-drugs.html.

Torre, Pablo S. "From Couch to Clutch." Vault, February 20, 2012. https://www.si .com/vault/2012/02/20/106161469/from-couch-to-clutch.

Travis, Kate. "Bernard Fisher Reflects on a Half-Century's Worth of Breast Cancer Research" *Journal of the National Cancer Institute* 97, no. 22 (November 2005): 1636–37. https://doi.org/10.1093/jnci/dji419.

Tversky, Amos, and Daniel Kahneman. "The Framing of Decisions and the Psychology of Choice." *Science* 211, no. 4481 (January 30, 1981): 453–58.

"Van Helmont JB (1648)." The James Lind Library. Accessed August 2018. http:// www.jameslindlibrary.org/van-helmont-jb-1648/.

Viera, Mark. "For Lin, Erasing a History of Being Overlooked." *New York Times*. February 12, 2012, Pro Basketball. https://www.nytimes.com/2012/02/13 /sports/basketball/for-knicks-lin-erasing-a-history-of-being-overlooked.html ?mtrref=mail-attachment.googleusercontent.com.

Virtanen, Reino. "Claude Bernard: French Scientist." Encyclopaedia Britannica. Updated February 6, 2019. https://www.britannica.com/biography/Claude-Bernard.

Wagner, Sarah. "Poop Pills: Fecal Microbial Transplant Offers a Promising Treatment for Obesity." *The Scope* (blog). *Yale Scientific Magazine*, April 19, 2016. http://yalescientific.org/thescope/2016/04/.

Waldeck, Andrew, and David W. Johnson. "Gawande's Gift: Re-imagining Corporate Wellness and Healthcare." *System Dynamics* (blog), 4sight Health, July 11, 2018. http://www.4sighthealth.com/gawandes-gift-re-imagining-corporate-wellness-and-healthcare/.

Walker, Peter. "The Oldest Person in the World Says 'Being Single' Is the Reason She's Still Alive." *Independent*, November 29, 2016, People. https://www.independent.co.uk/news/people/oldest-person-alive-italian-emma-morano-celebrate-117th-birthday-a7444951.html.

Wathen, Jordan. "Index Funds vs. Mutual Funds." The Motley Fool. Updated January 9, 2018. https://www.fool.com/investing/2016/08/27/index-funds-vs-mutual-funds.aspx.

Wingfield, Nick, Katie Thomas, and Reed Abelson. "Amazon, Berkshire Hathaway and JPMorgan Team Up to Try to Disrupt Health Care." *New York Times*, January 30, 2018, Technology. https://www.nytimes.com/2018/01/30/technology/.

White House Office of the Press Secretary. "Remarks Made by the President, Prime Minister Tony Blair of England (via satellite), Dr. Francis Collins, Director of the National Human Genome Research Institute, and Dr. Craig Venter, President and Chief Scientific Officer, Celera Genomics Corporation, on the Completion of the First Survey of the Entire Human Genome Project." Press release. June 26, 2000, 10:19 a.m. EDT. https://www.genome.gov/10001356/june-2000-white-house-event/.

Wolf, Hal. "What Health Systems Can Learn from Kaiser Permanente: An Interview with Hal Wolf." *Health International*, no. 8 (2009): 18–25. https://www.mckinsey.com/~/media/mckinsey/dotcom/client_service/Healthcare%20Systems%20and%20Services/Health%20International/HI08_Kaiser_Permanente.ashx.

Yeh, Robert W., Linda R. Valsdottir, Michael W. Yeh, Changyu Shen, Daniel B. Kramer, Jordan B. Strom, Eric A. Secemsky, Joanne L. Healy, Robert M. Domeier, Dhruv S. Kazi, and Brahmajee K. Nallamothu. "Parachute Use to Prevent Death and Major Trauma When Jumping from Aircraft: Randomized Controlled Trial." *BMJ* 363 (December 2018). https://doi.org/10.1136/bmj.k5094.

Zeldovich, Lina. "The Magic Poop Potion." Narratively, July 30, 2014. https://narratively.com/the-magic-poop-potion/.

Zetlin, Minda. "Want to Be Happy? Do These 6 Things, According to Warren Buffett." Icons and Innovators. Inc., June 28, 2017. https://www.inc.com/minda-zetlin/6-things-warren-buffett-says-make-him-happy-and-will-probably-make-you-happy-too.html.

Index

About the Author

 Travis Christofferson, MS, author of *Tripping over the Truth* and founder of a cancer charity, received his undergraduate degree in molecular biology from the Montana State University Honors Program and a master's degree in material engineering and science from the South Dakota School of Mines and Technology. He is a full-time science writer and lives in South Dakota.

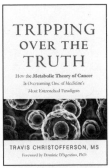
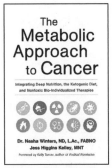
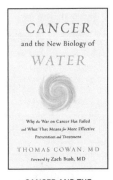
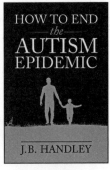

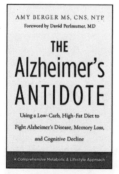